CASS LIBRARY OF AFRICAN STUDIES

AFRICANA MODERN LIBRARY

No. 6

General Editor: PROFESSOR E. U. ESSIEN-UDOM
University of Ibadan, Nigeria

A Humanities Press Book

We are pleased to send you a complimentary copy of

RENASCENT AFRICA
Africana Modern Library 6
by Nnamdi Azikiwe

. . . *for review*

We would appreciate two copies of your review.

Publication date . . . 1970

Price . . . $10.00

HUMANITIES PRESS, Inc.
Publishers & Importers of Scholarly Books
303 PARK AVE. SOUTH NEW YORK 10, N. Y.

Renascent Africa

by

NNAMDI AZIKIWE

Humanities Press

New York

FRANK CASS & CO. LTD.
1968

Published by
FRANK CASS AND COMPANY LIMITED
67 Great Russell Street, London WC1
by arrangement with the author

First published	1937
Third impression	1968

SBN 7146 1744 X

Printed in Holland by
N. V. Grafische Industrie Haarlem

RESPECTFULLY DEDICATED TO
THE HEROES AND HEROINES OF
RENASCENT AFRICA

PREFACE

To-day, the continent of Africa is the focal point of European territorial ambitions.

France, Great Britain, Italy, Belgium, Portugal, and Spain have colonial possessions in Africa. They are among the " have " nations.

There are other States which have no colonial possessions in Africa. They are among the " have not " nations.

A clash between the two groups is inevitable.

Amidst these conflicting ambitions of Europe for territorial expansion in Africa is the human factor—the fate of indigenous black Africans who dwell on this continent.

They constitute an extraneous element, so far as European imperialism is concerned. Their raw materials mean more to Europe than their existence to enjoy the fullest of life, as do the Europeans, on their own continent, respectively. Their man-power seems only valuable for the machinery of European imperialism and militarism.

That the indigenous black Africans are not destined to accept the old idea of imperialism as revealed law handed down to Moses on Mount Sinai; that the twentieth-century African is bound to be renascent; and that this Renascent African must be reckoned with as a concrescent factor in the peace of the world, is the theme of this book.

In view of the revolutionary concept of *Africa* and *Africans*, some terminologies employed in this book deserve clarification:

Old Africa refers to the Africa of yesterday.
Renascent Africa refers to the Africa of to-day.
New Africa refers to the Africa of to-morrow.
African refers to any indigenous black person.

The Renascent African exists in a transitional stage between the Old and the New Africans. He refuses to view his future passively. He is articulate. He is destined to usher forth the New Africa.

To avoid ambiguity, it is necessary to explain what is meant by the New Africa.

Naturally, the continent of Africa cannot be reshaped. Geophysical phenomena were responsible for its fixity, etc. It is, therefore, beyond human power to change the physical map of Africa.

The term is used in a psycho-social sense. It is the renascence of Africans and the reformation of African society.

History is full of movements which brought about a new social order. The Renaissance, the Reformation, the Counter-Reformation, the American and French Revolutions, the Bolshevist Revolution, exemplify the verdict of history with reference to sociological dynamics.

In Africa, outside of the immortal contributions made by the ancestors of the African, in antiquity—when Ethiopia was at the height of its majesty—and their forebears, during medieval times—when Songhay was in its splendour—African society has remained stagnant.

The Slave Trade and some of the evils of imperialism have helped to perpetuate the static condition of Africans. These offer a challenge—that the New Africa must come to pass.

The philosophy of the New Africa hinges itself on five bases. These are indispensable to its realization.

1. *Spiritual Balance* must be cultivated by Renascent Africans. This means respect for the views of others. Difference of opinion should not destroy friendship. In the Old Africa, difference of opinions intensified the wide gap between the various sections of the communities. Voltaire said that although he might disagree with his opponents, yet their right to state their opinions must be conceded, even if it cost his death in so doing. It means that the feelings of others must be taken into consideration, and that no ulterior motives should influence one's criticisms of others.

2. *Social Regeneration* must be experienced in African society. African conventions cannot be said to be consistent with what is ethical, just, and equitable. African society must be democratic. The ills of the present social order hinge on the

continuation of the forces of man's inhumanity to man. Let the Renascent African take upon himself the burden of looking at his fellow African as a man, nothing more, nothing less. Tribal appellations cause tribal idiosyncrasies ; these lead ultimately to vanity and superciliousness and disharmony.

A regenerated social order must come. Fanti or Ga, Temne or Mende, Yoruba or Ibo, Bantu or Touareg, Bubi or Hausa, Jolloff or Kru—all are Africans—all are human beings. "A man's a man for a' that."

3. *Economic Determinism* must be the basis of African economic thought. The quest for food, shelter, and clothing has been the primal motive in the establishment of society. It was responsible for the formulation of the social and political institutions of society. It is still the determinant factor in African contemporary history.

The Renascent African cannot create a new social order without an economic foundation. No longer must wealth be concentrated in the hands of the few. No longer must the profit motive guide and control the aims in life of the African. No longer must the wage-earners be told of a dignity that does not seem to exist in labour.

Let the Renascent African make to-morrow secure for posterity, and a milestone is reached toward African economic interdependence with the rest of the world.

4. *Mental Emancipation* is necessary in order to crystallize the New Africa. This includes education of the sort which should teach African youth to have faith in his ability : to believe that he is the equal of the people of other races of mankind—mentally and physically ; to look at no man as his superior simply because that man comes from the Antarctic or Arctic regions. It means that the Renascent African must be rid of the inferiority complex and all the trappings of hat-in-hand Uncle Tom-ism.

Educate the Renascent African to be a man. Tell him that he has made definite contributions to history. Educate him to appreciate the fact that iron was discovered by Africans [1] ; that

[1] *Journal of Royal Anthropological Institute*, vol. 43, pages 414-15. See also the views of Dr. Franz Boas in *Atlanta University Publications*, No 17 (1912), pages 26-27.

the conception of one God was initiated by Africans[1]; that Africans ruled the world from 763 to 713 B.C.;[2] that while Europe slumbered during "the dark ages" a great civilization flourished on the banks of the Niger, extending from the salt mines of Terghazza in Morocco, to Lake Chad, right to the Atlantic.[3] Narrate to him the lore of Ethiopia, of Ghana, Melle, Mellestine, Songhay.[4]

Let him relish with the rest of the world that while Oxford and Cambridge were in their inchoate stages, the University of Sankore in Timbuctoo welcomed "Scholars and learned men from all over the Moslem world", as Sir Percy puts it.[5]

The Renascent African will be better off with men and women who are trained to appreciate these facts of African history, than with those who spend a lifetime in Europe or America, for purposes of mis-education and devaluation of African culture and civilization.

5. *National Risorgimento* is inevitable. When the Renascent African has cultivated spiritual balance, regenerated his society, planned his society economically, and has experienced mental emancipation, his political status cannot be in doubt. It is from within that the element of national greatness springs.

Let Renascent Africans usher in a New Africa, and Africans of to-morrow need not continue to be in political servitude. The forces of nationalism are automatic, especially when factors leading to them are intelligently directed. The right of self-determination is a phenomenon which defies human ingenuity.

Forces which were responsible for the birth, growth, and decay of Ethiopia, Egypt, Babylo-Assyria, Phœnicia, Greece,

[1] E. W. Smith, *The Golden Stool* (1928), page 89n. See also Sir J. G. Wilkinson, *Manners and Customs of Ancient Egyptians* (1878), vol. III, pages 1-2.

[2] E. A. W. Budge, *Egyptian Literature*, vol. II, "Annals of Nubian Kings" (1912), pages xi-lxxxix and pages 1-88. See also A. C. Sayce, *Records of the Past* (1882-1892), and J. H. Breasted, *Ancient Records of Egypt* (1906), five volumes.

[3] Es-Sadi, *Tarikh Es-Soudan* Publications de l'école des langues orientales vivantes. (1900). Traduit de l'Arabe par Professeur O. Houdas. See also Felix Dubois, *Timbuctoo the Mysterious* (1897).

[4] Maurice Delafosse, *The Negroes of Africa*: *History and Culture* (1931), chapters II and IV.

[5] Sir Percy Sykes, *A History of Exploration from the Earliest Times to the Present Day* (1934), page 94. See also Dubois, *op. cit.*, pages 275-76.

and Rome will determine the fate of the West, the East, and Africa.

"For all I know," said George Bernard Shaw, "the next great civilization may come from the Negro race."[1]

This prophecy is enough for me, unless one cares to read Oswald Spengler's *The Decline of the West*.

January 23, 1937.
TROCADERO HOTEL,
ACCRA, GOLD COAST,
WEST AFRICA.

NNAMDI AZIKIWE.

[1] *The New York Times*, April 13, 1933, page 19.

CONTENTS

RENASCENT AFRICA

Chapter I

AFRICA IN RENASCENCE

1. *DÉBRIS OF THE OLD AFRICA*

Human nature is so remarkable that its make-up is still unfathomable. One may orate on certain phases of human nature. One may theorize on other phases of it, but in the final analysis it is impossible to make a categorical statement as to what constitutes human nature.

At one time, human nature becomes an easy task for the quack—say the physiognomist, the mesmerist, the hypnotist, the palmist, the fortune-teller, etc., but when it comes to a showdown, none, not even the scientifically trained psychologist, can explain, without reservation, the constitution of human nature.

It is a phase of human nature for Old Age to becloud the aspirations of Youth. It is too evident that throughout history a secret battle has been waging between Old Age and Youth.

The remarkable part of this secret battle is that it was caused by pride, and the struggle still rears its horrid head through unwillingness to admit the inevitable, graciously, on the part of Old Age.

Youth is said to be aflame. Youth is regarded as rash, uncontrollable and irresponsible. Those who emphasize these, in their denunciations of Youth, do so because they believe that the rôle of Youth is to obey and to take orders.

But Youth is also the golden age of man. It is a phase of man's life when the flames of passion burn within. It gives to the world some of the best poems imaginable, some of the finest dramas read, some of the most intriguing novels written, and some of the finest specimens of humanity, physically speaking.

In view of this, it cannot be safely concluded that the period of Youth is inconsequential in the history of any people, black or otherwise.

Look at Old Age, on the other hand. See how the snowy hair rests on the skull-cap of those who wear it in so dignified a manner.

Look at the wrinkles on the faces. Do they not seem like the ripples of a boundless ocean, symbolic of the experiences of Old Age, from which Youth can benefit?

Yet there is something that one forgets at times when one tends to glorify Youth or Old Age.

It is the state of mind of the two.

Youth is immortal.

The thought processes are immortal.

No matter how old an individual may be, no matter if he is young or old, if he thinks in accordance with the times he is immortal and has carved his name in history.

One may or may not believe in the immortality of the soul. But it is too evident that it is immaterial whether Socrates lived until he had grey hair or wrinkled brow, etc. One thing is known; what he taught had made him immortal. *Gnothi seuaton*—Know thyself. Is there not immortality in these two words?

Youth and Old Age are not synonymous with the terms old and new. Some elders seem to be youthful perennially. Some young folks are senescent perennially. This explains the justification of the use of the terms "Young Old Man", and "Old Young Man".

The Young Old Man, despite his age, his grey hair, his wrinkled brow, knows enough history to yield to the demands of the times. The Young Old Man has not a "Sir Oracle" complex. Rather, he is co-operative, looking forward to a better society.

But the Old Young Man, despite his youthful age, his strength, his beauty, and his symmetrical form, is ignorant of the forces of human nature as was made manifest in the cross-currents of history. Consequently, he becomes a pawn in the hands of

Old Age, and he lives as a man in a man's shadow. To him the breezes merely hum, and he becomes a sort of tree in walking form.

I will publicly admit that I have never claimed to be a New Messiah, although for reasons best known to a section of the West African Press I have been elevated to that creditable and immortal position. It is possible that I may be one of the apostles of the New Africa, and I do not mind the ridicule with which my gospel is regarded. The term " Christian " is not an honourable one, genetically speaking.

Again, let me inform Renascent Africans that the New Africa is not a movement. Just as the Kingdom of God cannot be reckoned along material lines, so too must they not fall into a common error of expecting a new continent, geo-physically.

The New Africa is a state of society where the mind is brought into harmony with matter. And when such co-operation exists the old order (where matter is master of the mind) will have passed away. It is therefore a psychological conception which is deeply rooted in a material environment.

To achieve mental emancipation, the apostle or disciple of the New Africa must hurdle over barriers of race or tribe. One must be willing to be called names and to suffer persecution, so that truth may be allowed a chance to flourish on the earth.

In other words, the disciple must forsake mother and father and relatives and friends, and even homes, so as to leave Nazareth for Jerusalem and proclaim the truth from Mount Olives, if even though the goal may be Calvary.

Not oblivious of my handicap, in this century, there is no better means to arouse African peoples than that of the power of the pen and of the tongue. True it is that Japan has become materialistic, yet the people were first aroused from their deep sleep. The Press is an avenue. Schools are also important, but the Press is a much wider and more potent avenue for this particular mission. And the pen is said to be mightier than the sword.

Modern industrial society and the educational policy of European powers in Africa make any *direct* attack, at the present, suicidal. An African endowed and operated university, in Africa, may be a way out, but where there is no spiritual balance, social regeneration, and economic determinism, a university is out of the question.

I submit that people who are strangers to one another cannot experience mental emancipation, much more economic emancipation. If the New Africa must be realized, then the Old Africa must be destroyed because it is at death-grips with the New Africa, which should guarantee to Renascent Africans the enjoyment of life more abundantly. Sacrifices must be made. I may as well be offered as an oblation to usher in the New Africa.

2. *THE DEATH GRIP*

If by politics is meant the application of the principles of political science, I feel that it is an erroneous view for any section of the African Press to conclude that politics is not " the right business and aim of youth ".

The premises leading to such a conclusion are as follows: " It (politics) is intricate, perplexing and difficult, and for which is suited only those who have experience, the true value of things socially and economically important and are acquainted with human life and conditions. This is essentially the business and concern of only those who have assumed the *toga virilis*.

" The legitimate claims of youth are the pursuit and exercise of physical and intellectual training of virtuous life to fit them to be healthy men with sound minds in sound bodies to devote to the prosecution and protection of the virtual interests of the country after they shall have assumed the *toga virilis* and acquired mature experience, the acquisition of which is so essential for those to whom is entrusted the guiding, custody and directing of the destinies of the country."[1]

I disagree with these conclusions on three grounds: ethical, sociological, and historical.

Ethically speaking, it is an unnatural situation for one segment of society to do the dictation all the time. Since ideas of morality are based on the principles of right and wrong, it is ethically inconsistent with the principles of justice that youth

[1] *The Gold Coast Independent*, July 20, 1935, page 684.

should take dictation all the time, irrespective of the merits of the ideas of the dictators.

Moreover, the criterion of ethics depends on the evolutional nature of society. For one generation to use its ethical criteria as a permanent standard of the ethical criteria of the coming generation is unethical, because it strangulates the *mores* and folk-ways of the group.

Sociologically speaking, youth is generally regarded as a leavening process in any society, be it primitive or advanced. This dynamic nature of youth enables society to be progressive. Otherwise it will devolutionize.

I must admit that society is like a stream. The spark which generates the power to enable the stream to flow is the spirit of youth.

Let any society be composed exclusively of old men and women. Let a group of octogenarians and centenarians live by themselves, give orders and take no heed of youth, for a while. It is needless to remark that the Dead Sea with all the alleged putrefaction thereof will be better than such society.

New ideas imply new minds, and these in turn imply a new order. On the other hand, old ideas imply old minds, and these in turn imply an old order. That is why Lord Tennyson wrote that the old order must change yielding place to new, lest anachronistic customs might corrupt the world.

Again, youth acts as a sort of catharsis to society. It is the revolt of youth against injustice of the old which enables Old Age to realize that it needs a new set of values, morally or otherwise.

If youth should acquiesce in certain evils of the social order it would become immunized, and so, despite its juvenility, its ideas would be old, and so that type of youth must be classified as an old man. And if there is an old man who believes in thinking like a youth, no matter if that individual is a centenarian, he is a young man. After all, it is the mind which generates the power over matter.

Rivers are better than lakes because they flow. It is true that lakes are the source of rivers, at times, but without the dynamic action of the river in flowing from place to place the lake would remain stagnant, torpid, and contaminative.

So is society. The old folks are the lakes. The young folks are the rivers. Let the lakes cease to be a source of the river and there would be no basin, no watershed, no valleys and no vegetation.

But let the lake be a source of a river, and the river is seen coursing through plains and mountains and valleys, blessing mankind and the beast of the field with vegetation.

Without the youthful in mind and in body, the politics of society will degenerate, contaminate, corrupt, defile, taint, and pollute the African socio-economic fabric. There will be all the evidences of man's inhumanity to man. There will be greed, selfishness, avarice, covetousness, and unnecessary prejudice, be they tribal or racial.

Readers will agree with me that were it not for the old, youths of Africa and youths of Europe would have understood one another better. But the old heads continued to pollute young minds with their old prejudices, hence the present dilemma.

It is too evident that from a sociological point of view the argument that youth must reach a certain stage before wearing the *toga virilis* is untenable, because it is based on artificial and superficial reasons.

Historically, the argument must be renounced. The pages of history are filled with narratives of the exploits of youth in the realm of politics. Neither Alexander the Great nor Julius Cæsar had grey hair, wrinkled brow, honours, etc., before they set out to see and to conquer.

The same is applicable to Boadicea, Joan of Arc, William of Normandy, Richard the Lion-Hearted, Antar, Taharka, Clive, Nelson, Napoleon, Chaka, Garibaldi, Peter the Great, Frederick the Great, Thomas Paine, Lord Lugard, Menelik, Ras Nasibu, and the other great men who have left their political achievements in history.

There is no need to belabour this point. Historically, politics is the game of youth. Think of the most sensational manifestation of the revolt of youth to-day in the idea of Nationalism.

Think of the names of Stalin, Ataturk, Mussolini, Hitler, Pilsudski, Mosley, Eden, Morley, Rex Tugwell, Matsuoka,

Chiang-Kai-Shek, Gandhi, Nehru—these men either reached the climax of their political careers or were great statesmen before they attained old age.

Because it is ethically inconsistent for one section of the community, from the standpoint of age, to do the dictating from time to time ; because it is not in the cards for society to stagnate sociologically ; because the verdict of history from 4241 B.C. to A.D. 1937, is that youth is a *sine qua non* in the political evolution of the various nations of the world, I submit, with all due deference, that the conclusion that the rôle of youth in politics is extraneous, is not only unconvincing but also heretical.

Old Africa is at death-grips with the New Africa. Renascent Africans must be equal to the task and must salvage the débris of Old Africa through the supreme efforts of Youth.

3. *A KNIGHTED AFRICAN*

" We have heard so much of a ' New Africa ' coming to birth. The protagonists of the New Africa are spreading doctrines which can only tend to cause trouble in this Country. . . .

" But if the youth of the Country are to be taught and educated to disrespect and to show open contempt to their Chiefs and Elders and leading public men with those views or with whose persons those ' teachers ' are not in agreement, or for whom they have an animosity, then it is a real danger."[1]

The above statements were credited to Nana Sir Ofori Atta, K.B.E., Omanhene of Akim Abuakwa, during the February, 1936, Estimates Session of the Legislative Council of the Gold Coast.

After making this speech, the Colonial Secretary, Mr G. E. London, C.M.G., called the attention of the Nana to the fate of public servants who were subjected to criticisms often and who were used to it.

Of course, I do not believe in acrimonious criticism of a tendencious nature against Nana Sir Ofori Atta or other public men.

[1] *Legislative Council Debates*, Gold Coast Colony, Session 1936, Issue No. 1, page 122. See page 128 for Mr London's remarks.

It was in London, during August, 1934, that I met the knighted Nana in the flesh. The students of British West Africa, in London, were at loggerheads. They seemed to have agreed to disagree, and, to all intents and purposes, these future leaders of British West Africa had made London a training ground for mis-leadership and tribal mitosis. So it seemed to me, particularly.

At his hotel in South Kensington, delegates of the West African Students' Union and the Gold Coast Students' Association met so as to iron out their differences.

Dr J. B. Danquah, B.A., LL.B., Ph.D., and the author were selected by the factions to act as arbitrators, with Nana Sir Ofori Atta as Umpire. The Nana was able to settle the differences between the two groups temporarily by appointing a Reconstruction Committee, which I understand died a natural death after the members of that historic " peace " meeting at South Kensington had regaled themselves with refreshments worthy of an Omanhene of Akim Abuakwa, in the city of London.

After the meeting I was introduced to the Nana as " Mr Azikiwe of the *Ocansey* Press," with emphasis on *Ocansey*. Since I was ignorant of the practical problems of Gold Coast politics at that time, i.e., four months before the inception of *The African Morning Post*, of which I was to be Editor-in-Chief, it was not until I assumed duties that I appreciated the import of that introduction and the " hearty " handshake of the Nana on that occasion.

Going back to the speech of the Nana at the Legislative Council I feel that it is perfectly legitimate for the Press to criticize the conduct of public persons and public servants. Even the King of England does not enjoy an amnesty from the shafts of the Press. " To assert that the King takes an erroneous view of some great question of policy is not seditious, if it be done with decency and moderation."[1]

The same is also applicable to Members of the Cabinet, Members of Parliament, Judges, etc. The Freedom of the Press is guaranteed so long as it is not licentious and so long as the criticism is made within the ambit of the law.

I do not see how an African Paramount Chief can claim

[1] Odgers, *Libel and Slander* (6th ed.), page 416. See *Rex* v. *Lambert* and *Perry*, 1810, 2 Camp. 398.

sanctimony from public criticism, especially if that Chieftain provokes criticism by lowering his dignity from that of an Executive to that of a Legislator.

This, no doubt, was what Mr London might have unconsciously had in mind, and it tallies with the motion made by Dutch-Sekondi, seconded by British-Sekondi, at the 13th session of the Provincial Council of Chiefs of the Western Province asking for an amendment to the present Order-in-Council, "to make non-Chiefs eligible as Legislative Council representatives of Provincial Councils" in the Colonial legislatures.

In the Gold Coast law and custom, as in African law and custom, generically speaking, the people make the law, and the Chief administers the law. If an African Chief prefers to make the law instead of administering the law, there might or might not be revolution. If there is revolution it means that the people object to this travesty on immemorial practice. If there is no revolution, it means that the people have accepted the new practice, provided that such African Chiefs would not claim sanctimony and amnesty which were reserved to them by virtue of their executive position.

Bearing these considerations of Political Philosophy in mind, I am not wrong in holding to the point of view that Chiefs are entitled to respect, on the part of *all* members of the community, in the same way that they are subject to be criticized for their legislative acts, within the ambit of the law. Here, they have two functions, as executives and as legislators.

Now, if Nana Sir Ofori Atta makes a statement of public importance, it is for the public to decide whether he made the statement in an administrative capacity or in a legislative capacity?

If in the former capacity, then the principle of the *Rex* v. *Lambert and Perry* case must prevail, but if in a legislative capacity, then he is subject to be criticized just as would any M.P. or M.L.C. be, irrespective of the fact that he might be a Chief.

This should be the reasonable way of looking at the status of African Chiefs (a) as Executive Officials, and (b) as Legislative Officials, unless Colonial Government and Administration rule otherwise. The statement of Mr G. E. London does seem to indicate that Chiefs, as legislators, are subject to criticism, since they become public figures by accepting an inferior status in the political structure.

The Honourable Nana said that the protagonists of the New Africa were spoliating the youth of the land and that they were creating disaffection among the peoples of the Gold Coast. Then he concluded that danger loomed with such doctrines being disseminated, especially since they would tend to make Chiefs and elderly persons to be objects of ridicule, on the part of the youth.

I submit, with all due deference to the Honourable Nana, that he had overshot his mark if his aims were targeted towards the philosophy of the New Africa, as advocated since the advent of the writer on the Gold Coast, in 1934.

For the sake of fairness to all parties concerned, a review of the fundamental bases of the philosophy of the New Africa as indicated in the preface of this book, is essential.

(1) The Cultivation of Spiritual Balance; (2) The Experience of Social Regeneration; (3) The Realization of Economic Determinism; (4) The Creation of Mental Emancipation; (5) The Expectation of Political Resurgence. These bases were further developed as follows:—

1. *Spiritual Balance.* Respect for the opinion of others; conceding to others the right to state their opinion whilst admitting one's right to state one's opinion. Cultivation of a spirit of tolerant scepticism for the views of one's antagonists remembering the ideal set by Voltaire.

2. *Social Regeneration.* The jettisoning of all forms of prejudice, be they racial, national, tribal, societal, religious, political, economic, or ethical; the realization that an African is an African no matter where he was born, whether at Kibi or at Zungeru, Navrongo or Cape Coast, Bathurst or Accra, Brazil or Manyakpowuno, Patagonia or Tuscaloosa, Mepom or Kukuruku, Nairobi or Amedica, etc., the breaking down of all barriers of tribal prejudice, be they inter-tribal or intra-tribal, which, so far, has postponed social unity of African peoples.

3. *Economic Determinism.* Realization that economic self-sufficiency on a sane basis is the ultimate means to the salva-

tion of the Renascent African. No matter how educated Africans may be; they may go to Switzerland, Cambridge, Birmingham, Heligoland, Oxford, Copenhagen, etc., for education; unless they are economically deterministic, they will fail to realize a stable society.

Under the circumstance, it was suggested that Africans should consolidate their interests towards an economic renaissance so as to prevent an over-production of any particular type of professionals.

It was suggested that education was useless unless it was an avenue for adaptation to environment, and since earning a livelihood was a form of adaptation, failure to provide employment for sons and daughters of Africans was to dent African social fabric. Economic determinism was, therefore, a way out.

4. *Mental Emancipation.* The African has not been in a state of incunabula throughout history. There is no scientific proof to sustain the idea of superiority or inferiority of any race, physically or mentally. For the African to cultivate an inferiority complex that he is inferior to other races, is to sign the death warrant of Africans. An emancipation is therefore essential.

Let the African know that he had a glorious past and that he has a glorious future. Teach the African to know his capabilities and his rôle in the scheme of things. Let the African realize that Burns was right when he said, "A man's a man for a' that."

Rid the African of all complexes which would retard his growth towards manhood on the theatre of nations. Let him follow Socrates: *Gnothi seauton* (Know thyself), and like a sleeping giant let him awake and harness his power for his own good and for the good of mankind. This will create mental emancipation, for mental slavery is worse than physical slavery.

5. *Political Resurgence.* The expectation of political *risorgimento* is not far-fetched if the Renascent African had cultivated *spiritual balance*, had experienced *social regeneration*, had realized *economic determinism*, had created a condition whereby he is *mentally emancipated* to appreciate his manifest destiny in the world.

Politics is a means to an end which is more glorious than

the means through which this end must be attained. Individually, the means are indeed glorifying. Socially, the end is a guarantee of social security, and a right to enjoy life, liberty and the pursuit of happiness, just as do other peoples.

Now that the Honourable Nana Sir Ofori Atta, K.B.E., Omanhene of Akim Abuakwa, has had the philosophy of the New Africa reclarified, as I conceive the idea, I shall proceed to give an account of my stewardship, i.e., a practicalization of this philosophy, which no doubt irked the Nana so as to elicit such pertinent comments he made in the Legislative Council.

1. *Spiritual Balance.* During the Subsidy Controversy I found myself drawn into a milieu of unnecessary dispute by two contemporaries of the local Press, which believed that *The African Morning Post* was a tool of the European to blindfold the Africans and to sell their rights for " a mess of pottage ".

The Times of West Africa (which succumbed after the controversy) and *The Gold Coast Independent* (which survived) were the principal actors in the attempt to place false values on my philosophical speculations. It was even mooted that the City Press, Limited, my employers, was subsidized in order to muzzle public opinion.

Because I had advocated the cultivation of *spiritual balance*, I did not silence my opponents. I gave them free rein to vent their spleen, and some of them were over-generous in the uncomplimentary adjectives used in rejoining or rebutting my points.

During the 1935 Gold Coast election compaign, *The Gold Coast Independent* found itself isolated against the majority of the Press of the municipality of Accra. I did not silence it in its aspersions and in its verbosities against me. Rather, the Gold Coast public will bear me out as to how I treated my opponents whenever I felt that there were grounds for disagreement of opinion.

I was called names. An Editor of *The Gold Coast Independent* wrote an open letter to a British subject then resident at Accra, in care of *The African Morning Post* which, in my opinion, was libellous, since the law precludes the use of newspapers as a medium to classify any individual as insane simply because he disagrees with his opponents, politically. I did not publish the letter. Even then, I had the spiritual balance to accept with equanimity the vitriolics and vituperations which followed.

If, therefore, by cultivating "spiritual balance" I respect the opinions of my antagonists and, at times, even publish articles which are not consistent with my editorial policy, does it not indicate tolerant skepticism, and is the Nana justified in saying that this phase of the New Africa will "tend to cause trouble" in the country?

I think that the Nana, in the capacity of a legislator, is wrong in this particular instance, and he is not justified to make such a generalization in the Legislative Council.

2. *Social Regeneration.* During the Election Campaign I had an opportunity to extend my attempts at social unity, so far as the West African tribes are concerned.

It is too evident that in the metropolis of Accra there are many persons with diverse tribal affiliations. Accra is, therefore, a laboratory of inter-tribal and intra-tribal relationship.

When now a candidate for re-election to the Legislative Council presented himself to the Accra public on a platform which looked upon certain tribes as inferior to the others, and branded certain denizens with uncomplimentary epithets and sobriquets, I opposed his candidature successfully because I felt that such a person lacked social vision, and was therefore a misleader.

I am quite sure that had Nana resided at Accra, as an ordinary denizen from Akim Abuakwa, he would have been branded a "stranger" just as other denizens were, and he would have seen the necessity for supporting a candidate who claimed that he was more interested in the social unity of West Africans.

Nana has heard of certain persons being called "strangers". Nana has heard of certain persons being called "Jekri", "Ibiobio", "Birds of passage", etc., and does Nana not agree that such appellations tend to hinder the tribal unity of Africa?

And if so, does the learned Nana think that those who oppose these tendencies by substituting a doctrine of *social regeneration* "are spreading doctrines which can only tend to cause trouble in this country"?

I think that the Nana, in his legislative capacity, has not been considerate in dubbing the protagonists of the New Africa with the statements he made at that session of the Legislative Council.

Again, take the offices of *The African Morning Post*, when I was Editor-in-Chief of that paper, for example. It was actually a miniature West Africa. As a means towards the practicalization of tribal relationship by experiencing *social regeneration*, I did transform the offices and the workshops of *The African Morning Post* into laboratories of inter-tribal fellowship.

In the staff there were persons who belonged to the following West African tribal or linguistic families: Ga, Fanti, Adangme, Twi, Ewe, Yoruba, Ibo, Kru, etc. There were persons from the following countries: Gold Coast, Sierra Leone, Nigeria, Liberia. These workers were from rural as well as urban districts. They worked together and tried to understand one another.

So that whilst Accra is a sort of macrocosm, the offices and workshops of *The African Morning Post* were parts of the microcosm. And does the Honourable Nana wish the truth-loving African or European Member of the Legislative Council to accept his remarks without a grain of salt?

3.—*Economic Determinism.* Since the doctrine of the New Africa was enunciated, I have tried to encourage Africans to become economically deterministic. I have never failed to support any attempt towards economic self-sufficiency on the part of the African.

When Mr. Samuel Duncan came into my office with his references and with samples of his product, I agreed with him that economic foundation is necessary to any tangible form of progress in this country. That is one reason why it was placed as No. 3 in my philosophy of the New Africa.

I satisfied myself that Mr. Duncan was sincere, and that he was honest in his attempt to do for his country what others would not do, even though I knew that he disagreed with me, politically.

I supported him in every way that the Press could. Not only did I give him necessary publicity, but I also pleaded his cause to the authorities, correlating the "back to the land" philosophy of Sir Arnold Hodson with this evidence of agricultural ingenuity on the part of the African.

In all seriousness, does Nana Ofori Atta mean to say that

I was spreading doctrines which "can only tend to cause trouble" in the country by backing Mr. Samuel Duncan, who was backed by the Provincial Council of Chiefs of the Eastern Province at the 22nd session of their meeting, held at Dodowah, on September 28, 1935, and whose resolution supporting Mr. Duncan was signed by "Ofori Atta, Omanhene of Akim Abuakwa," immediately after the signature of "Sri II, President, Eastern Provincial Council"?

The same is applicable to other attempts of the African to become economically self-sufficient. When the Ghana Model Farm idea was mooted, did I not back it by "spreading doctrines" regarding the necessity for looking at agriculture as a desirable vocation? The same is applicable to the Achimota Agricultural plan.

When an African company started to manufacture perfumery locally did I not lend whatever support I could to assist that industry? When an African started to manufacture confectionery locally, did I not lend a helping hand in my humble way so as to "spread the doctrine" of economic determinism?

According to the way of thinking of the Honourable Nana, is it to be concluded that my philosophy and practice of economic determinism would only tend to cause trouble in the country? Or shall I identify that portion of his speech as an example of oratorical phantasy? I submit, with all due deference to the learned Nana, that his utterance as a public man should have been toned down. It was too acrimonious an attack to make, especially when the charges border on vague generalities.

In addition to what I mentioned, I believe it fair to say that I have been urging the educated section of African society to invade the manual labour jobs and become efficient manual workers so as to better their economic plight.

I have asked those who have elementary education to offer competition to illiterate drivers, carpenters, printers, etc., and secure for themselves better economic conditions of living. Is this spreading false doctrines which would tend to cause trouble in the country? No, Sir Ofori, you have not been fair to me.

4.—*Mental Emancipation.* As Editor of *The African Morning Post* I laboured to emancipate the minds of Africans. Any impartial reader of that paper will agree with me when I say that my editorial methods had not been inflammatory, necessarily.

True, I had to be cautious, but in West African journalism, and in fact in journalistic practice anywhere, one cannot be over-cautious.

When I had reason to believe that a cause was worth fighting for, I exerted my efforts not in a vindictive way, but in a suasive and convincing way. When any injustice was done I did not necessarily blindly rave and rant and abuse and wreck my victims or my opponents. Rather, I conceded to them certain elements of human nature and then I tried to repay them in their own coins. With these in view I have always doctrinated that the African is not inferior to any race under God's earth. Is this heresy, as Sir Ofori's oration implies?

I have also doctrinated that the African is not doomed to be a wood-hewer and a water-carrier "from generation to generation, Amen". Is this a phase of my pernicious teachings, and is this a corruption of the mind of youth, so oratorically asserted by Nana Sir Ofori Atta?

Did I not attempt to emancipate the minds of Africans by telling them of their past? Did not "Antar", my other pen-name, reveal to Africans the lore of ancient Ethiopia? What about the names of Piankhi and Tirhaka who established the black man's dominion of the world in 763 B.C.?

Is it spreading false doctrines to tell the people of Africa that their grandsires were once rulers of the country which civilized Greece, which, in turn, civilized Rome, which, in turn, civilized Great Britain, which, in turn, believes it is its duty to civilize these selfsame Africans, to-day? Ye gods!

Another phase of the practicalization of this doctrine of mental emancipation may be envisaged in my policy so far as news value and arts are concerned. So many African papers devote columns to meaningless encomiums on unknown Caucasoids, and scanty columns to great Negroids. Is it not a form of mental slavery to believe that because a man's colour is pink (mistakenly identified as white) therefore he is superior to a person whose colour is coffee-brown (mistakenly identified as black)? And if I give to both races their due equally, is it to be concluded that I am spreading dangerous doctrines which tend to cause trouble in the country?

Again, it will be remembered that prior to the inception of *The African Morning Post*, most of the West African periodicals and newspapers specialized in carrying pictures of Europeans in the papers. It is artistic, true. But art is also a medium of propaganda. The aim of art is either æsthetic or utilitarian. In other words, art is either beautiful or useful. This is what I mean. A table may be an object of art, viewed from two angles, as an object of beauty or of utility.

Now, photography is a phase of art. A Chinese proverb says that one picture is worth more than a thousand words. If the people are shown pictures of Europeans all the time, they are bound to build certain complexes about the Europeans.

It is, therefore, essential wherever and whenever possible to show Africans pictures of black men and women in order to inspire them with racial self-respect. It is done by me with purpose—to emancipate the minds of Africans, although the contemporaries of *The African Morning Post* are wont to look at it from a commercial angle!

If these facts be the case, and the learned Omanhene, in his legislative capacity, knows or ought to realize these, why did he sink his javelin into my body, at the Legislative Council, that I was spreading doctrines which would tend to cause trouble in the country? Is it fair? Is it just? Is it equitable?

5.—*Political Resurgence.* In my philosophy of the New Africa, I submitted that the cultivation of *spiritual balance*, the experience of *social regeneration*, the realization of *economic determinism*, and the creation of *mental emancipation*, would automatically culminate in a *political risorgimento.*

There is no doubt that a *political resurgence* is in the offing. It must come, no matter how it may be postponed by the exigencies of Colonial Government and Administration. But the only means to usher it in is the successful practicalization of the four planks which are its foundation.

The part that youth plays in the politics of the world has passed the stage of stupefaction. It is a reality to-day, and if there are cronies who think that because they *have been*, therefore, they will continue *to be*, no more egregious blunder could have been committed. The days of the *have been's* are over. This is the day of the *will be's*. The sooner it is realized by fanatic worshippers of old age, the better will it be for co-operation between youth and old age.

When such a great empire as Great Britain has a youth of forty at the helm of its Foreign Office, it is a straw which indicates where the wind blows.

So far as I know, I have never denounced old age, *per se*. So far as I know, I have never taught youths to disrespect their elders, or to be contemptuous to them. So far as I know, I have always respected youth and old age, and I have garlanded the latter with a fitting classification, " youth-in-mind ".

This appellation is only applicable to the elders who do not belong to *the lost generation*. It is applicable to those elders who see things as they should be to-day, and not as they were in the 'nineties.

Now, the New Africa is not a movement. It is to be likened to Joshua's interpretation of his version of the Kingdom of God. Where my concept of the New Africa differs from the concept of others is that I believe that only *from within the African* must the New Africa become a reality and not through any other efforts, however noble and philanthropic, *from without*.

For holding this view, *The Gold Coast Independent* which, apparently, inspired Nana Ofori Atta's oblique view of my conception of the New Africa, has classified me with the " journalistic vampires and political frauds ", and has identified my concept as " the bastard New Africa ". Yet the bases of my philosophy and the successful practicalization of my ideal have so far proved unassailable by my antagonists.

If Nana Sir Ofori Atta, in his legislative capacity, is intellectually honest, after reading this section he would, I am sure, regret having made such vague remarks without trying to understand what he was criticizing.

After all, it is very easy to criticize by denouncing and wrecking, but it is very difficult to criticize by lauding, where praise is due, and by constructing.

As for the latter part of his philippics, I submit that on such a platform as that promulgated by me, for the realization of the

New Africa, it is impossible for elders and Chiefs to be disrespected, much more to be treated contemptuously.

Rather, young and old, having cultivated *spiritual balance*, would have learnt to respect the opinion of others. In this case, neither is youth nor old age a sort of Sir Oracle who, when he opens his mouth no dog dares bark or bay, even at the moon.

It is impossible for a spiritually balanced person to disagree with his opponent, and then abuse his opponent for holding different views from his own, or to distort his opponent's views.

I submit that the Nana, in his legislative capacity, did not cultivate spiritual balance before attacking " the protagonists of the New Africa ". If he did, he would not have distorted my philosophy by saying that I am among those who are spreading doctrines which can only tend to cause trouble in the country.

Again, I submit that the Nana was unfair to me when he misdirected his hearers by inferring that I taught disrespect and contempt of elders and Chiefs to my followers. Nothing can be farther from the truth.

On the other hand, the manner I have treated Nana's speech is a humble way in which I am trying to practise the cultivation of spiritual balance.

I conceded to the learned Nana his right to his opinion, and then I proceeded to show him how he was not justified in his opinions. But I am not trying to stop him from holding to his opinion. That would not bring about the New Africa. Rather it would continue to perpetuate the element of man's inhumanity to man which is part and parcel of the Old Africa.

One more word about how I try to live by the gospel of the New Africa, even at self-sacrifice. A well-known gentleman who enjoys the reputation of publicly maligning *The African Morning Post* as the cause of all troubles in the Gold Coast, found it necessary as a *sine qua non* to his life's ambition.

I did not question him about his overt acts of enmity. I did not consider him as a green snake in green grass. I did not call him a chameleon. And I did not proceed to debate with him so as to justify myself. I believed that his project synchronized with my doctrine of economic determinism, and I lost no time to concede to him his right to his opinions, and I did not scruple to place at his disposal my brain and brawn so as to facilitate the realization of his life-long ambition and dreams for the economic self-sufficiency of the African.

Of such stuff are the protagonists of the New Africa made, Nana Sir Ofori Atta, K.B.E., Omanhene of Akim Abuakwa, so that if you, in your legislative capacity, did not appreciate my views before you delivered your philippics, you are now in a position to understand me better.

Of course, I do not claim to be the sole protagonist of the idea of a New Africa, since there are others who see a New Africa in a different light.

For example, *The Gold Coast Independent* recently reproduced certain articles from a publication of Reverend E. W. Smith, regarding New Africa, which no reflective African will accept as satisfactory, but I will not question the right of any person to think of New Africa in the way that this scholarly President of the Royal Anthropological Institute and Editor of the *African Journal* thinks.

Rev. Edwin Smith is a fair-minded anthropologist. He was born in South Africa. He has written some good books of an ethnographical nature, but his views of a New Africa are challenging because the same missionaries who played a rôle in the imperialistic partition of that Continent are looked upon by him as a means to a realization of his concept of a New Africa.

No doubt I am reasonably justified in believing that the New Africa which was criticized by Nana Ofori Atta in the Legislative Council was the concept disseminated by me. And I do not scruple to place my facts of the issues involved before Nana Sir Ofori Atta, so that he may realize how he has attacked me, quite unprovoked.

4. *IT IS INEVITABLE*

Critics of the concept of the New Africa have often fallen into a common error of regarding it as advocating ultra-radical and ultra-revolutionary changes in the social order, by all means, fair or foul.

Some of these critics have their axes to grind. But to the honest critics, I aver by challenging them to re-read the sections of this book wherein the concept of New Africa is elaborated, and they will discover that they have been labouring under a misapprehension.

There must be changes in order to have a new order. True. There must be radical changes in order to have a new order. True. There must be revolutionary changes in order to have a new order. True. But I have never advocated that these radical and revolutionary changes should crystallize through foul means.

It is necessary that I make these pronouncements because there are some gratuitous critics of the New Africa who believe that the concept is comparable to the Spanish Revolution and other examples of European youth in ebullition. This is not true.

If the Spanish Revolution must be regarded as a criterion, in accordance with the view of some of these critics, then I submit that the Spanish Revolution is a direct antithesis to my concept of the New Africa.

The Spanish Revolution was engendered by Fascists and other ambitious persons who seek to prevent the crystallization of a new order in Spain.

The Spanish Revolution was caused indirectly because the Church and the State continued, for centuries, to perpetrate man's inhumanity to man, and when the sons and daughters of the New Spain challenged Old Spain to cultivate spiritual balance and experience social regeneration, they were faced with the forces of Fascism, which sought to destroy the vestige of democracy in Spain.

The New Africa is bound to be. Criticisms cannot destroy it. The conception of an idea is as indestructible as the concept and idea are capable of realization.

Evidences are not wanting of gradual encroachment of New Africa on the strongholds of Old Africa, despite misinterpretations and distortions so as to paint the New Africa in lurid colours.

Any person who reads the newspapers from the Gambia, Sierra Leone, Liberia, and Nigeria, and other parts of Africa, especially South Africa, will realize how these countries are adopting the practicalization of this ideology in the various institutions of their countries.

In Liberia, the people are clamouring for a New Liberia, and in a message to the Legislature of Liberia, His Excellency President Edwin Barclay did not scruple to challenge the honourable members to realize the fact that New Liberia was in the offing. Hear him:

" I think it is incumbent upon me at the threshold of a new era in the history of Liberia to direct your attention to, and to emphasize the fact that in the period of our national life now opening, old habits of political, social and economic thought and action must be discarded, and a new political ideology adopted and a higher moral conception of public and social duty and obligation accepted.

" This by no means implies that the fundamental principles of liberty and democracy which form the basis of our national organization should be abandoned, but that they should be given a new interpretation consistent with the urgent need to build up a strong, progressive State, each part and function of which shall be dominated by a definite national conception and motivated by a single will.

" Every step of the national progress and development must be planned in advance, and every social governmental function must be concentrated on the realization of the objective sought. No discordant voice should be permitted to break the rhythm of the nation's harmony, and a disciplined co-operation in all phases of the nation's life should be one of the principal and irrevocable aims of government. . . .

" I would again emphasize the fact that we are now entering upon a new era. Methods that have been outworn must be discarded, and it is hoped that this fact will be clearly realized by Members of the Legislature, that their co-operation in bringing about a complete revision and re-organization of our political, social and economic life and thought will be assured.

" The future is open to us. Only with a clear realization of facts as they occur from day to day will we be able to make that future secure for the people of the country.

" *I am quite sure that I can rely upon Members of the Legislature to give effect to every proposal that looks towards the realization of a New Liberia.*"

The above statements by His Excellency the President of

Liberia are inspiring. It is a challenge to the Liberians to realize a New Liberia, as part and parcel of the New Africa.

Let us see what Sierra Leone does with reference to this idea. In a recent issue of *The Daily Guardian* published in Freetown, a correspondent wrote as follows :—

" We are in a different age and things must be done differently ; it is fallacious to assert that only old age have wisdom to reason ; we forget that the child is the father of the man.

" Now, we are getting nearer to the New Africa and towards social regeneration. . . .

" There is need for spiritual balance in order to balance the rights of ethics ; unless this is forthcoming, our propensities might descend into licentiousness.

" There is nothing done to-day in which youth is not given a place. They are dominating the world and if we go into research work of highly advanced politics we would find that the world to-day is being ruled by youth. ' Blessed be the youth in mind, for theirs is the heritage of a new social order.' "

In Nigeria, the concept is being practicalized in many ways. For example, *The Nigerian Eastern Mail*, which is published at Calabar, is responsible for the following Editorial, when it announced the fact that the Calabar National Institute was being organized :

" The ideals that have brought to birth the Calabar National Institute, whose appeal is published elsewhere in this issue, is the common ideal of all race-loyal Africans to-day : these are the ideals on which the New Africa is to be brought into being."

Now, why have we taken the trouble to refer to these utterances and publications ? To point out to West Africans that the New Africa is destined to be realized, despite the unfair tactics of the Old Africa.

Renascent Africa honours and reveres the Old Africa. Renascent Africa takes the Old Africa into confidence and seeks for its advice. But Renascent Africa requests that the relationship between the two must also be reciprocal or the Old Africa must naturally be relegated to the background.

Radicalism and Revolutionism may be identified with changes, but these changes need not be the type usually connected with bloodshed and open disregard for law and order.

In my evangelisms regarding the New Africa, I have always emphasised the necessity for co-operation between all sections of the community and between the Government and the Governed.

This is to be expected of a person with spiritual balance. This is also to be expected of a person who has been socially regenerated.

The crystallisation of the New Africa is inevitable, but it can be realized after there have been a New Gambia, a New Sierra Leone, a New Liberia, a New Gold Coast, a New Nigeria, and a renascent social evolution in the other sections of black Africa.

God grant that the realization of the New Africa may not be far distant.

CHAPTER II

OUR EMERGENCE

5. *TO OUR FATHERS*

You brought us, Young Africans, into this world. You played your part from a biological point of view. God blessed your rôle and so we came into this world, just as you and your ancestors did.

It was not your intention to make our lot a hard and severe one. Yours was a noble philosophy of life—to make life worth while for your children so that they might enjoy life more abundantly.

It was not your motive to make our fate comparable to that of a slave whose future is blighted by the chains around his feet and his hands and his neck.

Rather, you desired a better world for us. You desired better conditions for us so that we might improve, at least, one whit better than you did in your days.

Allow us to assume, fathers, that you realized the incorrigibility of human nature, and that was why you made up your minds to do all you could to make life less tedious for us.

You also realized our innocence. You knew that as children we were immature in thinking. You knew that we could be advised to accept certain opinions and to form certain habits.

These, you understood to have a bearing on our character, yet you insisted that we should condition our reflexes and thinking apparatuses to them.

Now, dignified fathers, we are grown up, and we look forward to the better life which you have promised us, and behold our lot is far from being satisfactory.

Instead of economic security, we are faced with the hyena which howls and growls and threatens our very existence.

Instead of social security, we are faced with divisions and tribal prejudices which make it impossible for us, your children, to work together in harmony.

Instead of political security, we are faced with an era which goes back into the early beginnings of the history of worshippers of Democracy, who had to fight and grumble and complain ere they could enjoy their rightful heritage.

Instead of religious security, we are faced with divisions based on dogmas which affect our very philosophy of life, because they make us to regard our colleagues as different from us.

Abba, when you brought us into the world, did you foresee these socionomic cataclysms? Were you apprehensive that ours would be a lot of servitude and social disruption?

And now that we are in the milieu of social, economic and political catastrophes, and we look forward to you to extricate us, since you are responsible for our habit formations and character, are we wrong in asking you to save yourselves also from this difficulty?

What heritage did your fathers leave to you? What heritage do you propose to leave to us? And what heritage do you suppose we will leave to our children?

Historically, your fathers left for you a nobler and more glorious heritage. If we judge your fathers by their light, we believe that theirs was a life of self-sacrifice for the uplift of mankind.

But in these days of want, in these days of persecutions, in these days of tribal prejudice, in these days of slackness in morals, in these days of social irresponsibility, are we not justified in questioning your fairness to us?

Have you been fair to us? In your days, your fathers taught you to obey and to be patient, for good things came to those who learned to labour and to wait. You laboured and you waited. Your reward was a crumb from the master's table, socially, economically, politically, and religiously.

You had the opportunity of going through the mill. It cannot be doubted that your lot was better than the lot of your fathers, in view of the developments of the past century, but can you conscientiously say that you have laboured to make our lot better?

If you are of the opinion that you have made our lot better, due to developments in our social economy of a physical nature, we will not doubt you, because we have better streets, motor cars, railways, telephones, telegraphs, wireless, cinema, etc.

But do these by-products of material culture make for a glorious heritage? Who would have radios, telephones, motor cars, etc., in exchange for the liberties and privileges and rights which have been responsible for the progress of nations in history?

In view of present-day events in the world, as inhabited by black folks, can you conscientiously say that you have made our lot better than yours? Can you say that the rights and liberties and privileges of the citizen which formed the bedrock of the society of your fathers' days are the same to-day, so far as we are concerned?

Granting that as mankind progresses so are the limitations and encumbrances on its social ideology and practices, is it not an evidence of lethargy when you allow all claims of ours to a place in the sun to be eclipsed by the vanities of a material civilization?

That is why we are discontented. In Europe, in America, in Australia, in Asia, the younger generation have been privileged to study history comparatively. So too, in Africa.

In these continents, the younger generation have been privileged to probe into the philosophy and psychology of life of the older generation. They realize that their fathers have failed to live up to the glorious traditions of the past. So too, in Africa.

In these continents, the younger generation have been blighted by the passion of diplomacy and they have seen how this ogre threatens mankind with an Armageddon. So too, in Africa.

Don't blame us, fathers, if we seem rash and harsh on you. We know that in Europe, Asia, America, and Australia, things are different from conditions in Africa. But all we ask of you in Africa is that you should be candid enough to realize your inability to traverse the complexities of the modern world alone, without the invigorating blood of African youth.

We are prepared to co-operate with you and to concede

your wisdom. But we are not prepared to take dictation from you, under all circumstances, after these evidences of social chaos which depict the need for intelligent co-operation between old age and youth.

Now, fathers, we have been .frank to you. We have been respectful. Are you prepared to extend to us a helping hand and bless us and take us into your confidence? Or do you prefer to be vindictive? As a man thinketh so is he.

6. *OUR RAISON D'ÊTRE*

When in the vicissitudes of life, it becomes necessary that men and women of different tribes or races should aggregate on a definite territory for mutual support, it presumes a quest for happiness.

This quest is an historic one, because it is the *raison d'être* of life. Take away the quest for liberty. Take away the quest for property. Take away the quest for the pursuit of happiness, and life becomes dismal.

To every man or woman on this earth, there is one goal—the quest for enjoying life more abundantly.

Life would have no fascination for any person, were that person not fully assured that his or her life and property were secure and that that person's rights were not to be abridged in such a way as to incapacitate him or her politically, economically, or socially, for life.

If life offers more than these, then we know it not.

Consideration of these vital principles led to some of the great movements of history; for, without life, without liberty, without property, without freedom to pursue happiness in the best way possible, life is nothing short of oppression.

In view of the present situation in Africa, European nations would do well to re-study the history of the world and observe the psychological doldrums which capsized the ships of State of by-gone empires and created a new order.

No man or woman worth his or her salt, likes to live in an environment where liberty is a privilege. No true son or daughter of God likes to exist in a man's or a woman's shadow. If these are not axiomatic, then life is an illusion.

Liberty implies the right to live according to the choice of the individual, so long as that individual respects the liberties of others, as decreed by the State. Therefore, to enjoy liberty to the fullest, man must appreciate his worth to the community and what that community has to offer to him, so as to imbue him with a spirit of patriotism.

Liberty also implies the right to enjoy the amenities appertainable to any organized society. No matter how faithful to the cause of the community one may be, if that community deprives one of the essential rights of democracy, that community has no right to be labelled as libertinous in its institutions.

The right to live should be synonymous with the right to enjoy the fruits of liberty, else it is meaningless to say that the fullest enjoyment of life is possible without the fullest enjoyment of life's essential concomitant.

Give me life with liberty. Or give me death.

I cannot live without enjoying the fruits of liberty. If I live without enjoying the fruits of liberty, then I am merely dying a slow but sure death.

Social security implies a right to live and to enjoy liberty to the extent that one's right to pursue happiness is guaranteed, otherwise all is a sham.

How can the African exist side by side with the European, the American, the Asiatic, the Australian, without thinking in terms of liberty—the right to live and to enjoy life as abundantly as do his colleagues of other continents, with or without their co-operation?

If there is any African who disbelieves his capacity to enjoy the fruits of liberty, mark him well, he is not sane, he is destined to be the footstool of his compeers, and his doom has been sealed.

Woe to those who in the name of liberty destroy all that is good in the African. Woe to those who in the name of trusteeship postpone the enjoyment of liberty, so far as the Africans are concerned. Their days have been numbered.

Blessed is the African who faces his or her fate with his head up, chest expanded, hat on, and who strikes his blows from the shoulder, looking at other races face to face, without cringing and without sub-vocalizing. He is ideal and it were better that millions of traitorous Africans be cremated alive so that one such hero may live.

Let Africans resolve to create a sense of responsibility on the part of Africans, lest they continue to cut their noses to spite their faces.

Let Africans resolve to work so that African leaders may bury the hatchet, work together, march together, dream together, with a common objective—extension of the present rights and liberties of the African.

Dare Africans continue to live in the quagmire of spite, malice, selfishness, avarice, greed, and the other forms of man's inhumanity to man, and dare they wince when they are pierced with the shafts from the bow of public opinion?

Let Africans resolve to create in the African leaders of yesterday a spirit of youth so that they may live not as they lived in 1895 or 1905 or 1915 or 1925 or 1935, but as the exigencies and contingencies of 1937 demand.

Let the Africans resolve to usher in an era of sincerity instead of that of faithfulness to a cause, however worthless may be its idealisms and however crass may be its ethical foundations. Two rights cannot make one wrong. Two wrongs cannot make one right. Neither one wrong and one right, nor one right and one wrong can make two rights or two wrongs. Only self-analysis can determine the norm.

Dare you continue to live in the past when the present is a prophecy of the future? Dare you continue to identify yourselves with *the lost generation*—leaders of Africa?

Sires, there's the marble, there's the chisel, you can fashion a statue from these and you can also fashion a flint or a *coup de poing* from them.

But mark you, leaders, what you sow, you shall reap, to the fullest extent.

Old age is no disgrace. Youth is no shame. The two are not poles apart. The gulf between the two need not be widened into a bay by the activities of shallow heads. And the gulf need not be sand-banked into an isthmus by the activities of hot-heads.

What is needed is co-operation which reserves to old age and to youth mutual respect, and which concedes to old age the right to lead, co-operatively with youth, as a *primus inter pares*, when questions of national significance are broached.

The year 1937 will mean nothing to old age or to youth if their respective legitimate aspirations are not respected. Youth is not ungrateful to old age. There is no persecution of old age. A little use of the grey matter within our skulls will reveal to us that the battle is between *young old persons and young persons* on the one hand, and *old persons and old young persons* on the other.

To which of these four categories do you belong? If either of the latter two, then resolve to be a *youth-in-mind* from now on so that you may enjoy the blessings of life, liberty, and the pursuit of happiness abundantly, as a free agent of God on this paradise of stately palms.

7. *AGITATORS*

The term "agitator" does not find reception in high circles. It has become a sort of anathema to some Africans. When one is called an agitator, one feels that one is being derided, socially or politically.

An agitator, in Colonial parlance, is equivalent to a demagogue in Western domestic politics. But both terms do not necessarily denote the same thing.

So odious has this term become, that responsible persons are afraid to be dubbed as agitators lest their social prestige should be impaired.

The history of this word should be left to philology, but its actual results, in so far as the stream of human society is concerned, have been beneficial to mankind.

If there were no agitators, everything would be at a standstill. Society would be stagnant. Individuals would be so complacent that there would be no urge for change and improvement.

Some one must challenge social injustice. Some one must rouse society from its lethargy, if the forces of man's inhumanity to man are carried to the various institutions of society, be they political, economic, or religious. That is why "agitators" are born.

Just think of a lake. It has no opening. All is torpid. Life in that lake becomes dull and the activities therein are sluggish. In short, a condition of equilibrium has been reached. When matter reaches this stage, chemically speaking, it is the end. It is death. It is the physiological zero.

Again, think of the history of England in particular. Without the efforts of Watt Tyler and John Ball, would the iniquitous feudal system then in vogue have revised its attitude toward the serfs and the villeins.

If Savonarola, Wyclif, Erasmus, Luther, Melanchthon, Calvin, Zwingli, were quiet and accepted the *status quo*, would the world have experienced a religious regeneration? Had Ignatius Loyola acquiesced in the corruptions of the Papacy, would the world have experienced the Counter-Reformation and the founding of the Society of Jesus, which has done a great deal for the uplift of humanity?

Again, had Abbé Siéyès, Mirabeau, Condorcet, Marat, Abbé Grégoire refused to challenge the First and Second Estates, would there have been a French Revolution, whereby a French man became a French man and not necessarily an unprivileged person?

History is full of the records of individuals and organizations which have challenged society to assume a dynamic shape in order that "one good custom" may not "corrupt the world", as Lord Tennyson puts it.

Christianity is in full swing to-day.

In all the earth,—the outposts of Africa, the jungles of America, the bush regions of Europe, the wilds of Australia, the steppes of Asia, the name of Joshua, whom the Greeks called Jesus, is a household word.

Why all this reverence? Why teach this piece of Jewish history? Why emphasize the part played by the Renaissance, the Reformation, the Counter-Reformation, the Industrial, American, French, and Bolshevist Revolutions?

Behold the answer! *The individuals responsible for the change for a better society were agitators.*

The word "agitator" means to stir up. If you could stir up your generation into activity in the right direction, you should be proud to be an agitator, and posterity shall revere you as we honour and respect the agitators who are the makers of ancient, medieval and modern history.

8. *A BEATITUDE OF YOUTH*

Blessed are the youth, for theirs is the earth and all therein.

Blessed are the youth-in-mind, for theirs is the heritage of a new social order.

Blessed are the mentally alert, for theirs is the heritage of a society which calls a spade a spade.

Blessed are those who have social vision, for they shall leave their footprints on the sands of time for posterity to cherish.

Blessed are those who are not self-opiniated, for they shall be lauded by posterity.

Blessed is the New Africa, for it is the heaven of those who know that they have a rendezvous with life.

Blessed are you, Renascent Africans, when Old Africa shall castigate the signs of the new order and shall concoct all forms of accusations against you falsely; rejoice and be glad, for posterity shall appreciate and realize your dreams.

Blessed are the evangelists of the New Africa, who go from place to place, debating with the Scribes and Pharisees and Sadducees of the Old Africa, for they lay foundations for a new social order which is intangible and immutable and inevitable.

Blessed are the youth of Renascent Africa, who refuse to take a backseat on the saddle of the institutions of their society, for by exposing the graft, corruption, chicanery and incompetency of the Old Africa, they carve their names immortal in the annals of New Africa.

Blessed are the youth of Renascent Africa, who refuse to give way to dead-heads, for they shall enjoy what the Old Africa failed to enjoy.

Blessed are the youth of Renascent Africa, who believe in the cultivation of spiritual balance, for they understand their own problems and appreciate the problems of the Old Africa more sympathetically.

Blessed are the youth of Renascent Africa, who see the necessity for cultivating social regeneration, for they shall crystallize the brotherhood and sisterhood of mankind on the face of the earth.

Blessed are the youth of Renascent Africa, who understand that no society can exist without an economic foundation, for they shall inherit the earth and all therein, be it aquatic, bathyspherical, subterranean, terrestrial, aerial, stratospherical, etc.

Blessed are the youth of Renascent Africa, who are mentally emancipated, for they shall know who knows and knows that he knows, and he who knows not and knows not that he knows not, and he who knows and knows not that he knows, and he who knows not and knows that he knows not.

Blessed are the youth of Renascent Africa, who are politically resurgent, for theirs is the redemption of Africa and the reconstruction of this ham which has been carved by the sword of European imperialism.

Blessed are the youth of Renascent Africa, who have volunteered to exterminate all the bad relics of the Old Africa, to make way for the New Africa, for they have a rendezvous with life, and shall walk with God, and shall see God.

Blessed are the youth of Renascent Africa, who refuse to be intimidated, brow-beaten, cowed, mocked, mobbed by the Old Africa, for they shall grow stronger and sounder in spirit and in body.

Blessed are the Youth of Renascent Africa, who see in truth a virtue of virtues, and sacrifice even life so that falsehood and its concomitants may be eradicated from the face of the earth, for they shall be replenished with knowledge and wisdom.

Blessed are you, heroes and heroines of Renascent Africa, for you are men and women of destiny, and no force, however potent or subtle, shall deter you from your goal—the crystallization of the New Africa.

Blessed are you, heroes and heroines of Renascent Africa, for whilst you may suffer persecution at the hands of your friends and foes, you will be armoured with fortitude and courage so that your enemies will fall one by one.

Fear not, heroes and heroines of Renascent Africa, for the forces of the Old Africa are destined to pass away, to yield place to the New Africa, and no matter how they may harass or torment or abuse or deride or even kill you, the Old Africa is destined to die, and from its débris shall tower the New Africa.

Woe unto you, leaders of the Old Africa! You claim to have the sole prerogative to enjoy life more abundantly. Your days have been numbered.

Woe unto you, evangelists of the Old Africa! You do the bidding of the Old Order. You have no faculty to read the signs of the times. You have been weighed in the balance and found wanting.

Woe unto you, disciples of the Old Africa! You meet in strange hovels in order to hatch your diabolical plans against the harbingers of the New Africa. Your doom has been sealed.

Woe unto you, hypocrites who half-heartedly believe in the New Africa, whilst your deeds reveal you as part and parcel of the Old Africa. Your fate must be likened to the fate of the sailors of a submerged submarine boat which failed to emerge. You are doomed to a bathyspherical grave.

Woe unto you, self-centred leaders, who prattle about, dangling torches which are a beacon of destruction, hankering after vainglorious alphabets of a decadent civilization. You have eyes but see not. You have ears but hear not. You have mouths but speak not. Yet like dumb-driven cattle shall you be cast into the labyrinth of forgotten men and women.

Woe unto you, visionless leaders! You cut your noses to spite your faces. No plastic surgeon, however renowned, can save you from the judgment you have passed on yourselves.

Blessed are the youth of Renascent Africa, for they shall grow stronger, and shall aid the weak to become stronger, and shall extend the hand of helpfulness to their comrades who are still enslaved by the forces of the Old Africa.

Blessed are the brave and courageous of Renascent Africa, for they shall be heirs to the constructive heritage of the Old Africa.

Blessed are the youth-in-mind, for theirs is the heritage of a new social order.

CHAPTER III

IN THE GRIP OF IMPERIALISM

9. *THAT MAGIC WORD*

(a) *Causes of Imperialism*

WHEN a young English student asked his professor to define the word " Imperialism ", the instructor told him to look at the map of the world and notice the portions marked red. The young man did so and told his teacher that all the portions marked red represented the British Empire, an empire on which the sun never sets, and an empire to which he was proud to belong. And the professor said : " That defines imperialism ! "

In the language of the medical experts, the world suffers to-day from *map-itis*. If the map of the world is examined carefully, one would be astounded at the variety of colours which lends an air of reality to the cult of imperialism.

Red represents this State. Blue represents that State. Green identifies the colonial possessions of this State. Violet identifies the dependencies of that State. And *ad infinitum* !

Why all these colour demarcations ? Why must the British lad be proud to belong not only to England but also to an empire on which the sun never sets ? Why must the British soldier give his life to be buried somewhere in the world " *that is forever England's* " ?

Imperialism is a borrowed word from Latin. It comes from *impero*, and is interpreted to mean : to command, to rule, to govern, to hold in trust, to civilize, to educate, to Christianize, and all other ideas attached to it since imperialism became a factor in the course of human history.

It is a by-product of nationalism because without a sense of oneness which leads to co-operative existence in the attempt to formulate group control over any environment, the ideal of ruling and of conquering others would not crystallize.

Hence I will say that imperialism is an effect, and since there must be a cause to elicit effect, imperialism must have causes. As to the effect of imperialism, it must be identified with its ethics. And since ethics denotes morality, there must be good and bad sides of it. And since these are assumed, it must have problems and results.

In other words, to understand the significance of imperialism, it must be analyzed from the following standpoints: causes, ethics, problems, and results.

Now, what are the causes of imperialism? They may be social, economic, political, military, religious.

Socially speaking, I may refer to Darwin, Malthus, Spencer, Wallace, and other biologists, for giving me an idea as to the nature of the struggle for existence and the survival of the fittest. In this respect, the law of natural selection plays no less an important part.

In other words, the instinct of pugnacity (to dominate) is innate in man. It activates his emotions. It lubricates his intersocial actions. It fortifies his pride with a desire to conquer. Thus Lord Bryce reposited the *homo homini lupus* philosophy of Thomas Hobbes, by saying that "Every man is a wolf to every other man." [1]

Economically speaking, I may refer to Karl Marx, Friedrich Engels, and other economists for establishing the economic interpretation of history, through which one learns that the quest for food, shelter and clothing is the dominating factor in human society.[2]

In other words, since the Industrial Revolution has made society to manufacture goods and commodities by machine, and since mass production is the rule and not the exception, raw materials are essential to a stabilization of home industries. And since colonies produce raw materials, they are necessary to the economic life of the industrial countries.

Politically speaking, I am grateful to Jules Ferry (France), Friedrich Fabri, Dr Paul Rohrbach (Germany), Rudyard Kipling, Lord Lugard (Great Britain), and other advocates of colonial possessions who believe that in the imposition of the

[1] Lord Bryce, *International Relations* (1923), page 4.

[2] H. W. Laidler, *A History of Socialist Thought* (1927), chapters XII-XVI.

will of the superior on the will of the inferior, there must be a political symbiosis which will enable the inferior to graduate from tutelage.[1]

In other words, the strong are destined to rule the weak. The strong are destined to have empires coloured on the map of the world, so that the territories might be definitely delimited, to prevent any trespassing. But in so doing the flag of the strong must be flown at its highest, in order to confer on the weak the benefits of civilization.

From a military point of view, if the fittest must survive the struggle, and if economics motivate human life more predominantly than any other factors, and if the prestige of *map-itis* must be maintained, colonies are essential in order to co-ordinate the military organizations of the empire.

In other words, coaling stations are essential for the mercantile fleet of the imperialist countries; naval bases and fortifications are also of prime importance; not to mention the paramount need for using the colonial possessions as a reservoir of troops, and as a means towards the training of reserve soldiers for any unforeseen struggle, and of course, for preparing the Natives for the honourable rôle of becoming cannon fodder in case robbers fall out on the division of loot.

From a religious point of view, it is essential that the strong must weaken the weak, not only physically but psycho-physically. Physical slavery is one thing, but international public opinion is dead against it. Mental slavery is legitimate so long as it is done diplomatically.[2]

In other words, traders succeeded in having the flag to follow trade, but this could not have been successful without the most important phase of this trinitarian tragedy.

The religious man must, and did, teach the Native not to lay up treasures on earth; this enabled the commercial man to grab the earthly treasures; and this facilitated the rôle of the Government to regulate how these earthly treasures are to be exported for the use of the world's industries.

[1] P. T. Moon, *Imperialism and World Politics* (1926), chapter III.
[2] P. S. Reinsch, *Colonial Government* (1902) chapter III.

(b) *The Ethics of Force*

Subject peoples are destined to succumb to the ruthlessness and the might of their overlords. I have already pointed out the fact that Imperialism originated from social, economic, political, military, and religious causes, due to the *specialization*, *organization*, and *segregation* coterminous with the forces of Social Darwinism.

It remains for me to consider the ethical approach to this reality of imperialism, and the problems and results it carries in its wake.

There are two main doctrines in the philosophical analysis of imperialism, from an ethical point of view : (a) the Doctrine of Exploitation, and (b) the Doctrine of Trusteeship.

The Doctrine of Exploitation. Under this topic I have to consider : the right to exploit weaker races, the right to develop world resources, and the right to civilize backward races.

Premier Jules Ferry of France, a prominent journalist and politician, has been called an apostle of contemporary colonial renaissance. He posited that superior races have a right and duty to civilize the inferior races. In his opinion it was the right of France to stop the Slave Trade and to promote justice in maintaining material and moral order, equity, and social virtues in Africa.

Professor Alfred Rambaud, of the University of Sorbonne, urged the exploitation of backward races as " a great historic mission " of France.

M. Paul Le Roy Beaulieu, a former Colonial Governor, in supporting French imperialism, said that " Colonization is the expansive force of a nation, its power of reproduction, its dilation and multiplication across space ; it is the submission of the universe or a vast part of it to the language, the manners, the ideas and laws of the Mother Country."

The Rise of Our East African Empire by Lord Lugard (then Colonel F. L. Lugard) may be said to represent the apogee of the British section of this school of thought. Lord Lugard justified imperialism on the necessity of economic exploitation so as to develop world resources. It is significant to note that this political philosophy enabled him to be honoured among the Peers of the Imperial Realm, as one of the greatest Colonial Administrators of the British Empire.[1]

Under the leadership of Viscount Bury, the Royal Colonial Institute (now known as the Royal Empire Society) was founded in 1868, to promote the ideal of a United Empire. One of the early members of the Society made history when he correctly explained the objective of this group by saying: "I hope the day is not far distant when we shall see the Union Jack flying permanently in the centre of Africa."

The members of this society desired not merely to consolidate the existing Empire, but to expand it, on the ground that it is the right of a civilized State to develop the resources of the world.

As Professor of History at Cambridge University, Sir John Seeley won several converts to imperialism, by his influence on British youth, through his speeches and his writings. His book, *The Expansion of England*, which was published in 1883, is assumed by some experts to have earned for him his knighthood.

Other supporters of this ethics of imperialism are men like D'Israeli, Sir Harry Johnson, Sir Cecil Rhodes, Rudyard Kipling, and Joseph Chamberlain. The last-named was a vigorous protagonist of imperialism on the ground that such a policy of expansion and exploitation would be an avenue to solve the unemployment problem in Britain, and by civilizing Africans and Asiatics it would be profitable to England, for, in the happy phrase of Lord Rosebery, it is "pegging our claims for posterity".

Herr Friedrich Fabri, in *Does Germany Need Colonies?*, urged the diffusion of German *kultur* among backward races. As an Inspector in the Barmen Rhine Mission, he played his rôle effectively.

In 1908, Dr. Paul Rohrbach declared: "The rights of the Natives, which can be recognized only at a cost of holding back the evolution of the white races, at any point, simply do not exist." In other words, he was of the opinion that the right to civilize backward peoples was more paramount than the right of the Natives to remain in their primitive stage.

[1] Lord Lugard, *The Dual Mandate in British Tropical Africa* (1922).

Rudyard Kipling is better known as an apostle of " aggressive altruism ". He called upon his fellow Caucasoids to " Take up the white man's burden ". He urged upon his compatriots to govern and to civilize Asiatics and Africans, who were classified by him as " sullen " peoples, " half-devils ", " half-children ". One of his imperialistic songs reads :

> " Take up the White Man's burden—
> Send forth the best ye breed—
> Go bind your sons to exile
> To serve your captive's need ;
> To wait in heavy harness,
> One fluttered fold and wild—
> Your new-caught, sullen peoples
> Half-devil and half-child."

Supporting this ethical concept of the right to civilize the backward races, President William McKinley of the United States (1896-1901) declared that the annexation of the Philippine Islands was justified : " There was nothing for us to do but to take them all and to educate the Filipinos, and uplift and civilize and Christianize them, as our fellow-men for whom Christ also died."

I may therefore define " aggressive altruism " as the justification of the use of force, *brutal force*, to impose on unwilling Native peoples the " blessings " of British, French Belgian, Italian, Portuguese, Spanish, American and Dutch civilization.

There is only one conclusion which is inevitable after summarizing the points raised in the thoughts of the great thinkers and doers enumerated above. *It is a vindication of the philosophy of force.*

This philosophy is identic with that of Thucydides : " Gods and men alike always maintain dominion wherever they are stronger." [1] Xenophon also supported this view : " It is a perpetual law amongst all men that, when a city (i.e. State) is taken from an enemy, both the persons and property of the inhabitants belong to the captors." [2]

In other words, " To the victor belong the spoils ". And if man needs the pathway of the deer for the construction of a

[1] Thucydides, V : 105.

[2] Xenophon, *Cyropaedia*, Book VII, chapter V, 73.

highway or for any purpose whatsoever, the deer must surrender its path. *Therefore, the ethics underlying the Doctrine of Exploitation is a glorification of force as a means to an end.*

(c) *The Idea of Trusteeship*

Trusteeship, as distinguished from *Exploitation*, is an anomaly. But in order to be fair to the school of thought which disseminates the doctrine of trusteeship, let us examine the principal points in the philosophy of trusteeship.

This doctrine is more or less humanitarian in its approach. Its basis is a dual mandate. That is, a belief that exploitation involves a duty.

In other words, this doctrine is not opposed to exploitation, necessarily, but it suggests that exploitation should be a complement of responsibility. It says: Exploit the weaker races, develop their mineral resources, civilize backward peoples, but in so doing respect their rights and protect them.

The Doctrine of Trusteeship thus revolves around four categories: (a) The rights of the backward races, (b) Protection of the backward races from exploitation, (c) Appeal to a sense of responsibility on the part of imperialists, and (d) Tutelage of the backward races.

Dr. J. H. Oldham [1] admits that Europeans are in Africa from economic and not from humanitarian motives: "Their object is the development of their own industry and trade, but the benefit may be made reciprocal."

He advocates that the rights of backward people should be respected and their resources should be protected from unlimited exploitation. He insists that advantage should not be taken to exploit the weaker races, but that whatever is the nature of the exploitation it should be mutually reciprocal.

Moreover, it is his point of view that in case the interests of the exploiter and the exploited should clash, the issue should be decided, not through the arbitrary and selfish exercise of superior power, but on the basis of impartial justice.

[1] J. H. Oldham, *Christianity and the Race Problem* (1924), chapter VII.

These views are in accordance with the opinion of Edmund Burke in the eighteenth century: "All political power which is set over mankind ought to be in some way or other exercised ultimately for their benefit." Wilberforce was also a believer of this doctrine of Burke.

William E. Gladstone, former Prime Minister of England, who seemed to have opposed imperialism, warned Englishmen: "We shall never seek to extend the Empire by either violently wresting, or fraudulently obtaining, the territories of other peoples."

In a White Paper the British Colonial Office went on record as condoning the doctrine of trusteeship through respecting and protecting the rights of backward peoples, thus:

"Primarily, Kenya is an African territory, and His Majesty's Government think it necessary definitely to record their considered opinion that the interests of the African Natives must be paramount, and that if, and when, those interests and the interests of the immigrant races should conflict, the former should prevail. . . .

"In the administration of Kenya, His Majesty's Government regard themselves as exercising a trust on behalf of the African population, and they are unable to delegate or share this trust, the object of which may be defined as the protection and advancement of the Native races. . . .

"There can be no doubt that it is the mission of Great Britain to work continuously for the training and education of the Africans towards a higher intellectual, moral and economic level than that which they had reached when the Crown assumed the responsibility for the administration of this territory. . . ."[1]

With these admissions that backward races have rights which must be respected and protected, there is also the challenge to a sense of responsibility which naturally leads to tutelage of the ward by his imperialist master.

By 1821, the United States of America had realized that its responsibility over the Indian tribes must take shape in the policy that the relationship between the two "should be in its nature, parental—absolute, kind, and mild."

In 1837, the British Parliamentary Committee on Aboriginal

[1] "Indians in Kenya", *Cmd.* 1922 (July, 1923), page 10.

Tribes found that the responsibility and obligation of Great Britain towards backward races were implied and expressed because of Britain's ability to protect backward races and the inability of the latter to resist any encroachments, " however unjust, however mischievous, which we may be disposed to make ".

In 1879 Mr Joseph Chamberlain who had previously claimed that it was the duty of England " to take our share in the work of civilization in Africa ", added : " Our rule over these territories can only be justified if we can show that it adds to the happiness and prosperity of the people."

On February 26, 1885, the signatories of the Berlin Convention (which Convention actually legalized the scramble for, and the partition of, Africa) agreed in Article VI to act as trustees for the preservation of the aboriginal population and the betterment of their social and moral conditions, so that they might be instructed to understand and appreciate the advantages of civilization.

On July 2, 1890, the General Act and Declaration of the Brussels Conference confirmed the above ideals of the Berlin Conference. In Article II, the African races were admitted as constituting the wards of the Colonial Powers who should safeguard and protect them.

On September 10, 1919, during the Convention of St. Germain-en-Laye the Revised Act of Berlin was signed. This propounded a new deal, in Article XI, by making the Colonial Powers to adhere to the principle that they " will continue to watch over the preservation of the Native population and to supervise the improvement of their moral and material well-being. They will protect and favour, without distinction of nationality or of religion . . . undertakings created and organized by the nationals of the signatory Powers . . . which aim at leading the Natives in the path of progress and civilization."

In Article XXII of the Covenant of the League of Nations, which is a sub-division of the Treaty of Versailles, backward races were regarded as " a sacred trust of civilization " who are supposed to undergo an indefinite period of tutelage, before initiation into the " mysteries " of " civilization ".

This covenant urged the application of " the principle that

the well-being and development of such peoples form a sacred trust of civilization and securities for the performance of this trust should be embodied in this Covenant." Thus was crystallized the Mandate System.

Ethics of imperialism, as I have shown, narrows down to two main doctrines: (a) The Doctrine of Exploitation, and (b) The Doctrine of Trusteeship.

The Doctrine of Exploitation. Under this topic I discussed the following: (1) The Right to Exploit the Weaker Races, (2) The Right to Develop World Resources, (3) The Right to Civilize Backward Races.

The Doctrine of Trusteeship. Under this caption, I examined the following: (1) The Rights of Backward Races, (2) Protection of Backward Races from Unfair Exploitation, (3) Appeal to a Sense of Responsibility on the part of the Exploiter, and (4) The Tutelage of Backward Races.

The Permanent Mandates Commission of the League of Nations is an outcome of the Doctrine of Trusteeship, with particular reference to the tutelage of the backward races.

In Article XXII of the Covenant of the League of Nations, it is stipulated: "To those colonies and territories which as a consequence of the late war have ceased to be under the sovereignty of the states which formerly governed them and which are inhabited by peoples not yet able to stand by themselves under the strenuous conditions of the modern world, there should be applied the principle that the well-being and development of such peoples form a sacred trust of civilization and that securities for the performance of this trust should be embodied in this Covenant."

In view of Article XXII, three classes of Mandates were established: Classes A, B, and C.

Class A Mandates are inhabited by peoples who are alleged to have reached a stage of development where their existence as independent Nations can be provisionally recognized, subject only to administrative advice by the Mandatory until they are able to stand alone.

Syria and Lebanon (France), Palestine and Transjordania (Great Britain), Mesopotamia, i.e. Iraq (Great Britain), were classified as Class A Mandates with the countries in parenthesis as their Mandatories. These peoples are members of the Caucasoid race.

Class B Mandates are inhabited by peoples who are alleged to be in a backward stage and the Mandatory Power must be responsible for the administration of the territories, subject to certain guarantees.

Togo (Great Britain and France), Cameroons (Great Britain and France), Tanganyika (Great Britain), and Ruanda-Urundi (Belgium), were classified as Class B Mandates, with the countries in parenthesis as their Mandatories. These peoples belong to the Negroid race.

Class C Mandates are territories which owing to the sparseness of their population, or their small size, or their remoteness from the centres of civilization, or their geographical contiguity to the territory of the Mandatory, and other circumstances, can be best administered under the laws of the Mandatory as integral portions of its territory subject to certain guarantees.

South-West Africa (Union of South Africa), Samoa (New Zealand), Nauru Island (Great Britain), German Islands South of the Equator (Australia), German Islands North of the Equator (Japan), were classified as Class C Mandates with their Mandatories in parenthesis. S.W. Africa is peopled by Negroids, and the rest by Mongoloids and Negroids.

It will be seen that this development in the philosophy of imperialism from exploitation to trusteeship found Great Britain (or shall we say the British Empire) playing an important rôle. Of the *fourteen* mandated territories, the British Empire undertook to civilize, Christianize and care for *nine* territories ; France for *three*, Belgium for *one*, Japan for *one*, and Italy and other members of the Allied Powers for *none*.

Of course, the Mandate System is not regarded as spoils of war, but rather as an advance in the philosophy of imperialism ! But when one studies the distribution of the territories, one is astounded at the way territories were carved.

Mr E. Y. Becr. Boni, in an article, criticized the allocation of Mandated territories, without the knowledge and consent of the Natives. Said he : " There is a worse form of slavery. To place a person under the tutelage of another without the knowledge and consent of the person or persons so placed, is slavery pure and simple. This type of slavery has been legalized by the League of Nations, while at the same time it hypocritically accuses Liberia of slavery.[1]

Professor Clyde Eagleton regards the system as "intriguing", but to locate sovereignty in the Mandated territory is the problem which is racking the brains of international lawyers.[2]

Professor Edmund C. Mower and Professor Parker T. Moon are of the opinion that the policy of trusteeship and exploitation is fundamentally inconsistent. Success of the Mandatory system depends upon the application of the idea of collective responsibility in Colonial Administration, generally.[3]

Professor F. L. Schuman says: "So long as the great driving forces of capitalism, nationalism, and imperialism persist and produce the same consequences in the future as in the past, the Mandate System can scarcely become an ultimate solution to the problems of war and oppression created by Empire builders."

Summarizing the doctrine of trusteeship and its bearing on the Mandate System, the following are pertinent: Man is not necessarily a wolf to every other man. Backward races have rights to life, liberty and the pursuit of happiness. The existence of a ruler who exploits the resources of a country, inhabited by backward races, attaches responsibility for the welfare of the governed. If exploitation should be an aid towards a process of civilization, it is justifiable, but it should be carried out on the dual mandate principle—exploitation in exchange for the beneficences of civilization.

According to an authority, expressions on the doctrine of trusteeship are sham ambiguities: "All imperialists are disposed to issue mealy-mouthed and pious platitudes regarding their solicitude for Native interests. Such statements must

[1] *The Gold Coast Spectator*, May 20, 1933, page 665.

[2] Clyde Eagleton, *International Government* (1932), page 106.

[3] E. C. Mower, *International Government* (1931), page 449. See also Moon, *op. cit.*, pages 506-12.

[4] F. L. Schuman, *International Politics* (1933), pages 621-22.

always be taken *cum grano salis* as rationalizations and justifications of policies of exploitation."[1]

How these conflicting ideals and by-products of imperialism have given rise to various problems will be discussed in the following section.

(d) *Problems of Imperialism*

Many problems have been raised by the practicalization of the ethics of imperialism. They are racial, social, educational, economic, political.

Racially speaking, the contact of two races which belong to an imperialist country and an exploited country, respectively, leads to an arrogation of superiority and inferiority, respectively.

The race to which the imperialist State belongs becomes *progressive and superior* and that to which the exploited race belongs becomes *backward and inferior*.

Condition of this nature leads to clashes which do not tend to promote goodwill and inter-racial fellowship. Naturally, an Englishman considers himself superior to the African, because he rules the African. The same is applicable to the Japanese who considers himself superior to the Korean or Formosan because Korea and Formosa islands belong to Japan.

The bolstering up of racial prejudice or a Nordic complex by reference to "intelligence tests" has been concluded by eminent anthropologists to be false and misleading,[2] yet imperialist powers formulate their colonial policies on the data yielded by pseudo-ethnology, thus justifying the policy of racial discrimination.

Socially speaking, the policy which arrogates innate superiority to the race of the imperialist State, reinforces its social ideology by enabling such "superior" race to pass unfair measures directed against the Native races, to impress upon the latter their status of inferiority.

Throughout Africa, before and after the war of 1914, there

[1] Schuman, *op. cit.*, page 596.

[2] G. A. Dorsey, *Why We Behave Like Human Beings* (1925), page 119.

have been cases of brutality and debauchery. Africans have been flogged mercilessly, at times to death, by their masters. In South Africa, particularly, Africans are identified by the tokens which they wear on their necks like dogs. The Colour Bar is at its worst in South Africa and Kenya.

In the French colonies, a special body of rules applicable to Natives alone exists, known as *l'Indigénat*. In Korea, the Japanese formulated a penal code which was especially severe towards Koreans. In British colonies, there is a policy of segregation whereby the Natives stay aloof from the European official residential area.[1]

These observations are definite indications of how the seed of racial superiority has sprouted into a tree of social arrogance, which eventually bore fruit of snobbery and consequent results which must be disastrous to both the imperialist and the exploited.

Educationally speaking, the education of the backward races has been regarded as a "problem". In the attempt to solve this "problem", efforts have been made to reduce education to the lowest minimum, possibly *the four R's*—Reading, 'Riting, 'Rithmetic, and Religion.[2]

The restriction of the education of the Natives is based on fear, because the imperialist believes that the more educated the backward races become, the more will they demand for an increased share and participation in the governance of their countries, which is natural. This, the imperialist States are not prepared to grant, at least at the present time.

Even Lord Bryce went so far as to say that the diffusion of education among backward races must not be regarded necessarily as a passport to autonomy.[3]

In the French, Belgian, Portuguese, Spanish, Italian colonies, mass education is not encouraged. In British territories, there are more educated Africans than are in all the territories of other European powers in Africa, but the British Colonial system of education, despite its liberalness, cannot be said to represent the ideal.

[1] R. L. Buell, *International Relations* (1929), chapter XIV.

[2] See also B. N. Azikiwe, "How Shall We Educate the African?" in *The African Journal*, April, 1934.

[3] Lord Bryce, *Modern Democracies* (1921), vol. I, chapter VIII.

Economically speaking, the problems of imperialism are based on the following: production, distribution, consumption, and exchange. The production of raw materials is necessary to the manufacturing industries of the home country. There must be a large source of labour supply which consequently brings problems of wages, conditions of work, industrial accidents, forced labour, etc., to the fore.

In addition to this, goods and other commodities must be distributed to the Colonies, at prices which must pay appreciable dividends to the investors of the mother country, and the raw materials must be bought from Natives at the prices dictated by the imperialist firms according to their rate of exchange.

Native lands have also been confiscated on the ground of the right of eminent domain; and among some Powers, these unfairly acquired lands have been leased and subleased to plantation owners where Native labourers have suffered all sorts of inhumanity. The rubber plantations of Putumayo, and the activities of King Leopold II, on the Congo, are typical examples.

Politically speaking, the question arises whether the period of tutelage is definite or indefinite? If it is the former, who is entitled to decide when a ward is ready to assume the task of autonomy—the imperialist State or the exploited Native? If it is the latter, is it consistent with the policy of trusteeship, and must it be accepted as revealed law, handed down from Mount Sinai, without the Natives making just demands, in accordance with the verdict of history?

These are some problems which have been caused by imperialism. They must be solved, if the world must experience universal peace and goodwill, and if the Armageddon of the races must be averted or postponed, indefinitely.

The use of force, whilst practicable temporarily, will not settle these issues. Sympathetic attitude will not alleviate these conditions. There seems to the Renascent African to be one solution, and it is not palliative at that: the recognition by imperialist States:

That no races on the face of the earth are either inferior or backward to the other.

That the so-called backward races have as much right to aim towards the enioyment of life, liberty and the pursuit of happiness, just as the so-called advanced races.

That the so-called backward races also have a civilizing mission which must be performed even if it takes a century or a millennium to do so.

That the so-called backward races also have a place in the sun.

In other words, man's inhumanity to man must be replaced by the philosophy and practice of man's humanity to man.

Unless the Natives are allowed to participate in the governance of their own lands, on a sound basis of democracy, that is, the application of the doctrine of natural, civil, political, social, and economic rights and equalities, in the administration of their country, by a system which will not only educate them to make use of the ballot, but will also educate them to make it possible for them to *participate* in the higher political offices which are now restricted to Caucasoid foreigners, the future is not assuring.

(e) *Blessed are the Strong*

Writing on such a subject as imperialism, it is not academic to define it at the outset, in view of its nature. However, since the causes, ethics and problems of imperialism have been considered, it is safe to attempt a definition.

Imperialism may be defined as the imposition of the will of one political organization, which is backed by superior armaments, upon the will of another political organization or organizations, whose physical force is incapable of resisting the will of the State which is bent on a civilizing mission. This is a general definition, and some of the factors hitherto discussed come under its various ramifications.

In order to be rational in my approach I have withheld stating my opinion until towards the end of this topic. Had I presented my opinion concurrently, my conclusions might be lacking in scientific objectivity; and this is typical of the Old Africa, and it accounts for the reason why Governments and other responsible agencies have discounted African opinion. In the past, Africans have been too emotional and less rational in analysing any subject of vital importance to them and to their rulers.

Towards the end of the preceding contribution, I ventured an opinion on how the problems raised by imperialism could be solved. That was in order, for any problem anticipates solution. Now, I wish to present some of the pertinent results of imperialism and also to suggest how imperialism should be regarded by intelligent Africans for the mutual benefit of the Imperialist States and the exploited Natives.

One of the results of imperialism is the social factor. Association begets accommodation, assimilation and amalgamation. By accommodating the people from imperialist States, there is gradual assimilation, and possible amalgamation, of cultural patterns. It works both ways.

In this process, the so-called backward races may be imitative or emulative. If the former is the case, the crystallization of an inferiority complex is certain because there is a process of Europeanization and de-Africanization. In case of the Europeanized Native, he or she has contempt for the Native culture-complex, and the resultant experience is a disintegration of Native social institutions.

On the other hand, the process may be emulative. In this case, what seems to be the best of the imperialist's culture-complex is assimilated and, with the amalgam, there is an adaptive process which makes the Native to use his reasoning faculty to effect.

When the Native questions the inconsistency of the imperialist State, or challenges the dogma of racial superiority, or criticises any religious organization from abroad, or refuses to agree in principle or in practice with any policy of the imperialist State, it is an indication that the emulative processes are at work.

It must be admitted that religious and educational organizations have been responsible for the crystallization of the emulative and imitative complexes. With the education and conversion of Natives, there have been detribalization, diffusion of cultures, depopulation of the rural areas, thirst for learning, cultivation of the ethics of the West, the desire for political autonomy, intensification of the various aspects of social pathology (viz., crime, poverty, prostitution, liquor traffic), unemployment, etc.

Supplementing these may be mentioned the social amenities which came as a result of imperialism : hospitals, postal services, good roads, paper and metal currencies, coinage, the Press, the Radio, railways, cars, bicycles, manufactured clothes, European drapery, shoes, the Church, schools, ethnocentrism, nationalism, and all other by-products of " civilization " which have enabled the " backward " peoples to become mentally emergent and to look forward to a better day.

Historically speaking, imperialism is inevitable, Hobbes might be right when he postulated his *homo homini lupus* philosophy, for self-preservation is the first law of nature. Since imperialism is a *sine qua non* in the evolution of organisms, the main problem of Africans is to adjust themselves to it, for what cannot be helped cannot be helped, especially if it be an obeisance to the law of nature.

What is needed to-day to strengthen the constructive phases of imperialism is the unequivocal acceptance of the postulate of the equality of the races. Inability to organize a stable civilization does not necessarily imply inherent racial inferiority or lack of political capacity.

It is desirable, from the standpoint of universal order, for the stronger races to rule the weaker races (*it is inevitable and cannot be helped ; and since this is the predicament of the weaker races, they must cultivate tolerant skepticism to accept their fate, if even it may be temporary*) provided that the rulers will act merely as guides and guardians, on the dual mandate principle—exploitation for development, trusteeship and tutelage—and provided that the ruling Power is willing to surrender its suzerainty if and when the ward is convinced that he is fledged for political independence.

In this wise, both the Government and the Governed will have a sacred obligation which is reciprocal. And since the obligation assumes the nature of a *social contract* (impliedly speaking), there should be no postponement of the opportunity of the ward to profit by his tutelage—by the Government refusing to respect the opinion of the Governed, and by the Government refusing, consciously or unconsciously, to admit the Governed on a plane of equality in the governance of the country inhabited by the ward.

I proclaim without fear of criticism that, no nation can claim to be a model of civilization, even though it is conceded that Anglo-Saxon civilization is probably productive of a special degree of virility. A stage has been reached in the societal evolution of mankind, where the world must not view with alarm, fear or suspicion, the progress of the Negroid or other races. What the world needs to-day in contemporary political thought is the cultivation not only of " the international mind " but of *the inter-racial mind*, which knows no distinction in the racial classification of man, but regards man for what he produces towards the welfare of the world.

The plea that one country is unfit to wield the sacred sceptre of directing its own destiny is nothing but propaganda directed against the weak, to strengthen the strong, and to weaken the weak.

Society is not static. It is a dynamic stream which flows with each generation under the sun. With these changing conditions, man must liberate his outlook on the destiny of his fellow man ; and once man is able to remove the shackles of ignorance and prejudices from his vista, he will be able to see some good in the make-up of other races of the human family.

Not until then shall it be realized that imperialism, essentially based as it is on the ethics of force and duplicity, is like a boomerang, which is comparable to a two-edged sword, which ultimately destroys him who wields it.

This is how Renascent Africans should view this magic word, IMPERIALISM.

10. *OUR TRUSTEES*

(a) *A Wrong Perspective*

Sir Samuel Hoare distinguished himself as a great statesman in connection with the Indian crisis, and that is why he is regarded as a man of social vision, in some circles. In reality, he was not put to any acid test. All he did was to call a spade a spade.

In his official capacity, as Secretary of State for India, he correctly interpreted Indian opinion as definitely defiant. In other words, Indians were politically conscious.

It means that the flame of nationalism which was smouldered when Mahatma Gandhi was incarcerated still flickered in the darkness of the night.

When the India Bill was discussed in the House of Commons, he had the spiritual balance, not only to appreciate the point of view of Conservatives and die-hards like Winston Churchill and his ilk, but also to warn England that Burke might not be wrong after all when he asserted that great empires and little minds formed an unnatural combination.

Sir Samuel Hoare realized that the India of the days of Clive was a thing of the past. Education in British and foreign universities had made Indians to appreciate the essence of living and enjoying life more abundantly.

Despite attempts to misinterpret the India Bill, it is too evident that the goal of non-extremists, that is the non-Gandhi-ites, has been reached, *viz.* : autonomy within the British Empire, which is also an essence of Gandhi's *swaraj*-ism.

Applying the policy of India to West Africa may not be the prudent thing to do, but the Indians are related to Africans by blood, at least the Dravidians are, and they are also their companions in bearing " the white man's burden ".

Indians agitated for independence and secured some measure of it; this might not have been prolonged had not the personality of Sir John Simon stalked as chairman of the commission which bore his name. Moreover, the world has yet to appreciate the tact and statesmanship evinced by Lord Willingdon whilst in India. Lord Linlithgow may be better or worse.

Lately, Mr Malcolm MacDonald, B.A. (Oxon), thirty-five years old, then Secretary of State for the Colonies, made his maiden speech in Parliament. It took him fifty minutes to review the official reports contained in despatches forwarded by the various Governments of the Colonies. True to the ideal of economic imperialism, more emphasis was laid on what were squeezed out of the colonies in the nature of raw materials and mining products. The speech so assumed a Mercantilistic aspect at one time, that it was thought he was making a report of the economic conditions of the colonies.

Then he swerved and made remarks regarding education. As usual, Achimota and Yaba were lauded and the statements contained in the report of the D.M.S., which was passed to the Secretary of State, through the Governor, through the Colonial Secretary, formed the basis of the statement that the moral and material welfare of the people was improving. When he came to the political issues of the day, he admitted that some of the ordinances were made without tactful consideration of African psychology, particularly *Homo occidentalis africanus*.

He agreed that the Sedition Bill and the Asamangkese Bill created political misunderstandings and elicited adverse criticisms in the Gold Coast, but he was unable to answer his critics satisfactorily. All he was able to do was to assure the members of the House of Commons that although the Sedition Bill had been passed, yet the Criminal Code Amendment Ordinance of 1934, *alias* Sedition Ordinance, was not being enforced in the Gold Coast. He also admitted that no literature had been prohibited and that no prosecution had taken place.[1] When a member of Parliament asked him whether it was not ironical to have a law in the Statute book of the Gold Coast, without enforcing the same, this product of Oxford University was unequal to the task.

The Secretary of State for the Colonies and the British leaders of opinion should be in position to understand the temperament of the African from the tone of the West African Press, in particular. No longer are Africans prepared to be fed with milk when they know that they have arrived at the age of eating real stuff with vitamin content and enough calories to supply fuel to their bodies, politically speaking.

His hearers might have been motivated by other reasons

[1] Mr I. T. A. Wallace Johnson was fined the sum of £50 for publishing and possessing an article which was deemed seditious. See *The African Morning Post*, May 15, 1936, page 5, for this article. For the conviction of Mr Johnson, see *The African Morning Post*, October 14, 1936, *passim*.

to tantalize and criticize him. It was suggested that because the leadership of his father was " renounced " by his colleagues of the Labour Party, they were visiting his sins upon his son. Howbeit, the criticisms of the Right Honourables Mr Dingle M. Foot, Mr Kenneth W. M. Pickthorn, Sir Edward W. M. Grigg, Colonel J. C. Wedgwood, and *West Africa* indicate that the British people are beginning to realize that the New Africa is superseding the Old Africa, in that the African giant is waking up, alive to his mission and destiny.

If the handwriting on the wall were correctly interpreted, it seems as if the mission of the Aborigines' delegates should have been more successful and more fruitful than that of the Central National Committee. I say this because the C.N.C. delegation was not persistent enough to interest the British people in Gold Coast problems ; although it must be admitted frankly that the A.R.P.S. also failed in its mission.

In all probability, the mission of the Aborigines' and C.N.C.'s delegates may bring about the required commission of inquiry into certain political problems of the Gold Coast. Again, it may lead to disallowance on the part of the Crown of certain ordinances which have been forwarded to the Colonial Office, for His Majesty's assent.

No matter what happens now, the début of Mr Malcolm MacDonald is historic, in that it represents another stage in African political evolution. The trustees of the Africans seem more interested in them and are paying more attention to *African human beings* instead of devoting pages upon pages on African cocoa, palm oil, ground nuts, gold, diamond, sisal, hides, tin, as if material values count more than human values.

(b) *But They See Not*

The debate on the future of India in the House of Commons recalls to mind the existence of men in high positions who are morally bankrupt.

They exist like trees in walking form. To them, the wind

blows and whither it goeth, they care not. They have eyes but they see not. They have ears but they hear not. They have tongues, but they speak not in terms of harmony and co-operation, but in a vein which leads to the inevitable Armageddon.

Fortunately, there is a type of persons who can read the handwriting on the wall. They have eyes, and they see. They have ears, and they hear. They have tongues, and they lash out with honest convictions on the necessity of conforming with the movements of a dynamic society.

The British Conservatives—in the majority—typify the first category. They represent the most important families in England. But most of them are several centuries behind time with reference to the *raison d'être* of Colonies. They live in a sort of delusion.

Their political philosophy is definitely autocratic. Their economic philosophy is still Mercantilistic. And their social philosophy is coterminous with the fallacies of Count Gobineau in his *Essai sur l'Inégalité des races humaines*.

On the other hand there are still in England statesmen of the type of Edmund Burke. They look upon the colonies as destined to be co-equals in order that Inter-Imperial Unity may not be a mere topic for Parliamentary wind-jammers and long-winded orators.

These men are in the minority. They understand history. They appreciate humanity and are out to co-operate on all fours. This type of leadership could improve inter-racial and international relationships if they had the opportunity. But they make up for what they lack quantitatively, qualitatively.

The problem of India is indicative of the moral bankruptcy of certain men who have the audacity to call themselves Statesmen. India has been a challenge to the political honesty of English statesmen ever since that mercantile clerk, who later became Lord Clive, accomplished his dreams at the expense of General Dupleix, the French Governor of Pondicherry and Surajah Dowlah, the Nabob of Moorshedabad.

It was first a problem of economic nationalism with all the trappings of Mercantilism. Then imperialism became the basis of relationship between Bombay and Lancashire and this assumed a different aspect, economically. It was mutual at first, but now it is necessary that politics should defend its handmaiden, foreign trade. Hence the only alternative is for sociological problems to confound not only the civilizers of India, but Indians themselves.

Then came young Gandhi. Fresh from one of the British universtities. He was vain, supercilious and haughty. But with his university education, he was just a black man, in British society. In India, he was just an ordinary lawyer. That is nothing exceptional.

He went to South Africa to practise law. Then he realized that straight or wavy hair, and even leptorrhine nose do not necessarily make an Indian (the ancients classified some of them as Ethiopians) a European. South Africa opened the eyes of the founder of *Swaraj*-ism. The rest of the story is well known.

After a series of troubles, Lord Willingdon was able to appreciate the fact that four hundred million peoples led by persons like Gandhi, Pandit Jawaharlal Nehru and Mrs Sarojini Naidu and Mr C. F. Andrews, an English man, could not be wrong. Certain recommendations were made. These crystallized in Sir Samuel Hoare's pledge of Dominion Status for India. Sir Samuel was then Secretary for India. He ought to know.

But there are die-hards and bone-heads, even in the British Parliament. Eyes have they, but they see not—the handwriting on the wall. And so India was not deemed qualified for "Dominion Status."

(c) *Official Obstinacy*

Some men are vicious animals, no matter what may be their race or nationality. Place them in position of responsibility and they will show their true colours.

Some men are intolerant animals, no matter what may be their race or nationality. Place them in position of responsibility and they will show their true colours.

Some men are victims of the inferiority complex. Place them in position of responsibility and let them realize that their authority is unquestionable, and they will run true to form.

If these few examples portray what this curious animal called man is capable of doing, then there is no necessity to question why the world is in a state of topsy-turvy to-day.

The world has been saddled with some responsible men and women who have a one-track mind. They do not reason enough to realize the consequences of their utterances. They prefer to hide their diabolism under the cloak of technicalities.

But this cannot be an artificial world. Technicalities may have a place in the scheme of things in this world, but it is the finer objectives of life that undulate the cross-currents of history.

If some statesmen of the world are not so technically minded as to become slaves to formalities, there is no doubt that what is so realistic to the average man-in-the-street, when grave issues of internationalism are discussed, is often so apparent to the so-called experts. Why? Because they follow the shadow, leaving the substance alone.

As in international relations, so too in the relationship of Governments and their subjects. As Dr. J. B. Danquah posited, hollow power is not the final mandate of authority on the part of any institution of Government. Rather, it is "the substantial power that goes with responsibility, *the power that counts public opinion as its ultimate justification and sanction.*"

In other words, this is a paraphrase of the doctrine of leading political philosophers of the world that *Governments derive their just powers from the will and consent of the Governed.*

In its essence, that form of Government which respects the will of the Governed is democratic because the *demos*, that is, the people, are the ultimate criteria of the justness or unjustness of the acts of Government.

Where for example, an official is sympathetic with one particular philosophy of Government the policy of that official will correspond with his philosophy. The test of the sympatheticism or apatheticism of that official will finally lie in the way the *demos* think of that particular official.

In other words, an official may become popular or unpopular. The *populus* prefer an official whose tendencies are not antagonistic to the basic principles which bind the people with the Government. And naturally, the *populus* cannot be expected and will not be forced to worship any official whose tendencies are inimical to the continued friendly relationship between the Governed and the Government.

If these humble observations are accepted as being of universal application, then they must be presumed to have a particular application as well.

Unless the people who aggregate in a State have crystallised self-consciousness, the idea of sovereignty of the people is far-fetched.

Where there are countries existing as appanages of States, it devolves on Governments, which are the agents of States, to approach the people in a way which is mutual, reciprocally speaking.

There is also a challenge to the people to so conduct themselves as to impress the officials, who are the servants of Governments, which are agents of States, that a responsibility attaches to both the Government and the Governed.

This responsibility, put in lucid terms, is that the existence of a State depends on the goodwill of the people for the State, just as the existence of the people depends on the goodwill of the State, for the people.

If, by overt acts, either party to this implied *contract sociale* between Government and Governed fails to live up to expectations, the relationship becomes strained and unless wise and humanitarian judgment is used, it may create an historic catastrophe.

But Governments are nothing but an agglomeration of *persons* who are given powers to act on behalf of several units of the agents of the State.

If that be the case, it means that the human elements must be reckoned with as a factor in the relationship with human beings who are Government officials and human beings who are the Governed.

If the facts of history are reliable for the purpose of this theme, I may say that most of the blunders committed in the history of the world have been due to an abuse of power on the part of those who wield authority.

There have been great Government officials whose activities have been tempered with the human touch in the solution of human problems, and there have been Government officials whose activities have become notorious in history. As with Governments, so with peoples. There are some peoples who cannot and will not listen to reason. And the ultimate result is continual clashes between Government and the Governed. But the Government's responsibilities are so great that intolerance, vindictiveness, and official dogmatism must always yield to tolerance, forgiveness, and urbanity.

In looking through the history of Africa, particularly Colonial Africa, there is no doubt that some of the facts stated above may apply in part.

There are some officials whose names are engraved favourably upon the minds of the people of Africa, as humanitarian officials whose affection for their subjects have made them immortal. And there are some officials whose names are for ever anathematized so far as the people are concerned, and whose activities represent a sort of blot on the genuine and sincere attempts at co-operation between Government and the Governed.

Why is it that Gold Coast brags of Sir Gordon Guggisberg? It is because this administrator, during his régime, attempted in his humble way to solve human problems in the only feasible way—*the human way*. Why are some officials considered sacred and reverent in the history of colonial administration in Africa? It is because the officials in question realized that they had power but were conscientious of the fact that it was tyrannous to use their power as giants, because authority intoxicates a certain type of officials who, being human, are prone to become Neronic and Nebuchadrezzaic in the prosecution of their duties.

By all means let Governments exist. Let the people also co-operate with their Governments. But let those who wield the sceptre of authority forget their human failings and shortcomings in the prosecution of their duties, lest they destroy the foundation which must continue to support the superstructure which made it possible for them to labour for, and with, the people.

Officials who fail to adapt themselves to the solution of human problems in a human way are usually vindictive by nature. They become slaves of certain complexes which are acquired and not necessarily inborn. If they are x-rayed biographically, it would be found that at some stages of their lives they had cultivated certain habits and complexes which were often difficult to break.

Such ilk were the officials whom Edmund Burke faced during the American revolutionary days. Such type did William Wilberforce and other English humanitarians face in the attempt to abolish the traffic in human beings.

But they are usually like comets which flit in the firmament and vanish into the obscurity of history, unless their notoriety has made them to become immortal like Nero and Nebuchadrezzar.

Vindictiveness is not an asset but a liability in the governance of human beings. It typifies man as the embodiment of all that is haughty, vicious, revengeful, intolerant, and inhuman. These traits have been responsible for the fall of empires in the past, and there is nothing to prevent them from becoming responsible for the fall of empires in the future.

II. *ROME BURNS*

(a) *And Nero Fiddles*

In romantic literature, Claudius Caesar Nero is portrayed as a carefree ruler who delighted himself at the misfortunes of others. Whilst Rome burned, Emperor Nero asked that fiddle be played in order to amuse him.

Whilst Christians were sent to the lions he was engaged in wise-cracking with his numerous concubines.

Whilst the gladiators were battling, he laughed and quaffed, and as soon as a gladiator fell, he was the first to put his thumbs down.

And so reigned good old Nero, believing himself to be the greatest figure in history, believing Rome to be the mightiest empire on earth, believing the Romans to be the elect of God.

But lo, with all the grandeur that was the City of the Seven Hills, it is to-day the refuge of carrions and fossils.

Rome of the Caesars has passed into oblivion and neither all the Mazzinis nor all the Garibaldis nor all the Cavours nor all the Mussolinis will resurrect the ancient glories of the Caesars.

Rome had its day. It fiddled. Now it is a page of history; not even a chapter.

The visit of Lord Plymouth to British West Africa may be likened unto the reign of Nero.

True, the Plebeians of Rome were oppressed by the Patricians and were ignored; laws were made to stratify them into the scums of society, yet they were able to rise beyond the acceptance of the fiat of the Grachii, or of Sulla or of the Caesars.

In Africa, the Natives are hospitable, friendly, and impressionistic. They have welcomed the descendants of the Romans, even at the point of the sword.

In their munificence they have accorded to them a place to stay, something to eat, and the wherewithal to keep body and soul together from the ravages of the elements.

Instead of giving Africans the best that could be had, laws were made, shibboleths were rationalized, and their social fabric was distorted so that some of their sons and daughters have lost faith in the capabilities of the black man.

Instead of harmony, Africans have disharmony.

Instead of social unity they have selfish individualism.

Instead of a patriotism which knows no clan or tribe, they have a parochialism which has stratified them into water-tight compartments.

Some of them have carried this tribal prejudice to its logical conclusion that they are like the proverbial ostrich in the desert. Africans bury their heads in the sands, believing in their safety and perfection. They cut their noses to spite their faces.

How long shall Africans be overlooked by Nero? How long shall Rome continue to divide and rule and command

and govern and control and direct and impress upon them its omnipotence?

Lord Plymouth was not in West Africa on business. He said that he made the trip with Mr G. H. Creasy in order to visit the dependencies and see for himself the progress made since the days of Lugard.

Like Nero, the Colonial office prefers to play the fiddle whilst Rome burns.

The delegations sent from the Gold Coast to the Colonial Office have been given the cold shoulders.

There is a spark of fire smouldering in British West Africa regarding taxation without representation.

There is the mumbling of a river which may eventually transform itself into a flood.

If the Natives could not be amply represented in the Legislative Council on a par with the official majority; if they could not have the final word on the way their revenues should be disbursed; if when they pursue the constitutional way and appeal to the King to grant them redress, and the Colonial Office refuses to recommend or countenance their petition, then a definite challenge is being flung at their faces.

Yet Lord Plymouth was out here on a flying visit.

The fate of millions of people is at stake. Nero must not fiddle whilst Rome burns.

I appeal to the omnipotent Colonial Office to be more sympathetic in dealing with Colonial peoples.

British West Africans are loyal. They cherish British traditions of justice, of fair play, and of equity.

Their unbounded loyalty to the British Empire has been proved often.

While Canada, New Zealand, Newfoundland, Australia, Union of South Africa, the Irish Free State, and India are considered as having reached a status where democracy has passed an experimental stage, West Africans should not be ignored.

They too are human. They have feelings.

They understand what prompted the drafting of the Magna Charta, the Petition of Rights, the Bill of Rights and the other great documents of British constitutional history.

Behold West Africa! There are all sorts of peoples—the Uncle Toms and the stalwarts.

But remember that this historic visit will be a failure unless the Colonial Office could perceive the yearnings which throb in the breast of the average British African for a greater share in the governance of his country.

It is still a truism that *taxation without representation is tyranny, even in Africa.*

But then Rome burned! And Nero fiddled!

(b) *Colonial Status*

It is true that there is no necessity for Africans who are resident in sections of the British West African colonies to be unduly proud of their present constitutional status within the British Empire.

I say this because one of the most vital reasons why citizens are patriotic depends on the rights which are conferred on them by the Government to which they owe their allegiance.

Since it is accepted by all authorities of constitutional law that allegiance and protection are reciprocal, it implies that acceptance of the nationality of a foreign State presumes the conferment of political benefits of a progressive nature.

In the British West African colonies this is not the case. Through mis-education, some of the leaders of the Old Africa were not intelligent enough to appreciate what legal relationship between the mother country and the colonial possessions overseas connoted.

Some of them passed through the temples of London devoted to the exclusive studies of legal institutions, but they came out like parrots, reciting what they neither understood nor were they in a position to appreciate, excepting as an avenue for livelihood.

Some of them accumulated wealth and were able to foist their flag of leadership on the innocent African public. Being products of mis-education most of them became victims of alphabetimania.

Some African leaders thus followed the veneer of British aristocracy without understanding the basis of British form of diplomacy, especially in dealing with so-called subject peoples.

For an A.B.C., a legally trained mind bows and cowers before the diplomatically trained mind, no matter what may be the social and/or educational background of the latter.

Is there reason to doubt the ease and facility with which unknown men and women came out to "the white man's grave" and within a quarter of a century transformed the same into a "white man's paradise," even though the paradise is not permanent for their residents, yet it is permanent for their posterity?

I repeat again that the conditions which exist to-day in the four colonial possessions of British West Africa are due to mis-education and particularly to the lack of mental and moral resistance on the part of some African leaders.

Participation in politics is not the exclusive right of any demi-god, black or white. Since polititcs is defined to embrace the political relationship of individuals within a State or a quasi-State, it is the prerogative of all, whether they are connected with the First, Second, Third, Fourth or Fifth Estates of the Realm. That is one reason why some soldiers are classified as politicians and some physicians as well, etc.

Realizing the maelstrom which mis-education has dragged Africans into, I believe that the time has come for a reconstruction of the Beatitudes.

No longer must Africans be taught to believe that the meek are blessed to inherit the earth when it is too plain that the strong in mind and body are inheriting every inch of the earth's surface.

There is no need for Africans to exegete on this particular section or all of the Beatitudes, but the Renascent African must believe that for him to survive the struggle of existence he must now repeat with verve: "*Blessed are the mentally emancipated Africans, for they shall enjoy life more abundantly in Africa.*"

Despite the incongruencies of the African social order, those of them who brave castigations and meaningless flapdoodles which come from quarters whose mental virility is questionable, much more their moral and natural right to leadership, believe that the crux of their problem with their rulers, on the one hand, and with their mis-leaders, on the other, is a dispassionate, studied, efficacious, and scientific approach.

What is the constitutional status of Africans? Must they accept eternally the doctrine of the official majority? Must they allow Windbags, Nincompoops and Dead-Heads to continue the mis-leadership?

No, Africans must not. If they do so, then it is indicative of a lack of social capacity.

What then is their constitutional status? If they must reject the crumbs which the Government, in its beneficence, grants to them, if they see that most of their leaders are grossly inefficient, if they question the ethicality and the illegality of the present Constitution, what is the basis of it all?

To call Africans a Colonial people is one thing, and to treat them as Colonial peoples who reside in a Protectorate is another. A Colony is the property of a State. A Protectorate is not. That is why residents of a Colony are British subjects and residents of a Protectorate are British Protected Persons.

The Colony may not be a full-fledged State. The Protectorate may.

Africans as a whole are not disinherited political sons and daughters, which is the lot of peoples who live in Colonies. They have their rights as free men and women, and since they, as a whole, were neither conquered nor did they cede their territory to European Colonizers, I see no reason why their leaders have allowed these inequalities to remain so long.

Henceforth, the immediate problem of the Renascent African is fighting not so much for the right to enjoy a piece of measly bone, as it is for the right to throw to the Natives a piece of measly bone whilst they are entitled to the flesh as well.

The leaders who had gone before did what they could in the light of their knowledge. Unfortunately, most of them were alphabetimaniacs.

The leaders of to-day and to-morrow must know the legal basis of the constitutional status of their country, otherwise the people are in for another era of prosperity for Uncle Toms, Block Heads and Ciphers.

(c) *Whither British Africa?*

Certain writers describe Africa's contour to be likened to a ham-bone for the carving knife of Europe. Others depict it as a sleeping giant who will awake in the immediate or remote future. Dr. James Emmanuel Kwegyir Aggrey, M.A., D.D., described Africa with the continental island of Madagascar as a question mark. I agree in all these depictions but will supplement the same by remarking that Africa is a challenge to the twentieth century European civilization.

The contact of Africans with the British Empire dates back to the days of Mercantilism. The natural products of Africa were required in order to supply the demands of manufacturers precipitated by the Industrial Revolution. Moreover, the realities of international politics made it necessary for strategic locations to fall into the hands of certain powers.

The Conference of Berlin enabled Europe to partition Africa. Up to the World War, Great Britain together with France, Belgium, Portugal, Italy and Spain had succeeded in building up African Colonial Empires.

Despite problems of social, political, and economic import, Africans, especially those who are resident in West Africa, ought to be frank in the acceptance of this fiat: that under the British Empire their progress has been more rapid, on a comparative basis, than other sections of this continent.

The Briton is a born adventurer and his colonizing ability cannot be discountenanced. The nerve of a David Livingstone, the verve of a Mary Kingsley, the impetuosity of a Sir Harry Johnston, the diplomacy of a Lord Lugard, the philanthropy of a Sir Gordon Guggisberg, the imperiousness of a Sir Shenton Thomas, the humanity of a Sir Arthur Webber, and the reactionarism of a Winston Churchill—these lend romance towards the crystallization of the bonds of inter-imperial unity, no matter how diametrically opposite may be the policies of some of the personalities mentioned above.

In this mélange of conflicting policies, there is the emergence of a renaissance in Colonial Administration. Whereas in the Victorian and Edwardian days, the theme of imperialism was sung from the house-tops of the British Isles, and young Britishers were urged to think and dream of a corner somewhere in the world that was forever England's, and knighthoods were earned through the might and mane of the sword, the accession of His Majesty, King George V to the throne of England signified the dawn of a new era in colonial imperialism.

In the last twenty-five years, the relationship between Africa and the British Empire has been predicated by three stages:

Firstly, the era which disregarded the natural rights of the African on the ground that "Might" was "Right." This led to serious conflicts in which blood was shed and lives were sacrificed on both sides. The Fashoda Crisis might have been averted.

The second stage represented a period when Rudyard Kipling challenged his compatriots to "Take up the White Man's Burden." This was an era of extreme paternalism which found the African, at most, a sort of Lazarus, so far as administrative problems were concerned. The assassination of Sir Lee Stack was not inevitable.

Lastly, the era which followed immediately after the organization of the League of Nations in which the principle of trusteeship was enunciated.

The above explains in a nutshell the assumption and the application of the principle of trusteeship as enunciated in Article XXII of the League of Nations, with reference to localities inhabited by "peoples not yet able to stand by themselves under the strenuous conditions of the modern world". The reign of King George V is, therefore, a boon to Africans, in that the enunciation of the doctrine of trusteeship enabled them to have confidence in the integrity of the Europeans of British nationality within their borders.

The relationship existing between Africa and the British Empire is still evolutional. Just as in the last few months, problems of a political nature have arisen, so too do these challenge the Colonial Office and those in charge of Colonial Administration to experience a rebirth in so far as the political status of the African is concerned. The next logical step in this ladder of colonial evolution is the right of self-determination, among the African indigenes, within the Empire.

May it be possible for King George VI, or his heir or successor, to immortalize his reign in the political history of the African so that a concretization of this may not be remote.

12. *THE ACID TEST*

(a) *The Way of all Flesh*

Youth is at times puzzled at the way and manner mankind is inconsistent. One day, an individual stands by this conviction. And another, he shifts. These changes are said to be the avenue to success, by some, but in reality they represent lack of quality for leadership.

Men in the public's eye are often forced to take certain sides, not because it is their conviction, but because something which is a sort of sword of Damocles hangs over their heads. In their cowardice they yield.

To be a leader, there are circumstances which justify a retreat, but in the final analysis retreat must not mean surrender. The former is a means to an end. But the latter spells disaster if it be an end. It usually is.

Youth must not be disillusioned by the attitude of certain individuals who are as inconsistent as the proverbial rolling stone. It is due to the leadership material.

If the society worships the trappings and paraphernalia of ephemeral oddities, the leadership of that society would cower and seek to perpetuate that social ideology. Any attempt to change this evidence of mis-leadership receives severe joltings from within and from without. But the attempt will triumph eventually.

The continent of Africa is undergoing a transition. Some of those who are in power are remnants of the Old School. Others have caught the vision, but have not the sustaining influence to scrap the old order of things.

In other words, the spirit has experienced regeneration. but the flesh is still dormant and is in the process of moulding, Once the two processes are able to co-ordinate, the finished product is bound to reflect creditably on African society.

It is too disheartening for a young man to find himself in the presence of a highly touted humanitarian—yea a philanthropist; and, despite all the high hopes one may cherish and entertain, one faces the dilemma of this "great" man actually seducing the innocent young man to the path of crookedness and ineptitude.

How many times have Africans experienced a straightforward young person becoming a shell of his old self, simply because in his credulity he took too many things for granted. I submit that gold cannot be proved by the lustre of metals else brass would claim to be gold.

At times there are men of either race—officials or otherwise—posing as great humanitarians, whilst in reality their humanitarianism has a certain limit. One becomes a humanitarian so long as the *status quo* keeps him on the saddle; and as long as his underlings and immediate friends are paraded as saints and perfect beings.

But let there be a test. Let the Renascent African have the manhood to expose the quackery. All avenues of injustice and oppression are let loose, either to cramp the individual or to so disfigure his life's work that it would be a lesson to others.

So is this life of ours. Many a swallow might have made a better peacock. And many a fly might have made a better butterfly. But swallows are swallows and peacocks are peacocks, because they are what they are. Flies are flies and butterflies are butterflies, because they are what they are.

Renascent African! in whatever position you find yourself in life, aim to better your condition. But be yourself, young man or young woman. Once you attempt to be what you are not, you are going the way of all flesh. And you cannot profitably claim to be an evangelist of social justice no matter what may be your professional reputation and social standing in your community.

There are some Europeans who have been with Africans for decades. Their work enables them to come in contact with the

African community. They pose as friends of the African. They gain his confidence, and then they realize that they are firmly entrenched in his society.

As children, Africans grow up with the idea that they are saints and friends of the black man. But let a little shuffling of the cards take place. Let one of the friends of these so-called Negrophiles come under the lash and venom of the sword of truth; the situation changes.

The smile of yesterday becomes the anger of to-day; the preachments of love and social justice become an avenue to a doctrination of the idea of expediency. Falsehood is refurbished in all the trappings of convention so as to lend it a semblance of truth; then the machinery of the law is set in motion, and the true nature of the alleged Negrophile is vindicated.

The relationship of the races in Africa is a glorious one. Provided each race understands the ultimate destiny of Africa from its peculiar ideology, there is no need to be blindfolded. One destiny is before Europe and Africa. It is either Freedom or Servitude.

Europe leads Africa to Freedom, ostensibly, but Renascent Africans would rather be free mentally and be enslaved physically, than be freed physically and be enslaved mentally. Their present-day relationship with Europe does not indicate a rapid advance towards mental emancipation. That is the acid test of leadership in Africa to-day.

Despite oral protestations and official affiliation with all which appertains to the welfare of the community, I believe with the philosopher who said that, "It takes courage to speak the truth, when by a little prevarication you can get some advantage; it takes courage to be what you are and not pretend to be what you are not; it takes courage to refuse to do a thing which you think is wrong, because it is customary and done in trade; it takes courage to stand firmly erect while others are bowing and fawning for praise and power; it takes courage to do your duty in silence, obscurity, and poverty, while others about you prosper through neglecting or violating sacred obligations."

And it takes courage to battle wrong, and to retreat if need be, provided you are a seasoned warrior and dare not surrender, even though the odds may be against you.

Yes, the leadership of Renascent Africa must be tested by the above criteria. And without becoming outlandish, I dare say that very few of the leaders can stand the test. It is not wholly their fault. The spirit is willing, but the flesh is weak. That is the way of all flesh.

Chapter IV

AFRICA IN EBULLITION

13. *QUO VADIS?*

It is said that self-preservation is the first law of nature. This implies the fact that the individual loves himself so much that he will do all in his power to prevent any harm from being done either to himself or to his immediate relative or to his kind.

Throughout life, the objective of the individual is towards security. Although his ideas and practices may be motivated by the forces of economics, yet in the final analysis there is one philosophical basis—preservation of the group.

Once an individual is sure of his position in life, once he knows that his employment is secure, he fears nothing. He is not apprehensive of the unforeseen. There is social security. Therefore, there is satisfaction.

On the other hand, once the individual is made to realize the fact that he is just a cog in the machine, and that his position therein is temporary, he cannot be contented. The reason is because he is not reasonably sure of his security.

The chickens may wander far and near. So long as the hawk does not hover around, and so long as the sun smiles to make the atmosphere balmy, they will roam from place to place. But let the hawk stalk around them; let it rain, and you see these chickens fleeing to the hen's protective wings. It is because they know that once therein, they will be secure, if not permanently, then until the crisis passes. As with chickens, so with men and women.

Industrial psychologists have proved, from statistical observations, that individuals who prove efficient in their jobs are those who are almost dead sure and certain of their positions.

But as for those who comprise "the floating element" in industry, largely unskilled labourers, they are most inefficient because, not only are they underpaid, but they also are not sure of their positions. There is no security and consequently, there is no hope for continual employment.

When there is no security, we begin to worry. Instead of cultivating a spirit which should defy all the goblins of fear and apprehension, we become victims of psychopathic mania.

Self-preservation is, therefore, an important factor in our lives. It influences our mode of living, in so far as our social, political, economic, and even religious institutions are concerned.

An individual may be better qualified than another, but because his qualification may eclipse that of the other fellow, the instinct of self-preservation finds realization. Unfortunately, it is abused to such an extent that it becomes envy and jealousy instead of self-preservation.

An individual may hold a position which places him ahead of other individuals. There had been cases where Sierra Leonians, Gold Coastians and Nigerians were transferred to high positions in either of the above colonies. It becomes an economic and a social problem because of this instinct of self-preservation.

In economics, competition is a refining process, but when an individual who is alien to the community leaves his native haven for a " foreign strand ", he finds himself faced by unwarranted hostility which only time can mellow.

This hostility may not be necessarily directed against the individual because of his racial or linguistic or even cultural background, but because his presence intensifies the economic situation. The son or daughter of the soil looks on that individual's employer as " robbing Ladipo to pay Kweku ". As in Sierra Leone, so in the Gambia, Liberia, Gold Coast, and Nigeria.

It is time that Africans put away childish things. They have arrived. They are recasting their old fabric. They are building a new social order. Inasmuch as there are Natives of the Gold Coast intensifying the social and economic situation in other parts of the world, Gold Coastians must be tolerant to the denizens of other sections of Africa who are on the Gold Coast to intensify their own situation.

Civilization has made the nations of the world inter-dependent.

There is no section in West Africa where the Gold Coastian is not found earning his livelihood, and helping to ameliorate the conditions of the place of his temporary or permanent residence.

Go to Liberia, if you choose to. You will find Gold Coastians there. Go to Gambia, to Sierra Leone, to Nigeria, to Fernando Po, and other sections of Africa, even England for that matter. You will see ambitious sons and daughters of the Gold Coast developing themselves for the regeneration of Africa.

The same is applicable to the peoples who come from Liberia, Sierra Leone and Nigeria. We find them in different parts of the Gold Coast. Go to the Northern Territories, to Ashanti, to the Western Province, to the Central Province, and to the Eastern Province, and you will find them there.

Since it is exemplary of the instinct of self-preservation, Gold Coastians do not naturally cherish the intensification of their socio-economic problems by these foreigners. So too do the Natives of Gambia, Sierra Leone, Liberia and Nigeria. *But this way of thinking is suicidal and must not be allowed to flourish, else we are postponing the crystallization of the New Africa.*

Our philosophy of self-preservation must be universal enough to include Africans, no matter from what part of Africa they come. Once we are free to regard ourselves as one, our instinct of self-preservation would be concerted and could be directed more effectively against those who are non-Africans and who direct their own concerted efforts against us.

Whither are we bound? Towards a homogeneous and a united Africa for the regeneration of our race and individual countries? Or towards an heterogeneous and disunited Africa? Whatever we sow, we shall reap.

United, we stand upon the foundations of a New Africa, unshaken by the forces of envy, jealousy, greed, and evil. Divided, we fall and reel, from pillar to post, *exterminated as a race*, unwept, unhonoured, and unsung.

14. *BORN TO BE*

There is an eternal question mark which baffles the average individual of all ages. We are born into the world, not knowing whither we are bound or where we came from.

It seems as if our antecedents are unknown and our future is as mysterious to us as some of the phenomenal activities in our lives.

These set us thinking. We wonder whether there is a design in our existence. We question the rightfulness and wrongfulness of certain incidents.

At times we look into the spiritual nature of our lives to discover the solution to the eternal question mark. But the answer is sealed in the unknowable.

Sometimes we wonder whether there is any motive behind the creation or evolution of man. Then we think of the multifarious creatures, animate and inanimate, which grace the surface of the earth, the aquatic regions of the earth, and even the aerial hemisphere.

Certainly, there is a final cause behind these evidences of omniscience, omnipotence, and omnipresence. The ontological argument is enough to offset any bias in this respect. *Life is therefore a mission. A mission of happiness while it lasts.*

Mankind in various parts of the world has struggled to make life worth while. There have been attempts to render mutual aid so that life might be worth living. Yet, the world is still a place of make-believe and the Millennium is as far away as the earliest geological epochs.

Considering these evidences of intellectual bewilderment, the English novelist, Hugh Walpole, said that " Life is a comedy to him who thinks, and a tragedy to him who feels."

Thinking and feeling are amongst our choicest gifts. We think because we exist in a world punctuated by question marks. We feel because we live in a world of realities and unrealities. What a heritage to mortal man!

Life becomes a tragedy when our thinking carries us beyond the mere veneer of emotionalism, and when we balance our psycho-social with our bio-social selves we see the comedy of it all.

We have a rendezvous with life because it is our task to make a joy out of living. One of the greatest social philosophers of all times realized this rendezvous with life, and he postulated that he came into this world of question marks in order that his fellow-man might have life *more abundantly*.[1]

[1] St. John x. 10.

Our predecessors in the history of the world have attempted to fathom this Christological philosophy of life. How can we have life more abundantly? Or in non-theological language, how can mankind obtain a maximum of happiness from life?

Socially, religiously, economically, and politically, the great men who have left their footprints on the sands of time, have contributed their share towards the solution of the eternal question mark, yet we still have a rendezvous with life. It is a challenge to us.

Socially, there were times when one group believed that it was destined to impose its will on another. The Patricians of Rome stand out in bold relief. But the Plebeians would have none of this. And lo! the grandeur that was Rome is no more.

The nobility thought the serfs and villeins had no rights which were worthy of respect. But these serfs and villeins had a rendezvous with life. They were destined to enjoy a maximum happiness from life. And lo! the British aristocracy of yesteryears with all its trappings and paraphernalia has evanesced.

Nowhere in the world to-day can we find the existence of an idea of social superiority, unless the peoples, because of their mental retardation, have failed to realize that they have a rendezvous with life.

Religiously, it took man several centuries before he disentangled himself from superstition, ecclesiastical or secular. A realization of religious toleration which would be an avenue to enjoyment of life more abundantly led to the founding of the Protestant Faith, and the ecclesiastical organizations of indigenous African origin.

The individuals who distinguished themselves from the rank and file, reached a stage where they realized that they had a rendezvous with life; and behold the dawn of religious toleration, even in the vastness of Africa!

Economically, mankind groped from darkness to darkness. Barter, Mercantilism, individualism, free trade, bi-metallism, capitalism: these are some evidences of the economic shackles which prevent us from enjoying life more abundantly.

But just as social proscriptions and discriminations became mere historical incidents, so too did the workers of the world propound a new economic philosophy that the labourer was not only worthy of his hire, but must also share in the profits of his labour.

Thus the names of Adam Smith, John Stuart Mill, Karl Marx, Friedrich Engels, and countless others have been indelibly impressed upon the annals of economics, which neither the forces of time nor those of space can obliterate.

Politically, mankind ushered in an era of democracy whereby the people assumed the prerogative to make laws and to appoint their proxies for the administration thereof. They realized that they had a rendezvous with life, and that is why, to-day, they are free from being imposed upon by aliens within their gates.

Now, heroes and heroines of Renascent Africa: Have you reached a stage in your development to realize that you have a rendezvous with life, socially, religiously, economically, and politically? If not, it is now or never.

We have a rendezvous with life. The final cause which is responsible for our fleeting flame made us the equal of the other branches of the human family. If the others have realized their rendezvous with life, why not the Renascent African?

When we were born, we wept, whilst others rejoiced. And when we die, others weep, whilst we seemingly rejoice in peace perfect peace. Is your rendezvous with life to be likened to your birth or to your death? The solution is within you, Renascent African. You have the power, because you have a rendezvous with life.

> "*The morn that ushered thee to life, my child,*
> *Saw thee in tears whilst all around thee smiled.*
> *When summoned hence to thy eternal sleep,*
> *O mayst thou smile whilst all around thee weep.*"
> (An Arabic Poem)

Recent events in Colonial Administration indicate where the wind blows. These show that once a man is on the saddle it is difficult to unseat him. The love of power is inherent in man. That is why the rich wants to be richer and the man in authority continues to concentrate all efforts toward making himself more secure.

The panacea for all the ills in the world to-day may be summed up in this phrase: *the human way*. All problems that confront us to-day are human problems. They can be solved in one way: *the human way*.

The acquisitive instincts of man make him to keep on possessing. No matter in what sphere of life man directs his attention, in the final analysis, the acquisitive instincts of man make him to be in a state of warfare with his kind. Competition, although it brings out the finer elements, yet is exemplary of what the acquisitive instincts can do to destroy what others are doing.

Thomas Hobbes thus thought that man was a wolf to man. In the nature of the trend toward acquisitions, man becomes a wolf. Under the plea of self-preservation, he begins to fight with the other fellow. He may be successful or he may fail.

In the case of the former, he justifies the same on the ground that life is a struggle, and only the fittest will survive. Thus if force or war is used to attain to this objective, militarism is glorified as a pruning hook.

In case of the latter, it is taken for granted that life is evolutionary, and all must be dynamic and not stagnant. Hence, even though evil means are used to attain to a goal, the end is justified.

This acquisitive instinct has been responsible for the revolutionary ideas of history. The man with the capital proceeds to amass more wealth. The man without capital proceeds to fight those in his status so as to earn a livelihood and also to encourage the acquisitive instincts, even though on a small scale.

Considering these facts, it was thought fit to postulate the theory of the economic interpretation of history. That is, that all the movements of history were directed by the economic urge, or in the psychological sense, the acquisitive instinct—the desire to eat, to wear clothes, and to have shelter.

In turn, these have created changes in our societal structure. It made some people to leave their original homes in the attempt to settle elsewhere so as to earn a livelihood in order to satisfy their acquisitive instincts.

However, not all the associations established thereby may be said to have been ethical. Again, in discussing ethics we have to be careful because norms and criteria are not universally standardized. But speaking in a broad sense, ethical considerations of right and wrong have not always motivated the relationship between the aborigines and individuals who are migratory in their attempts to satisfy the acquisitive instincts.

Colonies are exemplary of this type of relationship. The persons who settle in the colonies face a different set of problems. If they have stereotyped ideas, it would be impossible for them to adjust their mentality in order to clarify these human misunderstandings. In other words, they are not prepared to employ the best panacea: *the human way.*

That is why there have been problems and super-problems. Men refuse to be re-educated from their mis-education. They prefer to continue in the *status quo*, believing that temporary suzerainty is destined to be eternal.

The verdict of history gives a negative answer to such form of mental abnormality. People are not destined to be oppressed, suppressed, repressed, and impressed for ever. Not if they are born free and equal. Not if they believe in themselves and in their capacity to reclaim the foibles of the past.

Africa is undergoing a very crucial period in its annals. The cause of this may be laid squarely and fairly on the acquisitive instincts of man. The man who owns gold wants more gold. The man who owns cocoa wants more cocoa. The man who directs and governs and protects these resources wants to do so for ever.

The problems arising out of these contacts are faced in a way which justifies the *homo homini lupus* philosophy of Hobbes. To what purpose? Whither are we bound? Are we to remain in such a form of bondage for ever?

A recent delegation from a British West African colony to the Colonial Office was virtually led to believe that the Bible, even though it may be a history of the Jewish peoples, yet has a maxim worth recollecting: "To him that hath shall be given, and to him that hath not, even that which he hath shall be taken away from him."

Africans, besides Liberians and Egyptians, are political inferiors. They are paying taxes, direct and indirect. They are not represented, proportionately. They have no rights which European Parliaments can respect outside the veneer forms of protection accorded to all protégés.

There is such a thing as destiny. The races of the world are destined to realize their destiny. So too are the African races.

Search through the records of history, and you will find that the races which have dominated other races have been those which believed that they had a destiny.

In Africa, through centuries of oppression, the black races have been cowed to a point where they seem to have lost all sense of vision towards a destiny.

The world mocks at the African, because there is nothing to show that he is prepared to face even death in order that a principle which he believes to be coterminous with his destiny may be preserved.

The world leers at the African, because there is a tendency on the part of the African to shirk his responsibility when the stark realities of life face him.

Take the life of Mahatma Gandhi for example. Here is a young Indian who was educated in London University, preparatory for the legal profession.

Mr Gandhi is a high-caste Hindu. By birth and by education there was nothing to hinder him from continuing the heritage of his forefathers.

But it took oppression, repression, aggression, and depression of the spirit, soul and body, in the Union of South Africa, to make Gandhi realize that Indians have a destiny.

Gandhi never wavered. He returned to India and reinforced the Nationalist movement with a view to placing India in the sun.

He was paraded before his rulers on a charge that he was fomenting the *Swaraj* movement into an organization which would change the sovereignty of India, and he was sentenced to prison.

After serving for about two years, Gandhi was saved from becoming a martyr by being released from prison, due to ill-health. He conceived other means whereby the destiny of India might be hastened.

What Rev. C. F. Andrews called "the irresistible might of meekness" was postulated by Gandhi. This is the use of spiritual force against physical force.

It has been partly successful and partly unsuccessful. The successful phase of it brought on the head of Gandhi another term of imprisonment. His followers, Pandit Jawaharlal Nehru and Mrs Sarojini Naidu, shared with him sentences to prison, because of the ideal which they cherished most—the ideal of liberty.

Now, Africans are capable of achieving their place in the sun provided that they discard the spirit of individualism which has so far prevented social cohesion. It cannot be doubted that one reason why Africans seem destined to serve other races for ever is because they have no sense of oneness.

If in a continent like Africa, where there are about one hundred and fifty million souls, social unity is made difficult by linguistic and cultural differences, why cannot educated Africans bridge this gap by crystallizing a sense of oneness for the ultimate destiny of the country ?

Is it a fiction of history that Sierra Leone, Gambia, Liberia, Gold Coast, and Nigeria are far apart, linguistically, culturally, and nationalistically, due more to factors from within than from without ?

What has happened to the National Congress of British West Africa ? Did it perish with the late Hon. J. E. Casely Hayford ? Why is a sense of oneness which is responsible for the realization of our destiny so dormant ? Are we not able to rise beyond thinking in terms of self and pelf, and to think in terms of nationhood ? Why must it be shameful for an African to dream of a place in the sun, whilst it is not shameful for a European ?

I fail to appreciate the trend of thought among certain Africans who allow alien races to do their thinking for them. It is inevitable that contact with other races must aid Africans in their societal evolution, but they are not bound to be imitative. They can be emulative.

Have you ever noticed a group of Africans during any period of national calamity ? They sit down, groaning inwardly with pain, and by the looks on their faces, you can see that they are in trouble, for they seem helpless.

But it is a challenge to manhood for any group of men to become helpless in this world. Their destiny is within their power. Marcus Garvey, one of the most far-sighted persons of African descent to walk upon God's earth, chose as his motto : " One God, One Aim, One Destiny."

This motto is universal in its application. There is a fatherhood of God for mankind. The aim of mankind is towards the enjoyment of liberty to live and to pursue happiness. These two predicate the crystallization of man's destiny.

It is time for Africans to cease from laughing at the calamities of other Africans, no matter how divergent may be the views of those so ill-fated.

There is no need for Africans to victimize themselves in order to soothe their vanities. Once they allow these agents of dissension to become a part of their social philosophy, they are doomed to eternal servitude.

Renascent Africans, to you is given the power to crystallize your destiny. No matter how devious may be the path before you, no matter how trying may be the trials to which you must be exposed ere achieving the destiny of the great African races, you must be prepared for any fate.

Sighing with those in distress will not enhance the crystallization of this destiny. Smiling at the misfortunes of others will not. Regretting the circumstances which necessitate the act of yours which may dent the career of your fellow African, will not.

But when the African has learned to bear the burden which is universally the burden of the Negro race ; when the African realizes that there is a place in the sun for him or her to carve a niche ; when the African wakes up from his deep sleep and realizes that he is a giant with strength which has not been harnessed, his destiny is within realization.

May God grant the hastening of that day !

15. *WE MARCH*

Life seems to be a mission in which each individual is bound to play his or her part, however small, however great. In this performance, we either make history or we leave no footprints on the sands of time.

The mission of any individual is to make this life better for others. If by gift of the pen or of the tongue or of the brain or of brawn, or by a combination of any or all of the above, this can be achieved, well and good.

Life must flow on because none, whether high or low, can escape the inevitable doom of death, if and when any person is summoned "to join the inumerable caravan which moves to that mysterious realm, where each shall take his chamber in the silent halls of death".

The criterion by which we must judge the efficacy and sincerity of one's mission in this life is one's attitude towards union with "the innumerable caravan".

If one should render account of one's stewardship without a Socratic will, one must, of necessity, be likened to "the quarry-slave at night, scourged to his dungeon".

But if, on the other hand, one approaches one's doom "sustained and soothed by an unfaltering trust . . . like one who wraps the drapery of his (*sic*) couch about him, and lies down to pleasant dreams", the mission of life would have been satisfactorily discharged.

Renascent Africa is at the cross-roads. Old Africa is at the cross-roads. And the New Africa is on the threshold to usher forth the dawn of a new era.

There is no need for one to expect perfect peace and perfect contentment when the forces of Old Africa clash unfairly with the forces of the New Africa. There can be no "peace perfect peace" when Renascent Africans are disillusioned by the inability of those whom they look up to for example, and who fail them at the crucial test.

It took Socrates seventy years to complete his mission ere he marched to that uncharted region whence the traveller returns not.

It took Joshua, whom the Greeks called Jesus, thirty-three years to complete his mission and to move towards his Thanatopsian doom.

What was the crime of Socrates? What was the crime of Jesus? Perverting the youth. Perverting the nation.

These were the excuses used in order to vent the spleen of certain enemies of Socrates and of Jesus.

In order to appreciate the mission of Socrates, let us peep into his biography. He was born in Athens in 469 B.C. He served in three campaigns during the Peloponnesian War, as a soldier.

At the age of seventy, Socrates was accused of *corrupting the youth and denying the gods.* According to a text-book writer, "*The enemies of Socrates accused him before the assembly of the people of having introduced new gods, and of denying the ancient divinities of the State, and other practices*; *it was alleged he had corrupted the minds of the young.*

"His particular accusers were actuated by personal animosity. Behind them were many others whom his efforts at reform and his bitter irony had made hostile. Behind all was the voice of Athenian conservatism against the Athenian culture movement. . . . Yet his death was a judicial murder."[1]

After having been found guilty, he had the option of being acquitted, provided he placed himself at the mercy of his accusers, but Socrates said to them:

"Ye men of Athens, I honour and love you, but I shall obey God rather than you. . . . I am a man, and like other men, a creature of flesh and blood, and not 'of wood or stone' . . I am quite sure that wherever I go, there, as here, the young men will flock to me; and if I drive them away, their elders will drive me out at their request; and if I let them come, their fathers and friends will drive me out for their sakes. . . . The hour of departure has arrived, and we go our ways —I to die, and you to live. Which is better God only knows."[2]

And Socrates called for the draught of hemlock. He had refused to escape from prison because, according to him, to do the law wrong is worse than the obvious injustice which was meted to him. He drank the hemlock and died in the month of May, 399 B.C., at the Davidian allotted span of man.

The sacrifice of Socrates is an example that in the mission of life, reformers are not necessarily limited to one particular age-group.

Here was a man who lived for sixty-nine years without making himself immortal in history. At seventy, Socrates, a youth-in-mind, paid the supreme penalty which awaits reformers of history.

[1] H. E. Cushman, *A Beginner's History of Philosophy* (1918). Vol. I, page 79.

[2] See the latter portion of Plato's *Apology*.

The mission of Socrates is better appreciated when we consider it from the views of one of his biographers :

" His life and death constitute an irony. He stands for the harmony of opposite qualities. He devoted himself to the good of Athens, and yet Athens put him to death. In the service of the eternal he was sacrificed.

" His own personality is an exemplification of this irony . . . he was the most austere and yet the most sensitive of men ; he was always a serious moralist and yet always a jester, he was scarcely out of Athens and yet he was a world's man ; he was the world's philosopher and yet he had no system of thought and left no writings." [1]

And this is our destined end or way in life. For whether it rains or whether the sun shines, we must march to our destiny. It is our fate. We march !

Life lies before us like a dream. Our mission in life is to do our part and leave our footprints on the sands of time, as we march along life's rugged paths.

I have focused attention to the footprints left by Socrates on the sands of time. I discussed him as an example of what the youth-in-mind is capable of achieving in this grand and glorious march to our destiny.

I will now consider the efforts of a youth-in-body to follow the path of those who marched into the " silent halls of death " via Martyrdom Avenue.

Socrates made himself immortal at the age of seventy. Jesus immortalized himself at thirty-three.

In the year A.D. 62, Aesculapius Cultellus, a Roman physician, wrote to his nephew, Gladius Ensa, a Captain of the VII Gallic Infantry, who was with the Roman Army in Syria, asking for information about Saul of Tarsus and Jesus of Nazareth.

His correspondence and the reply thereto speak for themselves, inasmuch as they demonstrate how Saul (St. Paul) and Joshua (whom the Greeks called Jesus) marched to their destinies. The reproduction is *verbatim et literatim*, from its Latin translation : [2]

From Aesculapius Cultellus : " My dear Nephew : A few

[1] Cushman, *op. cit.*, 79-80.
[2] H. van Loon, *The Story of Mankind* (1926), chapter XXV.

days ago, I was called to prescribe for a sick man named Paul. He appeared to be a Roman citizen of Jewish parentage, well educated and of agreeable manners.

" I had been told that he was here in connection with a law suit, an appeal from one of our Provincial Courts, Caesarea or some such place in the eastern Mediterranean.

" He had been described to me as a 'wild and violent' fellow who had been making speeches against the People and the Law. I found him very intelligent and of great honesty.

" A friend of mine who used to be with the Army in Asia Minor tells me that he heard something about him in Ephesus where he was preaching sermons about a strange God.

" I asked my patient if this were true, and whether he had told the people to rebel against the will of our beloved Emperor. Paul answered me that the Kingdom of which he had spoken was not of this world, and he added many strange utterances which I did not understand, but which were probably due to his fever.

" His personality made a great impression upon me, and I was sorry to hear that he was killed on the Ostian Road, a few days ago. Therefore, I am writing this letter to you.

" When next you visit Jerusalem, I want you to find out something about my friend Paul and the strange Jewish prophet, who seems to have been his teacher.

" Our slaves are getting much excited about this so-called Messiah, and a few of them, who openly talked of the new kingdom, whatever that means, have been crucified. I would like to know the truth about all these rumours. I am, your devoted Uncle ——."

Six weeks later, Captain Gladius Ensa replied to his uncle as follows, the text of which is culled *verbatim et literatim* from its Latin translation, as the first letter reproduced above:

From Gladius Ensa: " My dear Uncle: I received your letter and I have obeyed your instructions. Two weeks ago, our brigade was sent to Jerusalem. There have been several revolutions during the last century and there is not much left of the old city.

" We have been here now for a month, and to-morrow we shall continue our march to Petra, where there has been trouble with some of the Arab tribes. I shall use the evening to answer your questions, but pray do not expect a detailed report.

" I have talked with most of the older men in this city, but few have been able to give me any definite information. A few days ago, a peddler came to the camp. I bought some of his olives and I asked him whether he had ever heard of the famous Messiah who was killed when he was young.

" He said that he remembered it very clearly, because his father had taken him to Golgotha, a hill just outside the city, to see the execution, and to show him what became of the enemies of the laws of the people of Judaea.

" He gave me the address of one Joseph (evidently Joseph of Arimathaea), who had been a personal friend of the Messiah, and told me that I had better go and see him if I wanted to know more.

" This morning, I went to call on Joseph. He was quite an old man. He had been a fisherman on one of the fresh-water lakes. His memory was clear, and from him at last I got a fairly definite account of what had happened during the troublesome days before I was born.

" Tiberius, our great and glorious Emperor, was on the throne, and an officer of the name of Pontius Pilatus was Governor of Judaea and Samaria.

" Joseph knew little about this Pilatus. He seemed to have been an honest enough official who left a decent reputation as Procurator of the Province.

" In the year 783 or 784 (Roman chronology, i.e. A.D. 32 or 31)—Joseph had forgotten when—Pilatus was called to Jerusalem on account of a riot. A certain young man, the son of a carpenter of Nazareth, was said to be planning a revolution against the Roman Government.

" Strangely enough, our own intelligence officers, who are usually well informed, appear to have heard nothing about it, and when they investigated the matter they reported that the carpenter was an excellent citizen and that there was no reason to proceed against him.

" But the old-fashioned leaders of the Jewish faith, according to Joseph, were very much upset. They greatly disliked his popularity with the masses of the poorer Hebrews.

"The 'Nazarene', so they told Pilatus, had publicly claimed that a Greek or a Roman or even a Philistine, who tried to live a decent and honourable life, was quite as good as a Jew who spent his days studying the ancient laws of Moses.

"Pilatus does not seem to have been impressed by this argument, but when the crowds around the temple threatened to lynch (*sic*) Jesus, and kill all his followers, he decided to take the carpenter into custody to save his life.

"He does not appear to have understood the real nature of the quarrel. Whenever he asked the Jewish priests to explain their grievances, they shouted 'heresy' and 'treason' and got terribly excited.

"Finally, so Joseph told me, Pilatus sent for Joshua, that was the name of the 'Nazarene', but the Greeks who live in this part of the world always refer to him as Jesus, to examine him personally.

"He talked to him for several hours. He asked him about the 'dangerous doctrines' which he was said to have preached on the shores of the sea of Galilee.

"But Jesus answered that he was not so much interested in the bodies of men as in Man's soul. He wanted all people to regard their neighbours as their brothers and to love one single God, who was the father of all human beings.

"Pilatus, who seems to have been well versed in the doctrines of the Stoics and the other Greek Philosophers, does not appear to have discovered anything seditious in the talk of Jesus.

"According to my informant he made another attempt to save the life of the kindly prophet. He kept putting the execution off. Meanwhile, the Jewish people, lashed into fury by their priests, got frantic with rage.

"There had been many riots in Jerusalem before this, and there were only a few Roman soldiers within calling distance. Reports were being sent to the Roman authorities in Caesarea that Pilatus had 'fallen a victim to the teachings of the Nazarene'. Petitions were being circulated all through the city to have Pilatus recalled, because he was an enemy to the Emperor.

"You know that our Governors have strict instructions to avoid an open break with their foreign subjects.

" To save the country from civil war, Pilatus finally sacrificed his prisoner, Joshua, who behaved with great dignity and who forgave all those who hated him. He was crucified amidst the howls and the laughter of the Jerusalem mob.

" That is what Joseph told me, with tears running down his old cheeks. I gave him a gold piece when I left him, but he refused it, and asked me to hand it to one poorer than himself.

" I also asked him a few questions about your friend Paul. He had known him slightly. He seemed to have been a tent-maker who gave up his profession that he might preach the words of a loving and forgiving God, who was so very different from that Jehovah of whom the Jewish priests are telling us all the time.

" Afterwards, Paul appears to have travelled much in Asia Minor and Greece, telling the slaves that they were all children of one loving father, and that happiness awaits all, both rich and poor, who have tried to live honest lives and have done good to those who were suffering and miserable.

" I hope that I have answered your questions to your satisfaction. The whole story seemes very harmless to me, as far as the safety of the State is concerned. But then, we Romans never have been able to understand the people of this Province.

" I am sorry that they have killed your friend Paul. I wish that I were home again, and I am, as ever, your dutiful nephew . . . ."

The above letters speak for themselves. They depict the story of the lives of two men who died that ideals of universal brotherhood and fatherhood might not perish from the face of the earth.

Just as Socrates drank the hemlock at the age of seventy, so too did Jesus bear the cross at the age of thirty-three. The one died at the allotted span of years (three scores and ten), and the other died in the prime of youth.

Ah yes, the life of Jesus is a challenge to mankind. His death is a beckon to the youths of the world, that in this struggle of right against might, youth must not be afraid to be plucked in their bloom, if by that the forces of man's humanity to man might prevail over the forces of man's inhumanity to man.

My destiny is before me. I march towards it full of hope and courage. Life is an empty dream and once my task has been done, the wide expanse of eternity is my ultimate destiny. But if, like Socrates, Jesus, and Paul, I go the way of all flesh, *I will continue the march*!

"Soon rested those who fought; but thou
Who minglest in the harder strife
For truths which men receive not now,
Thy warfare only ends with life.

"A friendless warfare! lingering long
Through weary day and weary year,
A wild and many-weaponed throng
Hang on thy front, and flank, and rear.

"Yet nerve thy spirit to the proof,
And blench not at thy chosen lot.
The timid good may stand aloof,
The sage may frown—yet faint thou not.

"Nor heed the shaft too surely cast,
The foul and hissing bolt of scorn;
For with thy side shall dwell, at last,
The victory of endurance born.

"Truth, crushed, to earth, shall rise again,
Th' eternal years of God are hers;
But error, wounded, writhes in pain,
And dies among his worshippers.

"Yea, though thou lie upon the dust,
When they who helped thee flee in fear,
Die full of hope and manly trust,
Like those who fell in battle here.

"*Another hand thy sword shall wield,*
Another hand the standard wave,
Till from the trumpet's mouth is pealed
The blast of triumph o'er thy grave."

W. C. BRYANT.

16. *A HEAVEN ON EARTH*

There is one distinguishing element in churchianity as it is organized in Africa and abroad. Whereas the Europeans and Americans originated ecclesiastical organizations, they continue to be original. On the other hand, the Africans, who are receivers of these religious cults, continue to be imitative.

The average individual who attends Church in England or in the United States of America goes there in order to be replenished spiritually. His interest is sought after and he is continually made to feel that he is part of the earth.

But in most of the African churches, so far as I have been able to learn from experiences in Gambia, Sierra Leone, Liberia, Gold Coast and Nigeria, Africans are still in the stage where the relics of medievalism form the basis of their Church beliefs. This may be true of other parts of Africa.

This is bad. It is enervating because it discourages the African with an alert mentality. It is an ignorant process because it keeps the African mind continually in the dark. He cowers at mysteries and thus the spirit of enquiry is inhibited.

By no means do I advocate the wrecking of the churches. I believe in the efficacy of the Church as an instrument for welding all sections of the community together, but when its dogmas become too orthodox and anachronistic then the Church is an instrument of reactionarism.

Let me be concrete. To-day, Africans are faced with problems of a political, social, and economic nature. What has the Church in Africa done to assuage these incompatibilities?

Without being ultra-radical, I venture to say that the Church in Africa has followed the policy of medievalism so far as the problem of living on earth is concerned. Unlike some of the European or American churches, the Church as it is organized in Africa is still living on earth but thinking of a place whose latitude and longitude are as vague as life on the other planets.

This should not be the case. But on second thought, I cannot denounce the ministers of the gospel. It is due to the type of education which Africans have been privileged to have.

I cannot afford to be satirical. I cannot afford to be vindictive. Life is too short. Our span on earth is numbered. I must therefore get down to brass tacks. That is why I feel that the Church, as it is organized in Africa has been, is, and will continue to be, a failure unless those at the helm would humanize their dogmas.

How can an unemployed African think of heaven as a land filled with milk and honey, on an empty stomach? Granting that Africa is so blessed by nature that Africans have not begun to feel the stress of life, so far as food and shelter are concerned, what dietitian would plan a menu of milk and honey?

What I am up against is the mental equilibrium of most of the religious and spiritual leaders in Africa. The modern world is revolting against medieval theology not because it is irreligious or atheistic, but because there is need for experiencing mental renaissance in the spiritual realm.

Why preach to the African to think of the world to come when the world that is, is filled with avarice, greed, selfishness and all evidences of man's inhumanity to man? Why teach the African to think of a home "Over There", whilst not one of the leaders who sing this song has ever been there and come back to tell the world that "Over There" is a better place to live in?

We believe that the religion which Joshua, whom the Greeks called Jesus, taught is empirical. It is based on deep devotion to the welfare of humanity. In other words, it is one of deep spiritual experience. Jesus never taught dogmas. He preached of the brotherhood of man and the fatherhood of God. He lived by this gospel as well.

It was left to Albertus Magnus and Thomas Aquinas to dogmatize so as to create a new study collected together from the paganism of Greek metaphysics and Roman epistemology. Then came the era of darkness—mental darkness, when the spirit of man groped and groped in ignorance.

Somehow, Europeans, under the leadership of Wyclif, Martin Luther, Zwingli, Calvin, and others revolted against these orthodoxies of dogmatic theology. But they have not wholly succeeded because denominationalism, with its perplexing dogmas, leaves the average African nonplussed as to which is the royal road to "Over There".

With all due deference to the followers of Christianity, I submit that it is because of its dogmatic nature, following its legalization by Constantine, that Mohammed revolted in order to humanize religion. Say what you please about Mohammedanism, you will agree with me that it is the basis of other great religious movements which aimed at humanizing and practicalizing religion.

The African must therefore cultivate a different attitude towards religion. Singing songs, praying, haranguing any congregation about hell and about the golden gates of heaven, may be all right in a way, but unless the human element is substituted in the Church, as it is organized in Africa, I am afraid that the Church will fail miserably.

The Church played an important part in the development of civilization. But now the forces of materialism seem to have overwhelmed it. What do the stories of Trinity, Resurrection, Immaculate Conception, Transfiguration, Immortality of the Soul, with their innumerable dogmatic interpretations and commentaries and exegeses mean to the average African youth when he is faced with problems of unemployment, taxation without representation; when his will as part and parcel of the community is flouted and he becomes an extraneous element in his society?

You may talk of heaven and hell and purgatory and all that. You may be right, but it may be a misdirected energy. I express no opinion. But, for the Church to be efficacious in Africa, it must humanize religion in the light of twentieth century civilization.

I want to go to Church to hear Reverend Candidus expostulate on social justice and how by cultivating this virtue I can build a heaven on earth. That is what Jesus meant by the New Jerusalem. And that is the Advent I look forward to. But you are entitled to your opinion, Renascent African.

I do not doubt that the Jews have been a factor in history because of their religiosity and because out of them came forth an agitator who shook the world to its very foundations and challenged social injustice.

Whenever men and women discuss man's inhumanity to man, the name of Joshua, whom the Greeks called Jesus, remains immortal. It is a *sine qua non*.

When this human lived, he was looked upon as a fanatic, an impostor, a braggadocio, an agitator, and a criminal; ultimately, he was convicted of sedition. All because he challenged the Sadducees and the Pharisees and the members of the Sanhedrim and the Scribes to rise from the quagmire of man's inhumanity to man.

They desisted. They called him names. They lauded him to the skies. They shouted "Hosanna to the Son of David! Blessed is he that cometh in the name of the Lord." Then they derided him. They spat on him. They jeered, mocked, and finally crucified him. All because of an ideal—the New Jerusalem.

What is this New Jerusalem? Has it any effect on the present day Christianity? Are Christians evangelists and apostles of the New Jerusalem? Are they also fanatics and idealists?

The New Jerusalem is a philosophic concept. It views the world as a State which requires re-birth. Since Jerusalem was the capital of Jewry, it was looked upon as the quintessence of this new society.

Consequently, from the days of the major and minor prophets, the doctrine of the New Jerusalem has been preached. Isaiah, Jeremiah, Ezekiel, Hosea, Amos, and other prophets and reformers encouraged the Jews to forget their captivity in Babylon. They challenged them to think of a new social order.

These men became Utopian Socialists. They dreamt of a new society where man's inhumanity to man would become a thing of the past. They believed that such a society was possible.

They visualized the millennium—the New Jerusalem where the desert would blossom forth flowers and vegetation, and rivers and babbling brooks and rivulets would yield their abundance and glorify the State. And the lion and the lamb would be friends. And the adder and the rabbit would be pals. And the tiger and boa-constrictor and mankind would be restituted to original perfection. And a little child would lead them to the New Jerusalem.

Leaving out the imaginary element of this concept, it is evident that the propagators of this doctrine were sincere. They suffered. They lived as slaves of an alien race. They were treated as if they had no rights. Their only refuge was to think of a New Jerusalem.

The idea of a Utopia did not die with the Jews. In the days of the Greeks, there were social injustice, corruption, selfishness, avarice, greed, and other forces of man's inhumanity to man. Some of the Greek sages kept quiet. Others did not.

Among the latter, Plato objected strenuously to the attempt to stratify Greek society. His book, *The Republic*, is an attempt to concretize his concept of the New Greece. In this book he attempted to solve the ills and problems of the social order.

In medieval times there was Augustine's *City of God*. This was a concept of a society where there would be perfection. Thomas More's *Utopia*, Francis Bacon's *The New Atlantis* are all evidences of the revolt against the incorrigibilities of the *status quo* in society.

In modern society Campanella's *City of the Sun*, Thomas Hobbes' "Social Contract" theory, James Harrington's *Oceana*, Francis Babeuf's *Code de la Nature*, Etienne Cabet's *The Voyage to Icaria*, and the writings of Saint-Simon, Fourier, Louis Blanc, Pierre-Joseph Proudhom, Edmund Burke, Jeremy Bentham, Thomas Paine, William Wordsworth, Samuel Taylor Coleridge, Robert Southey, Robert Owen, etc., propagated doctrines which challenged man's inhumanity to man.

In fact, most of these doctrines were identical with the challenge of the Nazarene: "Do unto others as ye would that they should do unto you." This doctrine preached catholic fraternalism.

Although Jerusalem is the name of a town, in their fanaticism or ignorance men still yearn and sing of "Jerusalem the Golden". They chant glibly of "Zion," "the holy city," "Sinai," as if to say these are supernatural towns reserved for the chosen ones.

To the heroes and heroines of Renascent Africa, I submit that these are evidences of mis-education. What do Jerusalem, Jehoshaphat, Methuselah, Zion, Sinai, and the catch phrases and other relics of the "Age of Faith" mean to the African under twentieth century imperialism?

By no means should one discourage Africans with respect to their religious beliefs. But the ministers of the gospel should now be emancipated and teach the doctrine, not of the New Jerusalem but of the New Africa. The former is Utopian. The latter can be realized.

The African child has nothing in common with the Jew outside the fact that he belongs to the same phylum and species. But be the African a Kru, Vai, Fanti, Ashanti, Hausa, Wangara, Ibo, Yoruba, Bantu, Kaffir, or what not, Africa is Africa.

When Jesus preached of the New Jerusalem, his outlook was universal. He was thinking of a new social order—the Kingdom of God.

He therefore requested that man should be born again before becoming eligible for citizenship in the Kingdom of God. The New Jerusalem was used symbolically by Jesus. Jesus is dead and buried. His thoughts are still propagated, thanks to the British and Foreign Bible Society.

But Africans are facing realities and must cease to think in terms of the abstract alone. If the Jews dreamt of the New Jerusalem when they could have possibly dreamt of the New Meroe or of New Napata, it is time that African Divines should guide Africans to think in terms of the New Africa. *Africa means more to the African child than Jerusalem, idealistically or realistically.* Selah.

17. "*IF WE MUST DIE*"

Death is the common fate of all. The kings of the earth may rule and govern, but in the end they share the common fate of all.

The angel of death spares neither the aristocrat nor the commoner; neither the black nor the white. The rich and the poor must meet on a common basis, when death comes.

It is the doom of humanity that all animate things must eventually become inanimate so that the cycle of existence may continue in its mysterious march.

What though a group may select itself as the lord of creation. What though it may oppress, suppress, repress, impress, and harness other groups. In the end, each member of this self-centred group must have his share of the wine of death.

Just as all men and women have a rendezvous with life, so too do they have a rendezvous with death. Life is the opposite of death and *vice versa*. So whilst men and women lay up treasures on earth to enjoy life more abundantly, they must remember that to-morrow finds them nearer to the grave.

Africans have reached the cross-roads of their history in Africa to give due consideration to some of the factors which affect their daily lives. If life must be made pleasant for them let them also have as their objective the necessity of living for others, because in the end they go away whilst others stay behind, to follow them to the unknown journey.

It is becoming too frequent for Africans to chronicle the boorishness of some of their non-African friends. These delight themselves in manhandling and maltreating their African colleagues and/or co-workers.

Quite recently, the African Press disclosed the intrepid way some of these persons, whether in the mercantile establishment or in the Civil Service or in the mining industries, had concentrated their efforts in insulting and assaulting Africans.

The African may be an ass, according to General Jan Christaan Smuts, of South Africa, but for some civilized Europeans to give evidence of kinship with the mule which delights in goring and kicking, creates a situation which is not only ironical but also calls for an immediate action.

I submit that all men and women are born equal, biologically speaking. I hold this truth to be the basis of a sort of universal kinship between the races, black or white or yellow.

If any of the races believes in its superiority, it is entitled to its opinion, but if it thinks that the way to demonstrate its superiority is by making a human football out of the African, then I submit that it is evidence of low mentality.

The body of an individual is inviolate. Men have no absolute rights. Their rights are relative. But if any person, black or white, thinks that he has a right to kick or to hit another person, he is a social outcast. Indeed, he needs a comprehensive mental examination as to his sanity.

When some Europeans assault Africans they give the African an impression of crudity of the worst magnitude. I admit that the type of individuals who indulges in this form of indoor or outdoor sports is feeble-minded, and a minute examination into his or her hereditary background will reveal facts which will warrant admission into a psychopathic hospital.

A Press correspondent at Takoradi recently reported the kicking and hitting propensities of one of the non-African beach-masters at that port. This individual should by now realize that boxing and wrestling are highly specialized professions which could be indulged in profitably in Europe or America, instead of allowing his talents to rot in Africa.

I must draw the attention of the Port Authority to this wretch who, it is alleged, has made it his habit to slap, hit, kick, and maltreat some of his African employees, literate and illiterate, at the slightest provocation.

The reason why these crude executives continue their barbarism is because some Africans are too cowardly. They are afraid of losing their employment. They are afraid lest a retaliation may lead them to prison. They dread the idea of becoming convicts. And most unfortunately, they have cultivated the inferiority complex.

I do not advocate a state of enmity between the races. I have always preached inter-racial co-operation and I will stand by this sane principle of human relationship. But I feel that the time has come when the African must no longer stand unnecessary assaults and batteries from other peoples.

I do not advocate the taking of the law into one's hands, that is, by administering to the culprit a severe beating, but *I suggest litigation on every occasion.* If possible, legal counsel and medical evidence should be secured so that the amount of damages to be awarded might have a beneficial lesson to the guilty ones. *African or European lawyers should be willing to render free services in this connection.*

Africans have been too humble and too mealy-mouthed. Death is the ultimate reality and the common fate of all. Knowing this, there is no need for them to be afraid. There is no need for them to stand the abuses and slaps and kicks and mauling of their employers, even if litigation or revenge means dismissal.

If Africans must die, let them meet the common foe with

a spirit which knows no defeat, remembering Claude Mackay's immortal lines :

> "If we must die, let us not die like hogs
> Hunted and penned in an inglorious spot,
> While round us bark the mad and hungry dogs,
> Making their mock at our accursed lot.
> If we must die, oh, let us nobly die,
> So that our precious blood may not be shed
> In vain ; then e'en the monsters we defy
> Shall be constrained to honour us, though dead !
>
> "Oh kinsmen ! We must meet the common foe ;
> Though far outnumbered, let us still be brave
> And for their thousand blows deal one death-blow,
> What though before us lies the open grave.
> Like men we'll face the murderous, cowardly pack,
> Pressed to the wall, dying, but—fighting back."

While Africa rues, the rest of the world proceed with ecstacy to enjoy a carefree life.

While Africa droops, the rest of the world stand erect, enjoying life, liberty, and the pursuit of happiness.

While Africa stoops, the rest of the world move with their chest forward in order to assume their rightful heritage.

Is Africa doomed to the sentences of rueing, of drooping, and of stooping ?

Must Africans rue for ever ? Must Africans droop for ever ? Must Africans stoop for ever ?

If Africans must rue and droop and stoop for ever, then there could be no reign of law and order in the universe.

If Africans must carry the burden of the rest of the world, day by day, as the sun rises and sets, then there could be no supreme creator.

If Africans must suffer, so that others might enjoy themselves day by day and night by night, as the moon shines and wanes, there could be no omniscient being.

If Africans are destined to be their own enemies, and to work for their own destruction, there could be no god.

But I believe in an omniscient being who knows all the rueings, the droopings, the stoopings, the burdens, the sufferings, the evil intentions, of Africans.

Therefore, Africans are not made to rue, to droop, to stoop, to carry the burden, to suffer, and to be their own enemies, for ever.

Therefore, there is a way out.

How can Africans escape from the present dilemma in which they are engulfed ?

They are forced to cringe and bow, when they should be brave and stand erect.

They flatter and acquiesce, when they should articulate with a degree of moral courage.

But are they destined to continue in this state of suspended animation for ever ?

Behold a continent which had stood the test of space and time !

Behold a continent which gave the universe the human race !

Behold a continent which produced and nurtured great civilizations !

Behold a continent whose majesty and splendour are now overshadowed by suffering and woe !

Are Africans doomed to this damnable destiny ?

No, it must not be. The spirits of their grandsires speak to them in language plain, that theirs is the power and the glory to revitalize their ideas and ideals of life, for the ultimate enjoyment of life more abundantly, for themselves and for other members of the human race.

Dare Africans fail the spirits of their ancestors which pine at the thought that the glorious traditions which they left to them have been desecrated, because they have eyes and they see not, they have ears and they hear not, and they have the will and they are impotent ?

Dare Africans sit still and feel that since they are able to solve problems which enable them to secure food, shelter, and clothing, therefore all is well that ends well ?

Is this not a form of racial suicide ?

Are Africans not doomed to extermination from the face of the earth because they are self-centred, and self-satisfied, and selfish ?

Do Africans not deserve extirpation because they have proved their incapacity to carry on and to disseminate the torch of civilization which their ancestors handed to them in the dim past?

Lo, the majesty that was Ethiopia!
Lo, the splendour that was Songhay!
Lo, the grandeur that was Benin!
Lo, the glory that was Dahomey!
Lo, the pomp that was Ashanti!
And lo, the dignity that was Zulu land!

Piankhi, Askia, Overami, Benhanzin, Prempeh, Chaka! Names immortalized in the annals of African history!

And how do Africans compare with these grandsires of theirs? Are they worthy enough to carry the shields, and the swords possessed by their grandsires when they were at the height of their glories, in the brave days of yore?

If yes, why do Africans still pine and sigh for the historic days when Princes came out of Egypt, and Ethiopia stretched forth her hands unto God, in token of victory over Sennacherib?

If not, why must Africans continue to wallow in the mire of lethargy? Why must the spirit allow itself to be stultified by the stupor and inactivity of the flesh?

Do Africans constitute an inferior race? No, a thousand times, no.

Then why do Africans accept the status of inferiority without proving their capacity to be considered better than they are now regarded?

Have Africans no mission to perform in the civilization of the world? No, a thousand times, no; Africans are destined to impose their civilization on the world. Then why are they asleep?

There is a destiny sublime for Africa and the Renascent Africans. And neither the forces of time nor the forces of space can obliterate this destiny.

Sons and daughters of Africa, to you is given the power to shape your destiny.

Sons and daughters of Africa, to you is given the chisel to fashion your destiny from the marble of human life.

It is up to you to produce something tangible in order to justify your existence. And it is up to you to cast your chisel away, waiting like Micawber for better times to come.

Renascent Africans! thine is the power to re-create a new continent! Renascent Africans! thine is the glory of a continent which was! Renascent Africans! thine is still the power and the glory which must flourish for ever and ever.

Are you capable, like Theseus, to lift the stone?

Are you capable, like Perseus, to capture the Gorgon's head?

Are you capable, like Jason, to regain the Golden Fleece?

Time and space are the exclusive possessions of no man or people or race on the face of the earth.

Thine is the power. Thine was the glory. Are you capable of justifying your past glory so that it may flourish for ever and ever, Amen?

CHAPTER V

ENVELOPED IN DARKNESS

18. *TOWARDS SPIRITUAL BALANCE*

THE right of free speech is inalienable in a democracy. It implies the right to express our opinions on any public question. It means that the gift of speech is not a privilege, so far as the candid expression of opinion is concerned.

It cannot be said to be a privilege. Indeed, the first test of democracy is whether privilege exists in any aspect of its society or not. If such there be, then that democracy is a misnomer.

In legal science, two terms are almost overworked. Yet they run a gamut through the legal relationship of individuals in their lives in any community. These terms are " absolute " and " relative."

An absolute term is conclusive. It covers a wide range. It has no limitations, mathematically or otherwise. It is definite.

A relative term is not conclusive. Its conclusions are subject to multiplications, divisions, additions, and subtractions. It is subject to certain limitations. But this term facilitates the extension of ideas and qualifications of the same, without making one's conclusions absurd or fallacious.

The two terms owe their origin to mathematics. Later, they found their way to the studies of philosophy, and to-day, they have been borrowed and used extensively almost in all fields of study.

Since logic is a phase of philosophy, and jurisprudence (i.e. the philosophy of law) is its handmaid, the terms when used legally are vitally essential to our socionomic existence.

The right of free speech is relative. It cannot be absolute because it has certain checks and limitations to prevent it from descending into licentiousness.

This is the reason why law exists, to prevent one person from enjoying his liberty, unchecked, at the expense of the other person.

This is also responsible for the existence of the legal institutions of society. There are the Legislative to make the law, the Judiciary to interpret the law, and the Executive to administer the law.

Reduced to its lowest common denominator, it means that no person may enjoy his liberty so as to jeopardize the liberty of his compatriots. That is the *raison d'être* of civil law.

This leads to that section of the law of tort which distinguishes between the limitations of the right of free speech in so far as it concerns the character and good name of others.

I may speak of others. It is a right. Others may speak of me. It is also a right. But no one has the right to speak of others in such a discreditable way as to jeopardize the reputation of others, unless it be a fair criticism, and even then it must be within the bounds of reason and within the limitations of the law.

I may write about others. It is a right. Others may write about me. It is also a right. But no one has the right to write of others in such a discreditable way as to jeopardize the reputation of others, unless it be a fair criticism, and even then it must be within the bounds of reason and within the limitations of the law.

The above explains in a nutshell why rights are not absolute but relative. Whilst it is true that within the great body of the law of torts there are technicalities which needs only the trained legal and judicial mind to fathom, it is too evident that no writer has the right to say or write of others, things which, in their simplest denotation and connotation, may mean a disparagement to one's reputation. In this case, the individual has a remedy in law.

Outside of public law, and the word "public" is used relatively, there is also what is known as public ethics. This means the moral mind of the community.

A number of people may aggregate in any environment after their ancestors had peregrinated. They have a code of ethics, which whilst not necessarily legal, yet has a binding force, even though there are no sanctions to enforce these codes.

In all advanced societies, this is known as a sense of decency. This means that a person, whilst the law allows him to ridicule his opponents, yet he or she must not be so lewd as to use his writing talents for besmirching the fair name of his society, so far as other societies are concerned.

In case this is allowed to happen, it means that that individual so guilty, from the standpoint of public opinion, is a traitor to his community, in that he gives the outside world reason to doubt the intellectual virility of his community and he berates his country's mentality, thereby.

There is need for spiritual balance in order to balance the rights of law and the rights of ethics. Unless this is forthcoming, one's writing propensities might descend into licentiousness.

Your right to state your point of view is admitted. But it is how you state it that matters. Nevertheless, how you state your view may be justifiable or may not be. That is the essence of criticism.

In case you are justified in how you make your statement then that criticism is fair. Otherwise, it is unfair. But to distinguish between fair and unfair criticism is a task which is most problematic.

Criticism, to be fair, must expersonate the critic, else one will allow one's personal idiosyncrasies to influence the criticism. In case the critic allows himself to be impersonate with the object of his criticism, he reduces his observations to an illogicality, popularly commented upon as a species of *argumentum ad hominem*.

Africans, in the majority of cases, are fond of impersonate criticism without attempting to expersonate themselves. Even among highly educated persons, the critical outlook is usually blurred by the forces of this type of criticism.

No people can hope to be spiritually balanced without cultivating respect for the views and opinions of others, even if they conflict with their own.

As soon as any community refuses to be impersonal in its critical outlook, it is a definite index of decline in the mentality of that group, particularly its leaders.

It is because in sections of Africa, I am formulating ideas which may run counter to the accepted ideas of yesterday that I find it necessary to consider the rôle of the critic in society. If the critic's rôle is that of praise or denunciation, it is all right, but the criterion of criticism must be fair, for the criticism to be justifiable.

In the history of literary criticism, there have been critics in many branches of literature. There are critics who have specialised in dramatics, in the novel, in the short story, in essay writing, in biographical writing, in historical and other forms of literature.

Some of these critics are devious, some are captious, some are carping, some are poignant, some are conciliatory, some are ambidexterous, and some are vindictive.

In these criteria of criticism, not all the criticisms are necessarily destructive. A carping criticism may redound to the credit of the criticized object and *vice versa*. On the other hand, a conciliatory criticism may lack honest efforts on the part of the critic leaving the criticized subject or object to share a lot of misunderstanding or misinterpretation.

Renascent Africans must, therefore, become fair critics in order to demonstrate their spiritual balance.

19. *TOWARDS SOCIAL REGENERATION*

If the brotherhood of man is a universal truth, then Africans are brothers, one to another.

If the brotherhood of man is a universal truism, then Africans are related to the inhabitants of Europe, Asia, Australia, and America.

Joshua, whom the Greeks called Jesus, did not study anthropology, so far as I know, but he doctrinated that all men and women on earth are brothers and sisters.

This doctrine is the noblest in the world, because it reflects leadership of a constructive nature. It demonstrates the fact that no individual can successfully distinguish himself from the rest of mankind, without proving his mental subnormality.

In anthropology, it is universally acknowledged that the human race has a common origin. If you prefer to trace it genetically, from the protoplasm, you cannot fail to reach your goal, for it will lead you through the biological steps and land you on Phylum Chordata.

If you prefer to make a functional analysis you may find palaeontologists and geologists enabling you to understand man's relationship with the *Pithecanthropus erectus*, *Eoanthropus dawsoni*, *Homo heidelbergensis*, *Homo rhodesiensis*, *Australopithecus africanus*, *Sinanthropus pekinensis* to the Neanderthal, Cromagnon, Grimaldi, Tzitzikama, and other precursors of the human race.

If you come to ethnology, you will take the nearest approach to present-day man, *Homo sapiens*, and you will sub-divide this into the Black, Yellow, and White races. The adjectives are used relatively, of course.

Coming to the black race, there are divisions as well, but there is no attempt to deny a common origin, unless one wishes to exhibit shallow mentality.

Here, there are the Bantu, the Sudanese, the Nilotic, and the Arabic groups. The above terms must be used with care, for some of them connote linguistic or cultural or ethnologic factors.

In West Africa, the tribes are either Sudanese or Semi-Bantu. But so far as the West African colonies, under the British, are concerned, *all* the tribes comprise the Sudanese group.

It will not be necessary to give the historical background of the ethnography of West Africa, prior to the Slave Trade, that is, before the Songhay Empire flourished, but after the slave traffic, there were tribal migrations; so that certain tribes peregrinated to settle in other sections of the great bend of the African continent on the west.

Without any attempt to offend, it should be clearly understood that the principal tribes who were the fountain head of all other tribes in West Africa from the days of Songhay to-day were the Benin, Dahomey, Hausa, and Ashanti peoples. Very few British West African tribes could claim descent from other unmixed tribes than the above.

That is why in formulating my concepts of the New Africa,

I suggested social regeneration as the second plank. I knew that the Ga and the other tribes of the Gold Coast had a common kinship with the Ashanti or Hausa or Dahomey or Benin peoples. Thus I thought that for one of these cross-cousins to arrogate to himself an idea of superiority or inferiority was preposterous.

Thus I pleaded for spiritual balance which would lead to social regeneration.

Renascent Africans must, therefore, regard all Africans as blood brothers and sisters.

20. *TOWARDS ECONOMIC DETERMINISM*

When Karl Marx and Friedrich Engels wrote *The Communist Manifesto* they introduced an idea which, in their time, was considered revolutionary.

By no means the first to originate that idea, yet they expounded and analysed the theory of economic determinism so that the average student of economics, be it in the field of history or philosophy or sociology, might grasp its fundamentals.

Reduced to its lowest common denominator, the theory of economic determinism posits that the quest for food, shelter, and clothing has been the determinants of history.

In economic philosophy, this theory is identified with the economic interpretation of history. It means that States exist because the individuals, after peregrinating, settle in a definite portion of the earth's surface, in order to earn a livelihood.

It also implies that why one State imposes its will on another State or on an undeveloped place, is due to economic motivation.

Therefore, it concludes that all the various aspects of societal life, throughout history, were affected by the forces of economics and that without the quest for food, shelter, and clothing, mankind might still be living in the Palaeolithic age.

This ideology is one of the corner-stones of Marxian or Scientific Socialism. Even capitalism with all its faults, real and fancied, cannot refuse to accept the fundamentality of the theory of economic determinism in society.

Applying this thesis to life in Africa, it cannot be done away with peremptorily. As it was efficacious in the life of mankind in the other continents, so, too, is it destined to be efficacious in the African continent.

Throughout British West Africa, the Natives of the four colonies peregrinate. In Gambia, there are Sierra Leonians, Gold Coastians, and Nigerians. They are all in Gambia seeking for food, shelter, and clothing.

The same applies to Sierra Leone, Gold Coast, and Nigeria. And among the leading lights of these communities to-day, are persons who have been forced by economic determinism to leave their homes to proceed to these places in order to earn a livelihood and then to return to their homes, to rest before stepping to the grave.

Those who realize that they must earn a living have found it difficult to do so. They appeal to the Government to give them employment. Government replies that it is not within its province to provide employment for its citizens.

They become eleemosynary, depending upon the charity of the State so that they may be economically self-sufficient. In the end, they are bound to fail, because they have been mis-educated.

On the dignity or indignity of manual labour I will hold no brief in this section. But I believe that the reason for the present unemployment scourge in West Africa is because mis-education has enabled one to lay wrong emphasis on superficial and artificial values.

Why one must complain of impolitic drivers and illiterate drivers, when there are thousands of literate men and women whose education can enable them to be politic and educated drivers is beyond comment.

Why one must complain of incompetent compositors, chase men, machine men, and proof readers, when there are thousands of literate men and women whose education can enable them to become competent and efficient workers in the printing trade, is, again, beyond comment.

Why one must complain of untrustworthy carpenters, masons, and painters, when there are thousands of educated men and women whose training in the elementary schools ought to obviate the necessity of such untrustworthy workers thriving is, again, beyond comment.

Why one must complain of inefficient, indolent, and unfaithful photographers, farmers, tailors, shoe-makers, barbers, goldsmiths, blacksmiths, electricians, mechanics, chemists, miners, labourers, and even traders, when the schools are gradually grinding out of their mill, thousands of their finished product, is a challenge to the mentality of the African.

The Government must not bear the brunt of unemployment. The employers must not be criticized for taking advantage of one's mis-education, thus paying the present workers a minimum wage of existence. Old Africa has allowed the inefficient and incompetent and un- or semi-educated workers to thrive.

Behold one way out of this economic maelstrom. Let the graduates of the schools embark upon the ocean of the world, forgetting the false values which were fastened on to their mentality during their school days: namely, that an educated person is destined to be a clerk all his life.

If educated men and women should enter and compete with uneducated drivers, printers, proof readers, carpenters, masons, painters, photographers, farmers, tailors, shoe-makers, barbers, goldsmiths, blacksmiths, electricians, mechanics, chemists, miners, labourers, and traders, the fittest would survive and the inefficient and incompetent would give way.

Having weeded out the undesirables who have hitherto profited by the mis-education, the way would automatically open for a better life for the worker, because intelligence commands respect. *Unionism* would automatically take place more effectively than the present era of exploitation.

Those who have been weeded out would go back to the land to join the better farmers, or secure an education, or die a natural death.

This is one practical way towards economic determinism. Leave your school and/or B.A. certificates at home. Put on your overalls and work with your hands and heads and hearts, and behold Renascent Africans shall become economically deterministic.

The economic history of mankind has reached a new stage

in its evolution. Its present status finds it sub-divided into two forces—rugged individualism and philanthropic socialism.

These two tenets have found multifarious ramifications that the world is beginning to feel the pressure of ignorance and intolerance.

Communism as an evidence of contemporary economic philosophy has been tainted with the colour which is devoid of intelligence on the part of certain propagandists.

In Africa, in particular, through the lack of balance, in certain respects, of some of the protagonists of Communism, it has been libelled and so, to the average African, Communism is nothing but a menace to the peace of the world.

I hold no brief for Communism or for any other " ism " which is being disseminated in the world, necessarily. But *I believe in academic freedom together with the liberty of conscience.*

It is my motto not to interfere with the right of any person to accept or to reject any dogma, ecclesiastical or otherwise, which may influence his or her environment, socially, politically, economically, etc.

I refer to the currents of contemporary thought, such as Socialism, Nationalism (Fascism, Nazism, Bolshevism, Chauvinism, etc.), Imperialism, etc.

However, it is high time that the average African should understand the basic factors which underlie any of the above " isms " so that he may not be unnecessarily rushed to form conceptions which lead to false conclusions.

One of the reasons which support the necessity for a formulation of the Gold Coast Criminal Code Amendment Ordinance, popularly known as " Sedition Bill ", is that certain Communistic literature which, according to the Legal Department, was seditious in nature, entered the Colony without check.

Since Africans in the majority of cases, have not been given a fair chance to understand the tenets of Communism, at least from an academic, if not from a practical, standpoint, some of them have laboured under misapprehensions as to the connotation of Communism. The letter of Dr J. B. Danquah supporting the opinions of Lord Charnwood and Sir Francis Lindley, is self-explanatory.[1]

[1] *The Times* (London), September 21, 1934, page 8.

The letters written by Lord Charnwood and Sir Francis Lindley to the *Times* cannot be regarded as authentic or authoritative, wholly. These men, like others, seem jealous of Soviet Russia as were certain Americans who opposed the recognition of that country by President Franklin D. Roosevelt. Like Sir Arthur Steel-Maitland, who opposed the admission of Abyssinia into the League of Nations, their objections are purely sentimental. In their socio-economic ideology, they are reactionary.

The Union of Socialist Soviet Republics of Russia is a political entity, with territory as large as a continent, and populated by about one-sixth of the inhabitants of the world. Soviet Russia is, therefore, a concrescent factor in international relations.

What crime has Russia committed to warrant the philippics of Lord Charnwood and the vitriolics of Sir Francis? Just this plain economic truth: *Russia is a successful Socialist State.*

What is Socialism? Is it a diabolical organization whose members must grow long beards, have their names ending in "ski", and become connected with plots to bomb buildings or to assassinate public officials? The above letters give me the impression that that is the notion which the writers have of Communism.

According to my limited knowledge, Russian Communism is essentially Marxian. In other words, it is what scholars term "Scientific Socialism", the tenets of which are as follows—

1. *The Economic Interpretation of History.* The quest of food, shelter, and clothing, has been the determinant factor in the history of civilization. Nationalism or Imperialism is basically motivated by economics.

2. *The Struggle between Capital and Labour.* In the attempt to answer the challenge of economic determinism, two groups arise: the land-owners or bourgeoisie, who are the capitalists, and the proletarians who are the workers. Having no capital, the latter become a permanent wage-earning class, of whom, the erstwhile serfs and slaves are the prototypes.

3. *The Theory of Surplus Value and Profit Motive.* Wage-earners are not paid according to their productive value. The profit motive makes it necessary to underpay the workers. The conditions under which most of them labour make it inevitable

that escape to the bourgeois class is not only difficult but jeopardizes their lives. They earn a minimum wage of existence and have a very low standard of living.

4. *The Dictatorship of the Proletariat.* Workers must have the right of collective bargaining. They must be allowed to use strikes and boycotts as media to secure higher wages, shorter hours of work, social legislation, and more leisure. But history shows that Governments have, at times, aided only the capitalists, and would not protect the workers to achieve economic emancipation. Here we have a parting of ways as to how this objective can be realized.

(a) *Utopian Socialists.* Men like Isaiah, Jeremiah, Jesus of Nazareth, Plato, Bacon, More, Saint-Simon, etc., suggested an appeal to the spiritual nature of man. This should bring about a Paradise where both capitalists and workers would live happily for ever.

(b) *Anarchists and Syndicalists.* Men like Kropotkin, Bakunin, Le Blanc, Abbé Siéyès, Condorcet, etc., preferred a society without Government, but more or less co-operative. Governments, they say, are necessary evils. The Syndicalists would commit sabotage in factories owned by capitalists to gain their objective.

(c) *Guild and Fabian Socialists.* Men like Graham Wallas, H. G. Wells, Harold Laski, George Bernard Shaw, Lord Snowden, Lord Passfield (Sidney Webb), Ramsay MacDonald, etc., suggested organization and orderly method in order to gain control of the political machinery. The British Labour Party is an exemplification of the strength and weakness of these brands of Socialism.

(d) *Communistic Socialists.* Men like Karl Marx, Friedrich Engels, Lenin, Stalin, Trotsky, Bukharin, etc., opined that the history of mankind was a record of force, that is, the imposition of the will of the stronger over the weaker. The Hobbesian philosophy of *homo homini lupus est* made an appeal to the spiritual or moral nature of man, abortive. Only one language was understandable by those who gained power through force. That language was force.

In view of this simple clarification of Socialism and what it stands for, I think that not all the attacks on Socialism are justifiable.

I believe that Africans should not be fed like children. Intellectual paternalism tends to emasculate Africans and it makes them spineless. I am aware of the pitfalls, fallacies, and incongruencies of Communism. But *African society is essentially Socialistic.*[1] Just because Lord Obesity or Sir Big Head says that Communism is good, bad or indifferent, that does not necessarily make it so.

. . . . .

Does it ever occur to the average reader why very few African companies are successful in business?

Have the Africans ever stopped to wonder why African business fails, whilst European and Asiatic business houses prosper?

In plain words, why is it that if an African should float a business organization, in seventy-five per cent. of cases, approximately, he fails, whereas the European, Syrian, Indian and other mercantile houses prosper invariably?

The African business man is egocentric. The African business man has no confidence in himself and so, he has no confidence in his business colleagues.

Again, the African business man thinks of profits in tens and hundreds of pounds, whilst the European thinks in thousands and millions of pounds.

The difference is too evident. Whilst the African is content to walk and fly, like the chicken, the European is desirous of flying high like the eagle.

Probably, the main reason for the difference between African and European business administration is the principle of *co-operation.* The two words, linked together, mean *working together.*

In the field of business, the European has not only annexed these two words into his economic dictionary, but he has also made use of the same to connote the type of business he conducts.

[1] In fact, *communalistic.*

In mercantile law, the word *corporation* denotes a business organization which is one body. It means, therefore, that instead of co-operating, as consumers, there is co-operation as producers. In the case of the former, the organization of co-operative societies has mitigated somewhat the problem of price-fixing, so far as the consumer is concerned, but in the case of the latter, persons have gathered together to work as one person.

The European, by pooling his financial resources together obtains a great capital with which to transact his business and to conduct his business relations.

With this capital, he gives employment to thousands. He organizes branches of his business in different places. He makes important contacts in different sections of the country. He has good banking references, and thus his business prospects are indicative of success, if not in the immediate, then in the remote, future.

The African, on the other hand, prefers to work alone. By spending a greater part of his life in accumulating capital, the African proceeds to control his business single-handedly. For a one-man's business, it will work out temporarily, but time will come when that one man will face problems which require many heads to solve. Solving it in a one-man's way is to precipitate an economic panic, sooner or later.

Whilst some of the Europeans are declaring dividends, some of the African business men are worried over their trial balance or profit and loss account. Whilst the European business man is expanding his business (postponing the dividends, in certain cases) the African business man is busy trying to cut down expenses so as to meet his liabilities, real or apparent.

In this connection, I am referring to certain African business organizations which do not understand what is meant by cost accounting. Because of this, they are at sea. They cannot tell outright the state of affairs of their business. They hardly keep books. They think that the employment of accountants and book-keepers is extraneous, and that since their grandfathers never employed book-keepers and accountants, there is no need for them to do so.

The result is that business which may have prospered, goes

to the rocks, because the African business man is too short-sighted to spend a little money so as to understand what it costs him every minute or hour of the day to keep his business going.

An important factor which must be reckoned with by the student of economics is that the African business man is justified, to an extent, in carrying on his business *alone*.

How many Africans have forgotten the bizarre schemes, the bubble propositions, the dishonest tactics, the defrauding propensities, of certain African business men, bringing ruin to many?

How many Africans have not known the African as a credulous creature who will give his land and his wealth in order to promote African business, only to become victimized by irresponsible criminals who are actually frauds in the guise of patriots?

How many Africans would not have sacrificed their lives' earnings or savings in order to back up a sound African business house, were they certain that the moving spirit of the company would be upright, honest, straightforward and industrious?

I know many Africans who are ethnocentric when it comes to the commercial world. But because of the past activities of certain African business men and women, they have become aware of these wolves in sheep's clothing.

Despite these set-backs, there is need for African business men to systematize their activities, by learning from their Western colleagues. Very few Europeans operate their business activities *single-handedly*—not if they want to make real money. Very few Europeans will be satisfied with three-figure profits. They would rather have four to five-figure losses for a seven-figure asset if they were sure that this asset, in time to come, would yield four or five-figure profits.

Because of this state of affairs in African business, the average African business liquidates with the death of the owner. Think of the great merchant princes of West Africa in the 'nineties and in the days of cocoa boom (1920); where are they to-day? Think of the great cocoa dealers of yesterday, where are they to-day?

But the United Africa Company, Limited, exists, even though Miller Brothers, John Walkden, A. & E.T.C., Niger Company and others have gone the way of all flesh. The United Africa

Company, Limited, is a lesson to the African. Notice the word *united*.

You may talk about monopoly, you may scream about fixing of prices, you may harangue about unfair competition until your epiglottis ceases to function, but unless the African business organizations learn to *unite* their efforts in a *co-operative* (working together) *combine* (union), African business will continue to be a one-man's affair, and the economic emancipation of the African is a long way off.

21. *TOWARDS MENTAL EMANCIPATION*

The education of the African in the past and present has prepared Africans for life in a social order which is stagnant and unprogressive. It made Africans to cultivate false values which are based on the veneer of a decadent civilization.

Their education is, therefore, anachronistic, for it makes them to live in the past. It enables the un-fits and mis-fits to thrive, and it facilitates the claims of Uncle Toms to leadership.

Their education, therefore, lacks moral stability. It makes them to be mere imitators and prevents them from cultivating that moral courage which is the basis of dynamic leadership. What is called character education is nonsense, because character, in the eyes of those who educate Africans, is nothing short of *emasculation*.

The education of the African therefore lacks perspective. It is interested in perpetuating the *status quo*. It sees in the present generation nothing substantial to make it to differ from the coming generation. Rather, Africans are becoming retrospective in their educational philosophy.

Their education, therefore, lacks permanency of values. It makes them to cling to artificialities and superficialities. They chase the rainbow of Occidentalism and allow its rays to strangulate them for want of constructive leadership.

Indeed, these postulates are severe indictments. But to lovers of academic freedom and to those who are intellectually honest, examples could be multiplied to support most if not all the points raised above.

Because the existence of these vitiating influences in the Africans' educational system has produced their kind, their leadership material lacks the moral stamina to balance the physical rigidity of the African, with his mental flexibility.

I cannot afford to be too general. But I submit, in all fairness, to the creditable side of the ledger of the achievements of Africans or peoples of African descent in West Africa, and with deference to their feelings, that present-day West Africa has failed to produce outstanding leaders.

Since leadership is the soul of any community, a community which lacks constructive leadership is destined to be the footstool of other communities with constructive leadership.

Search through the West African colonies. Point to me the self-appointed leaders who parade and kow-tow to the powers that be. Show me the men and women who have a list of alphabets behind their names, in token of appreciation of their "services" to the community, and you know, as I know, that they have no pretensions whatsoever to dynamic leadership.

This conclusion may be too general, but I will brave the ire of those who may believe that there are some holders of titular honours who are worth their salt to the aspirations of dynamic Africa.

But knowing human nature as I do, I submit again that the acceptance of honour on the part of any African gentleman who is in position to point to any State the way out of this interracial muddle, is a sort of acceptance of the fiat of colonial diplomacy.

I therefore feel that the system of education which encourages the existence of a privileged class of alphabetists has no prospect of producing real leaders to guide and counsel the type of Africans that must come into their own, *to-morrow*.

All that I have said can be summed up in these words: *Africans have been mis-educated. They need mental emancipation so as to be re-educated to the real needs of Renascent Africa.*

Their present-day society is shaped according to their educational perspectives and objectives. If one is educated to look up to titular alphabets as one's objective, it simply leads to the conclusion that one's perspective is tinged with the superciliousness and egocentricities of aristocracy. These, I submit, have no place in African society, if Africans must find their place in the sun.

A re-evaluation of concepts and values is necessary for a resurgence of the political society of Africans.

Peoples and nations are regarded great to-day because they are immortal. This by no means leads to the conclusion that they have not been physically dead. Rather, it implies that although the material side of their structures is no longer active, biologically speaking, yet the resultant efforts of their mentality have made them immortal.

Man being such a vain animal, has been engaged in seeking for immortality. No man is so self-satisfied that he would rather enjoy an epicurean existence and then leave the stage of life.

Such a form of existence is selfish. It holds out no inspiration for posterity. It destroys originality and the creative essence in man.

But when man dreams of the future and commits his thoughts through a process which must preserve his " brain-children ", he may be said to have carved a niche for himself.

Life in modern society is enriched by the contributions of the pen rather than the celerity of bullets. The one is imperishable. The other is perishable no matter how long it may be preserved in a museum.

Modern Europe has become an important factor in the history of the world because throughout its history—ancient, medieval and modern, it has been able to transfer its thoughts to posterity.

Before the science of printing was popularized by Lourens Coster, John Gutenberg, Aldus Manutius, and then later by William Caxton, there were other methods employed by the Egyptians, Assyrians, and by the Greeks to transfer their ideas to generations yet unborn.

It follows, therefore, that each epoch in human history realizes the necessity for immortalizing its thought, not necessarily for selfish aggrandisement, but as a means of preserving ideals and traditions, and also popularizing the urge for a progressive society through a panorama of the wisdom and follies of past ages.

Of all races of mankind, Africans have been non-literate, to a great extent. Whilst the Ethiopians had their hieroglyphics, and the Assyrians their cuneiforms, the Egyptians their papyrus, and the Greeks their parchment, and Western world their paper, Africans have still to invent their own system, not necessarily of alphabets, but of preserving their literary productions.

In the modern world, the African has an advantage. He is an inheritor of the rich classics of antiquity. He is able to go to school and transfer his thoughts either on slate or on paper. He has pencils and pens and ink. In other words, the African races are the luckiest in the evolution of man in this phase of society.

But with their vaunted knowledge obtained from the important educational centres of the world, what have Africans been able to produce, intellectually speaking? And by this one implies a literary output of such standing as to take its place with the classics or with contemporary authors.

Literature is the soul of any nation. Just as visionless nations are doomed to perish so too are nations without literature doomed to be imposed upon by the literary vandals of their contemporary society. After all, the mode of thinking and actions of the African are, to an extent, dictated to according to the type of literature they consume.

If they read books which portray them as inferior, their minds are conditioned to such a reflex. Hence it is this type of propaganda that should fire the African with a view to creative scholarship.

Why should Mr Touch-Me-Not content himself with citing Coke, Blackstone, Odgers, etc., every time he is in a jam? Why should he not study the law, make researches on all its aspects or on specific aspects, and then write a book on the law. Why should Sarbah and Danquah be the only legal scholars produced by West Africa?

In the field of medicine why should Africans be satisfied with Gray? Why cannot an African write a text-book on anatomy or otiology, or on any phase of medical science? Is it beyond their mental capacity?

I have yet to read an African text-book on engineering, commerce, carpentry, agriculture, etc. Piling up degrees or passing examinations mean nothing unless Africans are creative. The field is without competition. A text-book on African Law and Procedure is within human possibility. A text-book on African medicine is not impossible.

But the truth is that the African " scholar " is lazy. Probably his climate is responsible, they say. This is untrue. Are the Europeans who are resident in Africa not writing text-books on and for Africans? Why can an Achimota European master write a book on African Botany? Africans must be inferior. If not, what excuse can they offer?

Granting that for economic reasons it is impossible to publish books, how about the highly-inflated, self-centred individuals who are for ever resting on the oars of their University undergraduate days? Intellectual brilliance in the university is useless unless specific contributions after graduation justify them.

It is therefore encouraging to learn that an African who has never been abroad has written a text-book of shorthand. It is called *Pitman's New Era Supplementary Phrase Book*. May more of Mr Reffell's type hasten the dawn of creative scholarship in the New Africa.[1]

Greatness does not consist in things material alone. It cannot be an object of commercial transaction. It is not tangible. It exists but its existence is ephemeral, to the materially inclined person, yet it is an asset that can never be evanescent.

As with individuals, so with nations and races. The great man is not necessarily a rich man, much more a man of fashion. The great nation is not necessarily the richest nation on earth.

The criterion of greatness varies with the norms of society. But speaking catholically, greatness implies the ability of the individual or nation or race to so influence his contemporaries that he carves a niche for himself in the halls of fame.

Greatness, therefore, may be an ambiguous term, yet it signifies all the elements of success. To be great is to be successful, and to be successful is to be great. A limitation of my definition of greatness in this wise should obviate ambiguity.

Throughout the evolutionary history of man, there are two forces which, like the fates, gravitate in order to bring about a

[1] Mr A. G. Refell is author of the above book vide the review in *The African Morning Post*, April 17, 1935, page 5.

balance. At times the one over-balances the other. But in the final analysis, both are separate and distinct, but there is a sort of symbiosis existent between the two.

Society has two norms, generically speaking. One looks on things material as the criterion of success or greatness. It sees life as a mechanically designed mass for the gratification of man's hedonism. Contemporary African society is a pupil of this school of material determinism.

Another school regards things material as finite. They are phantasmagorical. There is nothing tangible, materially speaking. Matter is destructible. It is evanescent. It reaches an equilibrium. It has a brief span and it returns to its original state.

Thus the protagonists of this school of thought search for the intangible element which guarantees to man not necessarily the means to material greatness, but a means to an infinite atmosphere the vista of which is neither perceptible in whole nor within the limit of human comprehension.

Things material cannot do without things intellectual or spiritual. Although the mummies of the ancient Egyptians may still be available, yet the hieroglyphics are much more important in many respects.

African philosophy and life, in the past up till the contact of the African with the West, has been based on materialism. The concept of food, shelter, and clothing has made Africans materially deterministic that in certain vital respects, they have been under-developed from the neck up.

This has been responsible for the unfortunate judgment that the African races are children, and unequal in the scale of human evolution, so far as intellectual attainments are concerned.

When historical evidence throws light and shows that the most promising nations and races have been those which have so developed their mental capacities as to control the material universe, it seems that the critics of African mentality may be right.

Recent scientific investigations, however, have disproved the basis upon which Count Gobineau and other racialists posited this theory of the state of " suspended animation " of African mentality.

Universities have been responsible for shaping the destinies of races and nations and individuals. They are centres where things material are made to be subservient to things intellectual in all shapes and forms. No matter in what field of learning, at any university, there is an aristocracy of mind over matter.

Here the agriculturist learns to appreciate the soil, but by a mixture of certain chemicals, he " creates " a different object. By continually inter-mixing these compounds, he " produces " something more tangible, materially speaking, and intangible in the history of man.

The Universities of Europe and America have been responsible for the great movements in the national history of these continents. Universities could produce a genius like Hardy, who earned his B.A. with first-class honours at the age of twelve, and they could produce a " Frankenstein " or a " Dr. Jekyll and Mr Hyde " personality as well.

Black Africa has no university. Black Africa has no intellectual centre where the raw materials of African humanity may be re-shaped into leaders in all the fields of human endeavour.

With their vaunted wealth in things material, Africans are bankrupts beside the other races, in things intellectual. With a taxation of one shilling *per capita* throughout British West Africa, an endowment fund of more than twelve million pounds can be raised. This is capable of supporting three or four first-class universities.

Why should African youth depend upon Oxford, Cambridge, Harvard, Yale, Sorbonne, Berlin, Heidelberg, for intellectual growth? These universities are mirrors which reflect their particular societal idiosyncrasies.

An African graduate of these universities, unless he has developed his individuality, is nothing short of a megaphone, yea, a carbon copy of these societies. Hence, I say that he is mis-educated.

Give the Renascent African a University, you who are capable of financing the same. With twelve million pounds there is no reason why the best libraries, laboratories, professors, cannot be produced right here, and this continent can become, overnight, " A Continent of Light ".

22. *SUPERSTITION OR SUPER-SCIENCE?*

I do not propose to stir up a hornet's nest by making a generalization that African magic is pseudo-scientific, but I submit that continuous belief in the same is having a deleterious effect on African mentality.

I exist in the world, yet I believe that the same world is infested by beings which are destructive in their mission. This kind of thinking leads one to believe that a wicked man with " medicine " can dispose of a kindly man who has no " medicine " to stand the challenge of his detractors.

There may be an element of truth in certain practices connected with African magic, but unlike the scientific studies, they are in the stage which lacks classification and empiricism. If an African would only study the science of the West, and try to correlate the same with African science, an important contribution could be made to the studies of science.

The Western mind is one of enquiry. The enquiries lead to theories and hypotheses. These in turn lead to conclusions. But for the conclusion to be scientific, it must be empirical.

In other words, the Baconian era ushered in the critical spirit which took nothing for granted, but probed into the test-tube and the microscope, armed with a mind which could not be easily swayed.

Consequently, the who, what, where, when, how and why of matter were subjected to the most rigorous test. The result is a well-constituted field of studies divided into the physical, chemical, and biological sciences.

The physical sciences deal with the principles and applications of matter, mobile or inert. The chemical sciences consider the various changes which occur in matter. The biological sciences pry into the origin and nature of life in animals and plants.

These three divisions give a definite index to the nature of matter. It is in three forms : solid, liquid, gaseous. Land may represent the first, water the second, and air the third, although these in turn harbour matter in one or more forms.

On this basis natural science has been organized, systematized, tested, and collated so that there is real basis for formulizing conclusions.

If it is possible for an African to make " medicine " so that another African may go blind, or insane, or dead, the composition of the matter must be taken into consideration.

For example, an African standing five hundred yards away or more may make " medicine " to kill his fellow African. Granting that this is possible, the problem of the African scientist is to ascertain what form the " medicine " would take.

Could it be solid ? No. Because the African did not wish his victim to see him. Could it be liquid ? No. Because it is not possible to do so, for obvious reasons. Could it be gaseous ? Probably so, but would not contact with the air neutralize the gas and make it to dissolve in the atmosphere ?

Unless the African scientist could invent a fourth form or nature of matter which is unknown in the realm of pure science, whatever conclusions he had built up on the basis of his theories of " medicine " must fall flat. This does not mean that it is not true. It is simply this : That this brand of African " medicine " is *demonstrable*.

Again, in Africa it is taught that a man could " poison " another by shaking hands with him. It may be true. But the man who attempts to poison the other is physiologically identic with his victim. What poison can do to one man it can do to another. Therefore both individuals can be victims.

But you say that the evil-doer had immunized himself before administering the poison, and so it would not affect him, but would affect the other fellow. Granted that you are right, yet it is an unalterable law in science that once matter is neutralized it becomes neutralized. In other words, since matter has been neutralized not to affect flesh and blood of one, it would not affect the flesh and blood of the other.

This argument can be stretched. But in the interest of mental emancipation, Africans should either direct their attention to a systematic study *of their own science* or they should educate their children to study and to understand the science of the West. If they should follow in this way they would know the true causes of things and their effects.

There is no need for a professional man or any African for that matter, to think that he can " poison " his fellow man who lives miles away from him. It is possible to do so through the three forms of matter mentioned above. The victim must be near to eat, or to drink, or to feel one's weapon of death. Otherwise such credulous peoples deceive themselves.

African magic is either *superstitious* or *super*-scientific. What do you think ? Do you believe that an African can poison his fellow man without seeing him ? If so, why were the Sedition Bill and other unpopular bills allowed to remain on the statute book ? Probably Europeans are immune from African medicine ! If so, why are Africans not immune from European bullets ?

The African is born in an environment in which nothing is without a supernatural significance. The tree falls. The rain falls. The river flows and *ad infinitum*. None of these have a natural cause. They are mysteries and therefore supernatural—to the African !

Because the primitive educational system of the African is not empirical, he trains his mind to believe in a sort of super-scientific structure which may transcend the theory of relativity. If it is possible to reduce this African Super-Science to a scientific basis, a fifth dimension is possible.

In their ignorance or super-knowledge, Africans amass an amount of information regarding certain phenomena. And since these fail to stand the test of empiricism which is the basis of all scientific knowledge, they clothe the same with an attribute of supernaturalism.

Why does the tree fall ? It is not because the roots are unable to resist the force of gravity. No. It is because certain supernatural beings were aggrieved and so they " poisoned " that tree. This is an indication of African mentality.

Why does the rain fall ? It is not because of the evaporation which takes place. No. It is because " the medicine man " promised to " make " rain in order to destroy the ceremonies of a competing party. Another example of the curious mentality of the African.

Why do individuals die ? It is not because they were pathological victims or that they violated the laws of hygiene and sanitation. No. It is because their enemies " killed " them by poisoning them at a distance or so. Another example of the lack of spirit of enquiry on the part of the African.

In England, that is, at Oxford, certain courses referred to as the humanities, are nick-named " The Modern Greats ". In America, the collegians call these " The Bunkums ". These " bunkum " courses deal with the human side of life. They may be in the realms of history, economics, political science, sociology, etc. But " The Real Stuff " are the scientific courses, according to the American collegians. These consist of mathematics, biology, physics, chemistry and astronomy.

Because material science has become empirical, it makes the average student who is trained in the methodology of pure science to discount the classics, as comprising dead languages and dead ideas. To an extent, this revolution in the method and content of the curriculum has been responsible for the intellectual progress of human society.

Attend a university where more emphasis is laid on the classics and philosophy, and you will find there a group of young men and women who are living in the past and who are dead from their necks up, so far as contemporary problems are concerned.

Attend a university where emphasis is laid on the " Real Stuff " and you will come across mathematical minds who seek to interpret all phenomena according to set formulae and by means of the test-tube. To an extent, these individuals are not human in their approach to human problems.

Attend a university where emphasis is laid on the " Bunkums " and you will meet wide-awake young men and women who realize that they owe to posterity a heritage of better society, but who may be rather parochial in one way or the other.

But an ideal university, no matter where may be its location —in Manyakpowuno or in Kukuruku, is where you will notice that the curriculum is balanced and consequently, its graduates know a little of the classics, the humanities, and the sciences. This is the criterion of the efficacy of university education, in any part of the world.

When I consider the fact that throughout the continent of Africa there is not an indigenous university sustained through African initiative, I am in position to realize how most of the problems of Africa to-day are due to the intellectual poverty of Africans.

Had Africans universities, maintained at their expense, they could have had their curricula filled with the important divisions of knowledge which would have hastened their intellectual emancipation, and would have enabled them to make scientific researches into some of the quackeries which some of them are wont to elevate into an unmerited apogee by calling them a phase of " Super-Science ".

The recent news of Alabi, the " wonder " man of Abeokuta, who was alleged to have been imprisoned and to have used " super-scientific " means to escape from prison, has given the protagonists of African superstition grounds for articulation.

It was reported that by following a certain formula, it is possible for a man bound by iron chains to cause the same to drop on the ground, and to enable the prisoner to effect his escape immediately. It was also posited that with this Yola Formula, it is possible for a soldier to go to war, and bullets just breeze by him, whilst he escapes unscathed.[1]

" Spears and arrows will then fall harmlessly at his side. Knife-thrusts will have no effect. During a hunting battue, if he is outrun by a companion, as he nears the quarry, he has simply to twist the charm and his companion will fall," reports Mr Vanhein Wallace.

And all these supernatural things are supposed to happen provided one makes a certain charm and recites : " *It is nothing at all, koko-yam* ! "

Can there be any need for challenging the low mentality of any individual who relies on " *It is nothing at all, koko-yam* " in the field of battle, to save his life from a well-aimed bullet shot ? Hear ye gods ! And people who believe in such things are intelligent men and women ! !

I disagree with Mr Wallace and all those who trust in charms to save their lives. In mathematics, it is too evident that any solid will travel in a straight line, if aimed horizontally or vertically. In physics, it is too evident that matter in motion becomes inert when it comes in contact with another matter. But one has to consider the effect of velocity on the matter which is mobile

[1] *The African Morning Post*, September 18, 1935, page 5.

and that which is inert. In chemistry, it is known that any chemical which is not neutralized or immunized will have effect.

Bearing these generalizations in mind, how can a bullet which travels in a straight line, at a very fast speed, meet with the object aimed at, and fail to explode and eject its chemicals in that person's body, simply because that person says: "*It is nothing at all, koko-yam*?" If this is not the height of mental density, then mermaids exist!!!

Trust no charm, friend or foe. Trust the natural laws of the universe of which you are a part. Trust the objective realities of an objective world. It is true that subjective *realities* may be apparent. But the right to term them *realities* is questionable, in that a thing which is subjective is the opposite of a thing which is objective.

Charms may be useful, so long as they obey the physical laws of nature. But they don't, and that is why they are called charms. But when it comes to making a concoction which relies on a verbal command to cause matter to give way to matter, I think that it is stretching the point too far.

Again, the fact that Alabi's exploits were alleged to have happened in an inadequately supervised prison, and that the report lacks scientific proof, and that when Alabi was handcuffed and securely locked up in H.M. Prisons, at Lagos, the Koko-Yam charm failed to respond, makes the formula of the Fulani, as reported by Mr Wallace, still demonstrable. I will be glad to hear from any friends after they have tried to practicalize the efficacy of this charm, otherwise, it is a clear case that it is superstition, pure and simple.

Africa is a land of mysteries. Day by day strange tales are disseminated. These affect the thinking processes of the African, and if there is not a grain of truth in them, they do him more harm than good.

Imagine telling a child that witches and wizards inhabit a certain tree. Because that child is in a stage where his mind is impressionistic, nothing will make him believe that witches and wizards do not dwell in trees.

Unless that child is rescued by a broad educational training, he may be counted upon as an intellectual cipher.

I say this, because, when people of different interests, intellectually speaking, confabulate, there is bound to be a Babelism, and that child's intellectual vacuity cannot be a constructive factor in the societal existence.

Belief in witchcraft and wizardry is by no means confined to the continent of Africa. But its effect on the mentality of the African, on the whole, has been disastrous.

For example, very few Africans are able to diagnose ailments. They allow their acquired tendencies towards mental devolution (in that such a form of perversion of knowledge is devolutionizing) to dictate to them that witchcraft or " I know not what " caused the disease or death.

With a fairly good background in education, there is no reason why the foes of man—microbes, etc.—should be allowed to go scot free and innocent persons should be accused of being guilty of witchcraft, etc.

Are there witches ? Who has seen one ? What do they look like ? Did the witness see and know enough to describe one ? Is it possible to be in position to describe one, without that person being initiated into the order ? Is it a reality or is it the *reality* of an individual's mental imagery ? These are questions that must be answered by the African who believes in supernormalities in this physical universe.

Moreover, it cannot be doubted that some people who testify to having " seen " a witch have been victims of one of the various forms of hallucination.

Psychologists identify such form of mental imagery as an evidence of optic pathology. The eye is constantly under stimulation, which is due to the presence of action currents, the ideoretinal lights and hypnogogic images. The latter is a form which continues to linger in the memory after the original stimulus has made an impression and elicited a response.

According to Dr. John B. Watson, one of the founders of the theory of Behaviourism, one of the schools of thought in the field of modern psychology, " Visual impulses of a very simple character sometimes touch off complicated visual-motor habits. It is small wonder then, that in pathological cases where the retina is probably over-active so far as these internal changes are concerned, as in fevers, delirium tremens and the like, we see the subject *reacting apparently to a visual object to which other persons present do not react*." (His italics.)

In other words, when the nervous system experiences a sort of short-circuit, there is bound to arise fixations. These fixations may be initiated by the presence of any entoptic phenomenon and they linger so long that if even our eyeballs were removed, we continue to " see things ".

This attempt to explain African belief in witchcraft in psychological terms cannot be wholly successful. But of the two evils it seems to be the better one. Here are the two evils: the African claims to see witches (not all Africans have experienced this thrill or horror—so that the experience is not universal); the African who is beyond the pale of the " inner circle " becomes critical and submits a psychological explanation, imputing to " the inner circle " a status of mental aberration.

As in witchcraft, so too in " vision " of the dead. It is claimed that dead persons have resurrected and lived like human beings. If this is true, it is a direct disregard of the fundamental laws of biology.

Life is unexplainable, but the properties of life which generate matter are autonomic. What makes matter to be mobile is life. What generates the multi-cellular organisms including flora and fauna is life. But the biologist fails to define what is responsible for life after death.

However, when life is no more, matter begins to decompose. This form of decomposition guarantees the immortality of matter on the face of the earth. This is what I mean: through metabolism, the human body experiences certain changes, but these changes are cyclic from carbonic and nitrogenic standpoints. They are produced by bacteria in the processes which lead to chemosynthesis and photosynthesis.

But one thing is certain, once matter is lifeless, it is lifeless. So if a person dies, he stays dead, biologically speaking. Whether or not that dead person can become alive again, in view of the metabolic actions bringing about the Carbon and Nitrogen Cycles, bacteriologically speaking, is the issue between African superstition or " Super-Science " and the science of the West.

I submit that scientifically speaking, no dead person can live again. Whilst I admit that reports of apparitions and ghosts and biological selves of persons supposed to be dead have been current, and that upon recognition, they " vanished into thin air ", I posit that such phenomenon is still demonstrable.

I do not disbelieve in witchcraft. I do not deny that the dead can resurrect. I do not doubt that flesh and blood can " vanish into thin air ". But I assert that these are demonstrable, and must be proved empirically so as to warrant universal sanction that these beliefs have a scientific background.

Until the African has proved his theses and hypotheses on these supernormalities of the physical universe, it is better for him to learn the science of the West as a criterion to test the validity of the conclusions of African superstition or " Super-Science ".

If these fail to pass the test of the scientific norms, they should be discarded so as to usher in a new era of mental emancipation from the thraldom of ignorance and bigotry of superstition.

One phase of the lives of Africans in Africa is a desire for miraculous occurrences. Because the mind is so trained, the body behaves likewise. Thus Africans have been able to build up a series of shibboleths which may or may not have foundations of fact.

Explainable phenomena are defined as scientific. Unexplainable phenomena are regarded as superstition. A meeting place of the two schools of thought suggests another dimension in the study of man and his cosmology. This may be conveniently termed " Super-Science ", that is, observation of supernormal phenomena.

African society is one in which superstition or Super-Science reigns. Whether these are justifiable or not is still demonstrable, but one thing is certain, African supernormality in the realms of epistemology has not been a progressive factor in African society.

I must state my point of view clearly; African epistemology includes supernormal phenomena, just as the European, American, Asiatic, and Australian.

But whilst the other countries have disseminated their knowledge and have made use of the same towards their particular society for security, personal and societal, the African has used his for purposes which are responsible for his retrograde tendency.

In other words, the Caucasoid scientist or " Super-Scientist " makes use of his knowledge to safeguard himself and his society. His inventions are popularised so that the average person may understand, at least, its fundamentals.

On the other hand, the African restricts himself and confines his knowledge to a few who, on their death, may or may not have divulged their secrets. The ultimate experience is disastrous and catastrophic from a national point of view.

These difficulties may be responsible for the uncertainties that are connected with African " Super-Science ", and the certainties which demarcate between the science of the West and the superstition of Africa.

If African " Super-Science " is a reality, it is demonstrable. Otherwise, it is superstitious to continue to have faith in a reality which may be unreal.

To illustrate my point of view, I will say that to believe in the efficacy of a potion of medicine, judged by its empirical results, lends more authority to its realistic essence, than a belief that wearing a talisman made of parchment with a zodiacal sign engrossed thereon will chase away evil spirits, without empirically and universally *proving* the same.

The one is definite and certain, borne out by the experience of the experimenter. The other is indefinite and uncertain, not borne out by experience but may be an outcome either of mental aberration or mental subnormality.

If I must tout African " Super-Science " and habit African superstition in such a new garb, it is within my faculties to refurbish my beliefs by following the accepted scientific standards so as to prove my hypothesis.

It may be possible for an individual to travel through space without locomotion, physiologically speaking. It may be possible for a prisoner to curse a judge and cause him to remain stone-dead. It may be possible for a soldier to wear an amulet and go to war so that bullets stray from hitting him.

Again, it may be possible for a man to dig out sands from another's foot-prints and cause his death thereby. It may be possible for an adversary to obtain his victim's hair and cause him to become insane. No sane person doubts the possibility of anything on earth, but a critical mind will always challenge the validity of any right to believe in un-empirical phenomena.

Therefore, let the African believe in his superstition. But he must not categorize on it, until he has proved his thesis empirically.

To-day, the field of human knowledge is experiencing an evolution, a revolution, and a devolution. More inventions are being made. New discoveries are replacing older ones. New ideas in the realm of knowledge are discarding the cherished beliefs of yesteryears.

Science has been accepted, *universally*, as knowledge applied, tested, classified, systematized. In other words, anything to be scientific, must satisfy certain criteria as to its scientificity.

Speaking in scientific terms, *matter* is the basis of pure science. This matter may be reducible to atoms, electrons, protons, neutrons, etc. In whatever form it is reduced, one is told that matter must assume different essences, e.g., solid, liquid, gaseous.

Speaking in *material* terms, any component unit of the *material* universe must be reducible to the lowest common denominator of matter, be it in its substantive or derivative essence.

However, with the increasing amount of research studies in meteorology, astronomy, astrophysics, and advanced physics, the nature of the *ethereal* universe which had been a mystery which defied the attempts of science, is being gradually unravelled.

If, with the problems of science, I also consider the other realm which is a correlative of matter, namely, the mind, I may justify the right of a group of scholars who initiated the study of Psychic Research.

Here, prominence is given to the mind, just as prominence is given to matter, in Material or Natural Science. The claims of psychic science are as valid as the claims of certain fields of material science.

During one of the sessions of the Haverford Institute of International Relations, held at Haverford College, in Pennsylvania, in 1932, Dr. Hornell Hart, posited that since palaeontologists, archaeologists, geologists, and anthropologists were able to " establish " the existence of the *Pithecanthropus erectus* and other " ape-men races ", by digging up few skulls and bones, so too do the experiences of certain " mediums " with reference to their seeing ghosts, apparitions, etc., justify a psychological investigation which, with the aid of statistics, might justify certain conclusions.

Indeed, Psychic and Pure Science are fascinating studies for the average student of the West. For the African student, it would seem that his " Super-Science " may blend the two fields together, provided that the African has the mentality and the intellectual curiosity to make a definite contribution to the knowledge of the world.

If the African fails in this task, it is better for him to realize, immediately, that what he brands as " Super-Science " (an admitted evidence of his inferiority complex !) is nothing but superstition, ignorance, and for want of a better term, a form of mental slavery.

23. *ART OR PROPAGANDA ?*

Recently, a writer stirred a hornet's nest when he questioned the right of one group to portray the African as it pleases it in the name of art or literature. His point of view was re-echoed by others with particular reference to text-book writers.

Search through the artistic expressions which are available to mankind to-day, and with very few exceptions, you will see that the black man, as such, is portrayed as a hewer of wood and drawer of water.

In whatever field your researches may be directed—in literature, in arts (sculpture, music, painting), or even in religion, you will discover the fact that a series of shibboleths has been built making certain attributes glorious and others damnifying.

If the objective of aesthetics is to aid self-expression, then it must be art, but if the subjective personality is brought to bear in objectifying the arts, it ceases to be art but propaganda.

While I appreciate that propaganda itself is an art, it is taken for granted that my discussion of art is devoid of any attempt to beg the question. It pertains to the fields of paintings, sculpture, music, and literature.

Beginning with painting and sculpture, it is remarkable that the attributes which depict evil, wickedness, baseness, lewdness, ignorance, darkness, are generally black. Those which depict goodness, kindness, uprightness, righteousness, knowledge, light are generally white.

For this reason " black " is for mourning, and things relating to the dead and occasions for weeping. On the other hand, " white " is for jovialities and things pertaining to occasions which call for happiness in life, like marriages.

The devil is always black. The angels, the host of heaven, the Son of God, and even God Himself—these are supposed to be white. Where does this kind of artistry lead to ? How can a black man believe in a white God ? Is that not a form of mental servitude ?

Again, in the realm of literature, I find the black race portrayed as sub-human. In fact, some of the novels which have earned a great reputation have done so at the expense of the black races.

Take the modern novels in America and England, for example, you will never find a novelist who had the moral courage to give the black man or woman a position of respect in his characters. Blacks are either clowns, servants, or imbeciles, so far as their characterization is concerned.

It is true that there are characters like Rasselas, Prince of Abyssinia, and the Prince of Morocco, and even Othello ; but these are exceptions. Samuel Johnson and Shakespeare are among the few English writers who seem to have escaped from the bite of the bug of Negrophobism.

To-day, the most fascinating method of lending realism to a portrayal of the African as an ignoramus or coward or servant, is the cinematographic reels. Outside of an all-Negro production one hardly finds Hollywood or Elstree ready to portray an African man as a hero, or an African woman as a heroine.

Because some Africans still have a pride and have not been victimized by Western materialism to destroy their sense of respect, they have not always allowed their " talents " to be exploited at the expense of the race, compared with certain American and West Indian Negroes.

In the United States, men like Paul Robeson, Clarence Muse, Bojangles Robinson, etc., have sold their birth-right for a mess of pottage. Women like Nina McKinney, Ethel Waters, and others too numerous to mention, have followed suit. Where dollar calls, these " artists " follow.

According to the tradition of English writers, Edgar Wallace wrote his *Sanders of the River*, a novel of the variety which made him famous. True to his heritage, he found no attribute which could be said to be good in the African. It is the drunken coaster and over-rated official who take the palm for bravery, as usual.

This novel has been screened. Its cinema version was the " rage " of London. They praised it to the skies. One of the papers suggested that the Hungarian producer of the picture was an ardent imperialist, who deserved a King's Birthday honour.

I am not interested in the portrayal of the African as a god or as a devil, necessarily, in this instance. What is racking my brains is the mentality of those people of African descent who, on the one hand, would criticize the attempts of Europeans to undervalue African culture, and, on the other hand, would bow down to the almighty pound, shilling, pence.

Why did Mr Paul Robeson choose to play such an ignominious rôle to undervalue African mentality ? A man of his education (he is B.A., LL.B.), seems to be an enigma to me. As for Miss McKinney, the less said of her the better. Her education is not comparable to that of Robeson.

But for Mr Paul Robeson, a man who has been philosophizing about the destiny of the Negro race, to continue accepting parts in dramatics and cinemas which depict the Negro as something below human, is an indication of a lack of " foundations ", to borrow the terminology of my friend, Mr Kobina Sekyi.

The spirit may be willing but the flesh is weak. He did it in Eugene O'Neil's play, *Emperor Jones*. This piece of dramatic production was a definite insult to the African races. It was a caricature of Haiti, and it seems to me as if O'Neil used it as a propaganda to portray the Negro as lacking the capacity for self-government.

Paul Robeson made thousands of dollars for portraying the incompetent Emperor (apparently one of the emperors of Haiti, if not Emperor Henri Christophe !), at the expense of his race.

Sanders of the River may reach African shores for reproduction on the screens. Whoever sees this picture will be shocked at the exaggeration of African mentality, so far as superstitious beliefs are concerned, not to speak of the knavery and chicanery of some African chiefs.

Although I have not seen the picture, but having read the novel, and having seen parts of the picture whilst in process of production, in Elstree, and knowing some African students who proselytized themselves in order to earn three guineas a day, acting as soldiers of the R.W.A.F.F., or dancing the " Achiko ", I feel that what is being paraded in the world to-day as art or literature is nothing short of propaganda.

The will of the inferior is being substituted for the will of the superior, by potent means of propaganda camouflaged as art or literature.

24. *BORN TO BLUSH UNSEEN*

" Perhaps in this neglected spot is laid
Some heart once pregnant with celestial fire ;
Hands, that the rod of Empire might have swayed,
Or waked to ecstasy the living lyre.

" But knowledge to their eyes her ample page
Rich with the spoils of time did ne'er unroll ;
Chill penury repressed their noble rage,
And froze the genial current of their soul.

" Full many a gem of purest ray serene,
The dark unfathomed caves of ocean bear :
Full many a flower is born to blush unseen,
And waste its sweetness on the desert air."

Thomas Gray, whose immortality was made patent by his poem, " Elegy Written In A Country Churchyard ", has left the above for posterity. As it was in the eighteenth century when he lived, so is life to-day in the twentieth century.

Africa is a neglected spot. There are sons and daughters whose hearts burn with the celestial fire, and there are hands which are capable of swaying empires, yet they are doomed to flourish like the flower that is born to blush unseen, wasting its sweetness on the desert air.

Who will not agree that to-day there is a sort of chill penury which represses the African's noble rage and freezes the genial current of his soul, so that he becomes likened to many a gem of purest rays serene which flourish in the dark caves of the ocean, unsung!

That is the lot of Africans. Their talents are bound to be locked in that mysterious key of life, and unless they are in a position to unlock that key, there will be no opportunity for them to wake to ecstasy the living lyre within.

Renascent African, take heart, your lot is not that of a hod carrier. Your lot is not that of a canoe paddler. Your lot is not that of a fisherman. Your lot is not that of a porter. There is a far nobler destiny for you.

If in this irony of life and death, where the titled few are humbled with the many poor when they pay their Thanatopsian homage, man is able to achieve, thou too, Renascent African, could!

Take heart, Renascent Africa, the best is yet to be. If man could exercise his brains to invent a flying apparatus, thou too, could!

Take heart, Renascent African, your life is not a path of ignominy and oppression. If man could wield power over man, if man could subject to his wishes his fellow man, thou too, could!

Amidst the vicissitudes of life, the African seems to be impressed by the inventions and discoveries of others. He seems cowed and he believes that others have a superior genius.

No such thing exists, poor mortal fool. Remember Thomas Gray: "Full many a flower is born to blush unseen and waste its sweetness on the desert air".

The African is like a flower in a wild region. It blossoms and blushes—unseen. And it loses its fragrance in the great envelope of gas which protects this earth from the fiery balls in the celestial hemisphere.

Yet, that is not the end. Even a wild region can be transformed over-night into a modern city! Even a swampy region can be reclaimed to become a great city! And why not Africa?

Are Africans lacking the initiative to invent? Do they feel that they are incapable of inventing something that will be of benefit to the world?

Pin is a common object, but it takes brains to invent it. Matches seem to be commonly handled and regarded, yet it takes fully-developed and cultivated brain power to invent them.

Have Africans failed to exercise their brain power, in view of the fact that the possibilities of the human brain are yet untapped, by about ninety per cent., according to physiologists and psychologists?

Come now, Renascent African, believe in yourself. Believe that you have the talent, but it is latent. Believe, and it shall be done unto you.

Africa has produced geniuses in the past. Africa is producing geniuses to-day. And Africa can and will produce geniuses to-morrow.

Do you know that although Eli Whitney, a Caucasoid, is credited with the invention of cotton gin, which revolutionized the manufacture of cotton, yet Henry E. Baker, Examiner of the United States Patent Office, states that Whitney got the idea from a black slave?

Do you know that Norbert Rillieux, a black man, invented an evaporating pan which has since been the basis of refining and manufacturing sugar?

Do you know that Henry Blair, another black man, invented two corn harvesters in 1834-36, thus practically revolutionizing applied agriculture?

Do you know that Jan E. Matzelliger, a black man of Dutch Guiana descent, invented the Lasting Machine, by which the mass production of boots and shoes was made possible, and that he sold this patent in 1852 to the United Shoe Machinery Company, one of the greatest shoe producing concerns in the world?

Do you know that J. H. and S. L. Dickinson, black men, invented over twelve appliances which enable the piano to be played automatically? That Shelby J. Davidson, another black man, invented a mechanical tabulator (adding machine) which has been incorporated in modern comptometre machines?

Do you know that J. L. Pickering of Haiti, James Smith of California, W. G. Madison of Iowa, and H. E. Hooter of Missouri, all black men, have been granted patents for certain devices employed in airships?

Do you know that Granville T. Woods, a black man, made

the following inventions which are used all over the world: steam boiler furnace, an amusement machine apparatus, a type of incubator, electrical air brakes, devices for transmitting messages between moving trains, and that these patents have been bought and used by the following companies: General Electric Company, Westinghouse Air Brake Company, American Bell Telephone Company, American Engineering Company?[1]

Now these inventions were made by black persons through the cultivation and exercise of the gray matter in the skull which God gave to them, as it gave to you and other members of the human race. If they could, why not you?

Those shallow-brained persons who marvel at the exploits of others deserve to be called to order lest they infect posterity with the virus of inferiority complex.

Long before Europeans landed in Africa, Africans had been able to ascertain the nature and form of iron ore and to use the same.[2] Long before Europeans came, the material culture of Africa was a vindication of the mental equality of mankind.[3]

There is, therefore, no reason why the African should be satisfied with the inventions of others. Let Africans wake up and realize that they too have brains like others and that they have talents which are latent but can be developed.

"Let not ambition mock their useful toil,
Their homely joys, and destiny obscure;
Nor grandeur hear with a disdainful smile
The short and simple annals of the poor.

"The boast of heraldry, the pomp of power,
And all that beauty, all that wealth e'er gave,
Awaits alike the inevitable hour,
The paths of glory lead but to the grave. . . .

"Full many a gem of purest ray serene,
The dark unfathomed caves of ocean bear:
Full many a flower is born to blush unseen,
And waste its sweetness on the desert air."

[1] C. G. Woodson, *The Negro in Our History* (6th ed.), pages 230-31 and pages 461-7.

[2] See *infra*, page 9.

[3] P. A. Talbot, *Peoples of Southern Nigeria* (1926), 4 volumes; Leo Frobenius, *The Voice of Africa* (1913), 2 volumes; W. L. Hansberry, "The Material Culture of Ancient Nigeria", *Journal of Negro History*, Vol. VI, pages 261-95.

25. *OUR CIVILIZATIONAL CAPACITY*

Professor A. M. Carr-Saunders made a provocative statement at the last meeting of the British Association for the Advancement of Science, which was held at Blackpool, that I feel should not go unchallenged.

According to a newspaper publication the learned Liverpool University savant is reported to have said that the major groups which had provided civilizations of the world were: Nordic (white) five: Alpine (white) seven: Mediterranean (white); Yellow, three: Red, four. "The Negroes had contributed to none."

"*The failure of the Negro race is not evidence of incapacity, but of lack of opportunities. There is evidence that all the maior groups are endowed with a degree of intelligence for generating and maintaining civilization. Intelligence tests have shown that there is no difference between any groups of any colour.*"

It will be seen that this evaluation is made *racially* and *geographically*. The conclusive statement of Professor Carr-Saunders and his post-premises are conflicting. The learned gentleman did not realize that he made a conflicting statement when he said, on the one hand, that the Negro had not exerted any potent influence on civilization and, on the other hand, he admitted that "*There is evidence that all the major groups* (meaning races?) *are endowed with a degree of intelligence for generating and maintaining civilization.*"

Mr Carr-Saunders has not been logical in his conclusion, but his premises are *correct*! Is it not strange then that such a fallacious utterance could have proceeded from the mouth of so eminent a Demographer?

That Mr Carr-Saunders is an authority in the field of Demography is conceded. That as a Sociologist his reputation is nternational, is also admitted. But when he takes upon himself to wear the garb of the Anthropologist, he is thousands of miles away from his field.

Again, the subject matter of *civilization*, academically speaking, falls within the range of study of the Anthropologist,

Archaeologist and probably the Historian. Mr Carr-Saunders does not and cannot claim to be one of these.

The Sociologist depends on the data furnished him by the Anthropologist to formulate his premises and conclusions. The Anthropologist also depends on the Archaeologist, the Palaeontologist and Geologist necessarily. But I will say that his knowledge in these fields are limited and cannot be conclusive, if Mr Carr-Saunders admits that he is a specialist in the study of *populations*.

At this stage I wish to dilate on some points raised in the statement of Professor A. M. Carr-Saunders of Liverpool University. I shall discuss his premises, firstly, and then I shall reconcile these with his conclusion.

The learned Professor admits that there have been great civilizations in the past, but submits that not one of these constituted Negro civilization. Apologetically, he adds that this is not evidence of incapacity but evidence of lack of opportunity.

I say that this statement, coming from so eminent an authority in Sociology as Professor A. M. Carr-Saunders, is wrong and mis-leading on the following grounds:

1. Classical sources yield evidence of Negro civilizations.

2. Archaeological data substantiate to a very great extent the data yielded in the Classical sources.

3. Anthropological data substantiate archaeological evidence that is available.

4. Historical evidence does not puncture 1, 2, and 3.

5. Palaeontology is gradually revealing the validity of 1, 2, 3, and 4.

It must be stated that before A.D. 1442, the term *Negro* was unknown in history.[1] If there is any dispute as to this statement, I would welcome any rejoinder.

If it is accepted that black-complexioned peoples were identified as Negroes since A.D. 1442, what was the designation of black peoples before then? Any person who is able to answer this question should be able to shatter the thesis of Professor Carr-Saunders to smithereens.

I should not rebut Mr Carr-Saunders' statement without showing why. It is admitted that academic freedom is not

[1] *The Negro Year Book*, 1932, Division IV.

limited to a particular section of the world. It is also admitted that any person with my qualification, especially in the field of Anthropology is entitled to *competent* opinion on any subject pertaining to this field.

My right to criticize the thesis of Professor Carr-Saunders is not, therefore, questionable. A Fellow of the Royal Anthropological Institute who may have international reputation in this field, cannot remain mute when vital issues pertaining to this interesting study are discussed.

1. *Classical Sources.* Herodotus, Strabo, and Diodorus Sicullus, founders of History and Geography, identified black persons as Ethiopians in their treatises.[1]

2. *Archaeological Data.* The reports of archaeological expeditions led by Champollion, Volney, Heeren, Hoskins, Naville, MacIver, Petrie, Budge, Maspero, Sayce, Beard, Wilkinson, etc., indicate the important phases of Negroid civilization in periods of antiquity.

3. *Anthropological Data.* The researches and surveys and field studies of Sergi, Ripley, Haddon, Smith, Darwin, Gregory, Peringuey, Leo Frobenius, Heinrich Barth, Dixon, etc., yield evidence of the part played by black peoples in the evolution of civilizations.

4. *Historical Evidence.* The books on Ancient and Medieval History written by Eadie, Prichard, Erman, Maspero, Hall, Kenrick, Es-Sadi, Felix Dubois, Lady Lugard, etc., show the existence of Negro civilizations in Ancient and Medieval times.[2]

5. *Palaeontological Data.* Researches conducted by Andrews, Schlosser, Broom, Reck, Pigorini, Breuil, Boule, etc., yield data which no person of consequence can afford to overlook when discussing Negro civilization.

Now, in the face of the data yielded by classical, archaeological, anthropological, historical, and palaeontological scholarship, it is challenging to observe that Professor Carr-Saunders could have made such a generalization in a supposedly learned address before so eminent a group of scholars as the British Association for the Advancement of Science.

[1] Herodotus, II: 104; Strabo, XV, i, 13; Diodorus Sicullus, III, 1.

[2] Including the *Old Testament.*

I maintain that if the facts from which Professor Carr-Saunders made his generalization are reliable, my own facts are also reliable. Look at the eminent names mentioned in the various categories above and compare them with any names submitted by any person who speaks or writes on the intriguing subjects of Culture and Civilization. My authorities are just as valid, if not weightier.

I say that Negroes, i.e., the black races, enjoyed their day in Ancient and Medieval times. This is borne out by historical facts.

The climax of Negro civilizations in antiquity, was reached in the year 713 B.C. when Piankhi, the King of Ethiopia, conquered Egypt, Persia, Assyria, to crystallize the *black man's dominion of the world.*

During this period, five black kings, Piankhi, Shabaka, Shabataka, Tirhaka, and Tanutamon ruled " The Two Lands " (Ethiopia and Egypt) and made Napata and Memphis the capitals of this great empire.

The blacks also aided the Jews of Israel and Judah, by saving them from the onslaughts of Sennacherib, Ashurbanipal and Esarhaddon.[1]

In Medieval times, no trustworthy historian has as yet denied the Negro civilizations of Ghana, Melle, Mellestine and Songhay. Even Mr W. F. Ward, M.A., B.Litt. (Oxon.), of Achimota College, who wrote a thought-provoking booklet on this field of study, admits that our claim in this particular regard is founded.[2]

The fact that Tarik-bin-Ziad, the conqueror of Spain, in A.D. 711 was a black person, and that he was commander of the Moorish army which invaded Spain, and that Gibraltar was named after this black general, and that the great Turkish classic, *Tarik-bin-Ziad*, was named after him, indicates the potency of Negro civilization in medieval times.[3]

There is no argument about the Moors or Tarik-bin-Ziad being black or Negroid. Mr A. E. Houghton, author of

[1] See *infra*, page 10 n.

[2] W. F. Ward, *Africa Before the White Man Came* (1935).

[3] W. N. Huggins and J. G. Jackson, *A Guide to Studies in African History* (1935), page 48.

Restoration of the Bourbons in Spain, asserts that the Almoravides (conquerors of Spain) " were Berbers and were largely mingled with pure Negroes ".[1]

In the face of many facts which are available to show that black civilizations flourished during ancient and medieval times, it is discouraging to read the categorical statement of so eminent a Sociologist.

Now to the conclusion of Mr Carr-Saunders. I have shown in a sketchy but scholarly fashion that it is incorrect to say that the black race, i.e., the Negroid race, anthropologically speaking, has not, at any time, in the world's history, germinated and nurtured any civilization of its own.

That the black race has the capacity but lacks the opportunity, is the apology of Professor Carr-Saunders which must be dismissed contemptuously. The learned gentleman's premises that " *There is evidence that all the major groups are endowed with a degree of intelligence for generating and maintaining civilization* ", substantiates my contention that in the same line of reasoning, black civilizations have flourished and will flourish.

If the black race has the capacity to survive since the evolutionary history of mankind, there is nothing to prevent that race from crystallizing another great civilization as it had done in the past. The black race asks for no opportunity. It is apologetic for the black race to do so. All races are endowed equally, each according to its talents. May the fittest survive!

26. *TOWARDS POLITICAL RESURGENCE*

Ethiopia is the last vestige of black autocracy. It represents the type of government which the forefathers of Africans established on this continent.

That country will go down in history as one of the few survivals of the great powers of history. I am not superstitious but the continued existence of Ethiopia after its contemporaries and their descendants had vanished from political history, is, and should be, an object of admiration.

[1] *Encyclopaedia Britannica* (14th ed.), vol. XXI, page 128.

These historical facts purport to show that the black man, as demonstrated in the political history of the Ethiopians, has political capacity, and if in other parts of Africa the African seems to devolutionize, then a political resurgence is natural.

The Republic of Liberia is the last vestige of black democracy. It represents the type of Government which repatriated Africans brought with them after their contact with the New World. It is an advance when compared with the other types of Government, now prevailing in Africa.

Despite the difficulties in its way towards statehood, the Republic of Liberia has vindicated the political capacity of the black man. It has established a Government dedicated to the principles of security to life and property of the citizens and their enjoyment in all the political and civil liberties of righteous government.

In West African colonies, Africans are still living in a period of suspended animation, politically speaking. They have a form of Government which is neither conducive to democratic government nor does it hold out for them any distinct promise for political manhood.

In this circumstance, I have to consider why Africans are still the footstool of little Belgium, inconsequential Portugal, fourth-rate Spain, resurgent Italy and so on down the line.

Is it because they are lacking in political capacity ? It cannot be. If the Negro race produced a State which has existed from eons past, it cannot be logical to conclude that that race lacks political capacity.

Is it because they are lacking in political acumen ? Probably so. Most of those who are the self-professed leaders of the various sections of West Africa are, in reality, and with all due deference to them, worthy of one piece of job, that is, to commit *felo-de-se*.

In all sincerity and candour, the main reason why the shibboleth of the inferiority of the African for social and political capacity lingers, is due to the *imbecility* of most of African leaders. That word is not so musical to the ear, but it is the truth.

In Gambia, I find the people yearning for leaders, but who are at the helm ? A selfish prating clique. Mediocre personalities who are more interested in becoming foreign titlists than making an indelible imprint on the sands of history.

Gambia politics are just as corrupt as the politics of any other country. The only difference is that some of the self-professed leaders of Gambia are self-opinionated, lack social vision, and are wanting in mental virility.

All they seem to care for is the " privilege " to be addressed as knights, even though they can hardly wield a sword to defend their country.

The same is applicable to Sierra Leone. There one finds intelligent looking leaders pussy-footing with their hats in hands presenting their petition to His Most Excellent Governor reminding His Most Excellent Majesty that Her Most Excellent Majesty regarded Sierra Leone as the Most Ancient and Loyal Colony of Uncle Toms.

Is there any wonder that the youth of Sierra Leone are stifled and are made to be subservient to persons who have no pretensions whatsoever to leadership of ants, much more of men ?

Turn to Nigeria. The same thing holds true. After struggling to accumulate wealth, those who succeed, instead of using the same for the benefit of reconstructing their shattered national heritage, use the same to curry favours, bowing endlessly to those who are not entitled to the same, morally or otherwise.

The political situation in Nigeria is cyanogenic. Leaders who should be an emblem of courage and manhood to youth, cower before some swaggering officials.

Leaders who have been, seem to have lost the pep of continuing the fight, and they themselves go the way of all flesh.

Is there any wonder then that in a country of twenty-one million souls less than six thousand non-Africans seem destined to guide and control them for ever ?

As in the Gambia, Sierra Leone, Nigeria, so too in the Gold Coast. Some leaders perch on altars defiled with the stench of corruption, chicanery, egocentrism, tribal prejudice, cowardice, get-rich-quick philosophy, alphabetimania, and the relics of Uncle Tomism.

The youth of Africa believe that the time is at hand when

they should make a re-evaluation of their *raison d'être* on this continent.

Are Africans created to serve as slaves for ever or are they destined to impress their civilization on the world as they had done in the past?

Renascent Africa regards as youthful all Africans who believe in the cultivation of spiritual balance, the practicalization of social regeneration, the realization of economic determinism, evidence of mental emancipation, and the precipitation of a reverberation which will give them their lost place in the sun.

Renascent Africans, faint not, lose no hope. Although the Old Africa lingers, it is but a passing phase of your new lease of life. The era of ciphers and Uncle Toms is in transition. The days of hat-in-hand-me-too-boss political scavengers are numbered. The alphabetimaniacs have been weighed in the balance. You must now prepare for the inevitable so that you may fully appreciate your rendezvous with life.

Have you ever stopped to think that without biography history is incomplete? Have you dared to wade into the currents and cross-currents of history without being impressed by the lives of those who made history?

Yes, friends, no human history is complete without the narration, the description, and the exposition of human lives. Men and women make history. History does not make them.

Biography is an historical record of men and events. History is an analectum of biographies.

The study of life is just as historical as the study of inanimate objects.

If your field is astronomy, you study stars, moons, suns, the nebulae, comets, etc. But these have life. That is why they have motion. The nature of their life is the question mark.

If your field is mineralogy, you study stones, minerals, etc. But these have factors which lead to the conclusion that they *lived* once. The nature of their life is another question mark.

If your field is biology, you study life in all its forms, from the amoebae right up to the primates.

These are natural or physical history. The greatest history is the history of man—Biography.

When I consider the above and realize that without man,

no nation can progress or become historical, it is evident that the heritage that man leaves to man is the criterion of the greatness of any country.

Again, if I admit that man's biography is conterminous with human history, then the idiosyncrasies of men are responsible for the currents and cross-currents of history.

When Leonidas and his six hundred heroes faced the teeming Persians at the Pass of Thermopylae, it never occurred to them that their lives were at stake. They thought of country first.

Forget the physical courage exemplified by their heroic defence of the Pass, and think of the engraving on the spot where Leonidas fell: "*Stranger, go tell the Spartans that we are lying here, obedient to the laws which they have made.*"

And what was this law of Sparta which caused the obedience of Leonidas and his six hundred heroes, even unto death? Patriotism.

The Spartan had been trained to think of country first. The Spartan had been handed a heritage of freedom. This was the torch which Leonidas and his six hundred men sacrificed their lives to keep burning, so that posterity might profit by it.

But Sparta was a great country. Yet without the patriotism, without the moral and physical courage of Leonidas and his six hundred heroes, Sparta might have been forgotten.

Can you think of Greece without thinking of the biographies of some of the greatest men produced by Greece?

Without Socrates drinking the hemlock so that academic freedom might be safeguarded for posterity, would Greek philosophy have been so basic as to be the study of world's philosophy? I think not.

The life of Socrates is really the history of Greek philosophy. Take away the courage of Socrates, and you find a country which floundered until it was ready to be conquered by Rome. It is in the life of Socrates that one sees the moving spirit which prompted the Greeks, even in defeat at the hands of the Romans, to teach and influence the Romans, for posterity.

And dare you study Roman history without studying the lives of the men produced by Rome at the zenith of its existence?

"*I came, I saw, I conquered.*" True, but is that expression true of Caesar alone? Is it not typically the experience of Rome?

Caesar had to reach the bank of the Rubicon to arrive. *He came.* Caesar had to cross the Rubiçon to appreciate the glories of Rome. *He saw.* Caesar had to decide whether crossing the Rubicon was worthwhile or not. He did. *And he conquered.*

That is exactly the history of Rome. Rome came to the scene of a clash of the civilizations of the Near East and Greece. Rome saw an opportunity to leave a heritage of liberty and freedom to posterity. And Rome triumphed!

But just as Caesar came and saw and conquered and met his twilight on the day of the Ides of March, so too did Rome. Indeed the biography of Caesar is a symbolic history of Rome.

Bear with me through medieval and modern history. You will find the biographies of some of the leading lives the basis of medieval and modern history.

The candle which was lit at the stake by Cranmer, Ridley and Latimer, made religious toleration possible to be handed to posterity as a heritage.

"*Be of good comfort, Master Ridley, we shall this day light such a candle by God's grace in England as, I trust, shall never be put out.*"

Thus spake Bishop Latimer, one of the most popular orators of his day. And his conviction is now an added treasure to the torch of freedom handed down to posterity and which is jealously guarded to-day, even in England which sentenced him to an untimely grave.

During the American Revolution, was it not the spirit of some of America's sons that actually guaranteed for posterity popular liberty? Patrick Henry's biography is indeed the history of America. Read a part of his oration, on the eve of the Revolution of 1776:

"No man thinks more highly than I do of the patriotism, as well as abilities of the very worthy gentlemen who have just addressed this house. But different men often see the same subject in different lights and, therefore, I hope it will not be thought disrespectful to those gentlemen, if entertaining as I do opinions of a character very opposite to theirs, I shall speak forth my sentiments freely and without reserve.

"Mr President, it is natural to man to indulge in the illusions of hope. We are apt to shut our eyes against a painful truth, and listen to the song of that siren, till she transforms us into beasts.

"Is this the part of wise men, engaged in a great and arduous struggle for liberty? Are we disposed to be of the number of those, who, having eyes, see not, and having ears, hear not, the things which so nearly concern their temporal salvation?

"I have but one lamp by which my feet are guided, and that is the lamp of experience. I know of no way of judging the future but by the past. . . .

"*Is life so dear, or peace so sweet, as to be purchased at the price of chains and slavery? Forbid it, Almighty God! I know not what course others may take; but as for me, give me liberty or give me death!*"

And if any student of history disagrees with me that the biographies of the men and women of any country are the fundamental basis of the currents and cross-currents of that country's history, then let the study of biography be condemned: otherwise, let it be given its rightful place in the curriculum of the schools.

Coming nearer home, what is the importance attached to the biographies of the great men of West Africa? Outside of Liberia, pray tell me, ladies and gentlemen, where are monuments dedicated to the great men and women who lived and laboured and died that others might have this heritage of liberty, no matter how limited it might be.

How many school-children know the part played by Sir Samuel Lewis, Dr Edward Blyden, Rev. Attoh-Ahuma, Messrs J. M. Sarbah, Herbert Macaulay, Horatio Jackson, J. E. Casely-Hayford, and others in West African history?

Ah the times! Dare I forget those who laid the foundations upon which West African history was built? Longfellow's verses are a challenge to me:

"Lives of great men all remind us
We can make our lives sublime,
And departing, leave behind us,
Footprints on the sands of time.

"Footprints, that perhaps another,
Sailing o'er life's solemn main,
A forlorn and shipwrecked brother,
Seeing, shall take heart again.

"Let us then be up and doing,
With a heart for any fate,
Still achieving, still pursuing. . . ."

West Africans are faced with this challenge of biography. The lives of their illustrious men and women remind them to make their lives sublime, so that like they, they might make their footprints on the sands of time, still achieving, still pursuing . . . that heritage of freedom and that torch of liberty.

The rôle of the black man in contemporary international politics has been of the slightest sort that a modest survey of his status in different regions appears germane to a better evaluation of the factors involved.

According to one writer, there are less than one hundred and fifty million black persons in the world to-day.[1] Of these about five per cent. or more control their political destinies, and the rest have been absorbed in the sovereign States and colonial possessions of other world powers.

These small international personalities are so geographically separated that for decades it has been impossible to effectuate concerted action. The realities in the modern history of imperialism are gradually forcing them to align themselves together for mutual benefit.

The Kingdom of Abyssinia is the oldest of modern Negro states. The Republic of Haiti comes next, and the Republic of Liberia forms the latest addition to the list of international entities ruled and governed exclusively by black persons.

The form of Government of Abyssinia is aristocratic; those of Haiti and Liberia are democratic. The type of Government of Abyssinia is a constitutional monarchy, whilst those of Haiti and Liberia are definitely republican.

One thing is important, despite the difference, so far as form and type are concerned, there is a gamut in the three states which is translatable to mean that there is a universal identity of interest, in that *Government is based on consent of the governed through constitutional provisions*.

[1] Buell, *op. cit.*, page 85.

In the American continent, Negroes form a stratum of political society. They are somewhat articulate in their expressions and have a voice in the affairs of the State. Due to the practice of "Gerrymander", there is an inescapable process of geographic distribution of population so that the blacks have been submerged and they form a minority element. This is the fate of all minority groups and the Negro is no exception.

In the Caribbean regions and certain portions of European colonies in Central America, the voice of the black folks in the affairs of State is limited by certain weapons of colonial diplomacy, such as the principle of the official majority in the Legislative Councils.

In Europe, the black man has been such a negligible factor in politics that he is inarticulate. His rights are limited to civil and religious equality. His rights, so far as economic competition is concerned, are at times questionable. But in the actual formulation of the laws and policies, he is an extraneous element.

In Africa, outside of the independent states of Abyssinia and Liberia, the black man and woman are still regarded to be children of nature, and therefore to be in an adolescent state. They live under alien governments. They are vassals, not citizens. They are protégés, not citizens, with few exceptions. They exercise the rights of a *de facto* national and not a *de jure* citizen.

In the Negroid groups of Australia, Oceania, Polynesia, Micronesia, and Melanesia, they are generally regarded as protégés of their respective colonial masters.

Consequently, the majority of blacks are supposed to be undergoing a period of tutelage which would eventually qualify them for self-government. The criterion for such qualification is not indicated, however. It is generally concluded that the period of tutelage is indefinite, so far as the tutor-nation is concerned.

With the enunciation of the principles of the Mandates, vide Article XXII of the Covenant of the League of Nations, those groups of the world's citizenry (mostly blacks) were looked upon, with few others, as "not yet able to stand by themselves

[1] Abyssinia has since been conquered by Italy and reduced to the status of an Italian Colony.

under the strenuous conditions of the modern world ". Therefore, with the forces of international morality at work, they were regarded as mandates of civilized humanity, and " the tutelage of such peoples should be entrusted to advanced nations who, by reason of their resources, their experience or their geographical position, can best undertake this responsibility ".

Thus were some of the black peoples of West, South, and East Africa transferred to Great Britain, France, and Belgium, *to hold in trust* until they arrive at the age of political puberty.

From the foregoing summary of the political status of black folks in all parts of the world, I may fairly conclude that the black peoples, so far as international politics is concerned, present four classificatory categories :

1. *As a citizen of a Negro State.* Abyssinia,[1] Haiti, and Liberia, illustrate this category.

2. *As a citizen of a Non-Negro State.* Latin-America, the United States of America, and certain European states, exemplify this classification.

3. *As a protégé of a Non-Negro State.* The British West Indies and other colonial territories in Africa and Asia portray this division.

4. *As a protégé of the League of Nations.* The mandated territories, for example. Their position is mysterious because the League is neither a State nor is it clothed with attributes of statehood.[2]

From this, it is logical to conclude that the political destiny of black peoples as a race, is a challenge to their manhood. If out of a population of about 150,000,000 black persons, less than five per cent control their political institutions, it is indicative of racial devolution.

True, they must be tutored through the aid of their friends from across the sea, but if they must do so at the risk of losing their political identity, then it were better that they had not existed. The terms " tutelage " and " trusteeship " are, indeed, intriguing, if not challenging.

[1] Before its annexation by Italy in 1936.

[2] It was observed that the League of Nations " is not a State. It owns no territory, governs no subjects, and is not endowed with the attribute of sovereignty." See *Rex v. Christian*, South Africa Law Reports, 1924 App. Div. 101, *et seq.*

What qualifies one for the position of being a tutor? What are the norms for judging the capacity of one political entity to assume jurisdiction for an indeterminate period? What is the criterion to decide when the pupil has graduated from tutelage?

These are some of the questions that European and African leaders must answer satisfactorily in the twentieth century. *Satisfaction can be guaranteed when there is co-operation and mutual respect on both sides of the fence, else a Black or a White Peril complex must be inevitable.*

"Therefore, in the name of humanity, and virtue, and religion; in the name of the Great God, our Common Creator, we appeal to the nations of Christendom, and earnestly and respectfully ask of them that they will regard us with sympathy and friendly considerations to which the peculiarities of our condition entitle us and to extend to us that comity which marks the friendly intercourse of civilized and independent communities."

Thus reads the concluding portion of the Liberian Declaration of Independence which was signed and promulgated, ninety years ago.

Reader, bear with me as I survey the historic utterance made by black men and women, ninety years ago, when all the future that they could cherish seemed to have been blasted by the artifices and chicaneries of European diplomacy, and they braced up and asserted their right to life, liberty, and the pursuit of happiness.

July 26, 1847 *marked an important landmark in the annals of the black Republic of Liberia.*

July 26 is National Independence Day, when from the east to the west, from the north to the south, of Liberia, the sons and daughters of this Republic are reminded of their duty to posterity, just as the graves of their forefathers are evidence of the great foundation laid by them in the brave days of the nineteenth century.

Who would live in Liberia on July 26 and not feel like a man or like a woman—at least like a free man or a free woman?

Who would live in Liberia on July 26 and not dream dreams and see visions of a more glorious destiny! Beautiful! Wonderful!

That black men and women could exist in the nineteenth century and dream of laying down their lives for posterity, is indicative of the fact that the germ of nationality is not dead in the soul of the black man. Glorious! Splendid!

And now, why was it necessary for black men and women to so surpass the achievements hitherto made by their colleagues in the course of history?

This is the Declaration of Independence of Liberia, in part:

It recognized in all men " certain inalienable rights; among these are life, liberty and the right to acquire, possess, and enjoy and defend property.

" By the practice and consent of men in all ages, some system or form of government is proven to be necessary to exercise, enjoy, and secure these rights, and every people has a right to institute a government, and to choose and adopt that system, or form of it, which in their opinion will most effectually accomplish these objects, and secure their happiness, which does not interfere with the just rights of others.

" *The right, therefore, to institute government and powers necessary to conduct it, is an inalienable right and cannot be resisted without the grossest injustice.*"

The document then narrates the background of some of the founders of Liberia, i.e., those who migrated from the United States of America. It showed how these persons were segregated, discriminated and debarred " from all rights and privileges of man ".

" We were everywhere shut out from all civil office. We were excluded from participation in the Government. We were taxed without our consent. We were compelled to contribute to the resources of a country which gave us no protection.

" We were made a separate and distinct class, and against us every avenue of improvement was effectually closed. Strangers from other lands, of a colour different from ours, were preferred before us.

" We uttered our complaints, but they were unattended to, or met by alleging the peculiar institutions of the country.

" All hope of a favourable change in that country was thus wholly extinguished in our bosoms, and we looked with anxiety for some asylum from this deep degradation ".

Then this historic document proceeds to narrate the relationship between Liberia, as a commonwealth which was under the auspices of the American Colonization Society, and the United States.

Then it declares: " Liberia is not the offspring of grasping ambition, nor the tool of avaricious speculation. No desire for territorial aggrandisement brought us to these shores; nor do we believe so sordid a motive entered into the high consideration of those who aided us in providing this asylum from the most grinding oppression.

" *The people of the Republic of Liberia, then, are of right, and in fact, a free, sovereign, and independent State, possessed of all the rights, powers, and functions of Government.*"

Factors from without were responsible for this great document in the annals of West African politics. Forced to become a political nonentity, it was realized that political evanescence faced the fathers of that country and they were inspired to assume an independent national existence.

The Liberian Declaration of Independence is a critique of man's inhumanity to man. It is the tragic story of a free people who became victims of circumstances and who made up their minds to renounce for ever, even with their lives, a political inferiority status.

This Declaration is an historical epic and a literary masterpiece at that. It is destined to fire the imagination of Negro youth throughout the wide world.

In the words of Mr Justice J. J. Dosen: " With but little knowledge and insight into the complex machinery of statecraft, and with no other source whence to seek guidance but the philanthropic society which had launched the experiment, raised here on these shores the banner of Negro liberty and Negro independence, and bade the powers of Christendom to recognize the new bond and to admit the strange unique State into the family of nations while startled rulers gazed and marvelled that, from a handful cast upon these unknown shores there should have come within that brief space of time the embodied genius of human Government and the perfected model of human liberty. . . .

" What a record! What an achievement!

" Search history for a parallel and your search will be in vain.

" There is no other record, there is no other datum to be found in the annals of human history, where, within the brief space of twenty-five years (that is, from 1822, when the founders of the Republic landed at Mesurado, to 1847, when the Declaration of Independence was promulgated), a people, starting out from the very beginning, leaped the great bounds of national life, and assumed an independent status ! "

And on every July 26, His Excellency—the President—and his Cabinet revivify the nationals and residents of the Republic of Liberia with the lore of its history.

God grant that those who now live under the Lone Star flag of Liberia will so cherish this heritage of liberty and freedom, which was handed to them by the fathers of 1822-1847, that while the sun shines, and the days ebb, there will arise a greater Liberia, dedicated to the supreme task of preserving this glorious heritage of freedom.

God grant that the people of Liberia will not be satisfied with their present condition, but rather, to interpret correctly the handwriting on the wall of African destiny.

May Liberia continue to live. May it continue to be a sign-post to the black man and black woman everywhere in whose bosom burns the flame of liberty.

God grant that as the years roll by in ceaseless flow Liberia will continue to welcome into her fold sons and daughters of Africa who seek to enjoy to the fullest, the right to life, liberty, and the pursuit of happiness.

And may God grant that the motto of the Republic of Liberia will continue to be : " The Love of Liberty Brought us here ! "

27. *WHAT PRICE CIVILIZATION?*

Three Africans, representing three schools of thought, the Radical (the Leftist), the Eclectical (the Centrist), and the Conservative (the Rightist) are discussing the blessings and curses of European civilization in Africa. Questions are posed, and the three schools give their ideas, leaving the reader to form his or her own conclusions. Behold the symposium:

Have European influences improved or impaired the African people?

Rightist: European influences have improved the African people, materially and intellectually.

Materially speaking, there have been introduced into Africa metalled roads, railway, radio, telegraph, motor cars, European dresses and European style of architecture. The African enjoys the blessings of a sanitary environment, consequently his life-span has been lengthened.

Look at the hospitals built in many parts of Africa to save human life. Without the blessings of European civilization, could these have been possible? Africans also enjoy the benefits of all the amenities of European civilization which, under their own civilization, they fail to enjoy.

Intellectually speaking, the African has been educated to appreciate the cross-currents of human history. He is educated for the professions. He understands the various problems which face mankind and he uses his scientific knowledge to solve these.

See the liberty which the African enjoys under European civilization. Before the coming of Europeans, were African life and property secure? Africans should be grateful to Europeans for having made their lives secure.

Centrist: The views of Rightist are in order in certain respects. There is no doubt that the African has progressed materially and intellectually, but it is necessary that the African should eschew the worst phases of European civilization and emulate the best ones.

It is true that the African enjoys an amount of liberty, but it is also true that these are restricted at times. It is for the African to co-operate with his civilizers so as to bring about a better society.

It is admitted that the radio, telegraph, railway, metalled roads, etc. have brought advancement in our society, but then these have increased our taxation.

Let the African believe in African civilization and in European civilization. The process of time will bring about mutual adjustment.

Leftist: We submit that European influences have impaired rather than improved the African.

From a political point of view, point out to us any section of Africa, outside of the Republic of Liberia, where the African enjoys political privileges, unhindered and unrestricted, despite all the alleged amenities of European civilization?

From a social point of view, point out to us any section of Africa where the African, with all his alleged blessings of European civilization, is treated *equally* like a European?

In this connection may we ask how many African Governors are in charge of African colonies belonging to European countries? How many Africans are heads of departments in the Civil Services of European Governments? How many Africans are appointed to the High Division of the Civil Service of European Governments, and paid equally with their European colleagues—enjoying all the privileges which the European colleagues enjoy?

Economically, we may admit that some Africans may be regarded as wealthy, but can it be doubted that the economic system of the West has transformed the average African into a wage-earner so that he is now a slave of the machine, instead of the machine becoming his slave?

What is the position of the African producer, compared with the European middle man or the European consumer? Who fixes the price of the African product: the African or the European?

In the face of all these incongruities, dare any person conclude that European influences have redounded to the best benefit of the African? Is this not an example of mental slavery?

Educationally speaking, despite the ability to read, to write, to 'rithmeticize, to religionize, of what benefit has European educational system been to the African? Who writes the books that the African reads? What is the idea which motivates the theme of these books? Are these ideas supposed to justify the intellectual equality of the African with the European?

Religiously speaking, what benefit has European civilization brought to the African? The worship of one god? Was this unknown before the coming of Christianity? The liturgical ceremonies? Were these unknown before the coming of Christianity? Ethics? Was it unknown before the Europeans came?

Yet we are prone to think that because we can transmit messages over long distances, therefore, European civilization is better? Did we not have our own drum-language before Marconi dreamt of the wireless?

We are no destructive critics. We concede that European civilization has been of some material and intellectual benefits to the African, but we submit that these benefits have been of a superficial nature, because in accepting the amenities of European civilization, we have sold our birthright thereby.

What is meant by " Encouragement ? "

Rightist: This means that the African being a child of nature should be encouraged gradually—he must not be rushed into the sanctuary of political autonomy.

The African must remember that the great States of the world had to undergo a period of tutelage for many centuries, before they dreamt of becoming their own masters. The African must be encouraged in his evolution so that he may not err as did the other States?

We believe that the African is capable of administering himself, but the evidence upon which such belief is based is so scant that we must repose confidence in experience. If even the African does not measure up to the standards of other countries, he must be coddled, for after all he is a child of nature. He has no historical background outside the fact that he had been a slave in history. He must be trained. And the only training that is sound and practicable is sympathetic encouragement.

Centrist: It is true that the African is backward and therefore deserves encouragement. It must be conceded, however, that the training which the African should have, ought to accelerate his position so that he might claim his birthright when he is fledged.

It is also true that the history of the African is without any spectacular appeal as are the histories of the other countries of the world. This is not due to the fault of the African. He was enslaved in the days of Egypt, Greece, Rome, and even in the eighteenth and nineteenth centuries.

Encouragement is needed and should be pursued cautiously, but it should be remembered that the African is not the inferior of any race. All that the African asks for, is an opportunity to demonstrate his capacity.

Leftist: By encouragement is meant the desire to perpetuate the enslavement of the African mind and to prevent him from becoming mentally emancipated. The African needs no encouragement of this sort because it weakens his manhood. The more the African is treated like a baby, the more he acts like a baby.

We believe that the African is not being rushed, and we advocate that he should not be "encouraged" to walk like a snail in this age of aeroplanes. If the African demonstrates aptitude and capacity, let him take his place. There is no need to wait for the time when the African will be fit to graduate from his tutelage, because that time will never come, since the criterion of having shown capacity is undecipherable. Moreover, who is to decide: the African or his European master? According to experience, he who has, prefers to hold what he has, and to prevent the one who has none from having at all. We may be wrong, but it is the verdict of history.

We do not agree with those who say that because the great states of the world had to undergo a period of tutelage for many years, therefore Africans should also follow suit. We believe that the world has so progressed that centuries are being leaped in months nowadays, so far as material and intellectual attainments are concerned.

Those who say that the African has no history are vandalists of history. They refuse to concede to the African his worth. If Africans are black men, irrespective of what term they were designated in Egyptian, Greek, Roman, medieval and modern times, no intelligent person will dare deny the African a place in history, if that person is honest in his erudition.

The facts of history are there to be unravelled. The African has not been a slave from the dawn of history. The African had enslaved the European and the Asiatic in history. The African had ruled the world. And just as the European and the Asiatic had enslaved and ruled the world, at one time in history, and then declined, so too had the African. It is therefore groundless to continue the enslavement of the African by " encouragement " on the ground that the African has no history.

We therefore submit that if encouragement is at all necessary, then it should be of such a nature as to make the African realize that the impact of Western civilization is for his own *good* and not for his *goods*. To all intents and purposes, the latter seems to be the case. The African should not ask for opportunity: he should make his opportunity as did other countries in history.

Is African self-consciousness real or artificial?

Rightist: African self-consciousness is real. Since the World War of 1914, the crystallization of African nationalism has become a reality.

The Garvey Movement in the United States of America challenged the African to be proud of his race and to cultivate love for self-determination.

Moreover, the war transformed the psychology of the African so that he realized that the European races were not invulnerable. Since he fought side by side with the European, the African now has confidence in himself, and through this confidence he has expressed himself in arts and literature.

Indeed, there is a great intellectual awakening in Africa to-day, and if the statement of the present Primate of England is to be taken seriously, the West African is racially conscious, and this self-consciousness is becoming realistic day by day.

We believe that through the cultivation of self-consciousness the African will take pride in his heritage and thus adjust himself to the complex political, social, and economic problems which face him to-day.

Centrist: The self-consciousness of the African may be regarded as real, compared with the self-consciousness of other peoples.

Following the signing of the Versailles Peace Treaty, the principle of self-determination became an accomplished fact. Some European minority elements were granted autonomy; thus the existence of Poland, Czechoslovakia, Austria, Hungary, Yugoslavia, Lithuania, etc., was realized.

These changes have affected the political thought of the African, so that there seems to be some unrest and the Africans have begun to ask for participation in the governance of their countries.

With the founding of the National Congress of British West Africa, African Nationalism may be said to have become a *fait accompli* because this movement accelerated the granting of limited franchise to Africans, the establishment of a West African Appellate Court, and the appointment of Africans to the higher administrative branches of the Government, etc.

We believe that Africans should continue to secure their political privileges by constitutional means, remembering that good things always come to those who wait.

Africans should hasten slowly. Their racial self-consciousness should be pursued with caution and within the bounds of reason. They will ultimately reach their goal, sooner or later.

Leftist: We maintain that the self-consciousness of the African has been artificial. We cannot say that African self-consciousness is real, if we take into consideration the present condition of African society.

Self-consciousness implies interest in kind. It connotes mutual aid. It denotes an attitude of friendliness which should make African society safe for Africans.

If our definitions of self-consciousness are not far-fetched, we think that we are justified in holding to our negative point of view, because Africans seem to be enemies of themselves.

Where does the African show interest in his kind? From experience, is it not true that the African is more interested in treacherously betraying his fellow African so as to gain temporary advantage, materially or otherwise?

Where does the African practicalize mutual aid? From experience, is it not true that instead of co-operating in his economic institutions, the African would rather continue in his cut-throat competition?

Tell us how many African banks have been able to weather the storm of competition? Tell us how many African business houses have been able to survive, after the principal "proprietor" has succumbed?

Is it not true that most African business executives are Managing *Proprietors* instead of Managing *Directors*? Does not proprietary interest in the economic life of the African show that he has no idea of social-consciousness, and that he is more interested in *self* than in *others*?

Where does the African exemplify friendliness so as to justify the crystallization of self-consciousness? Is the African not the enemy of the African in any field of human endeavour?

Seek through the political institutions? Are Africans not prone to make themselves enemies for life simply because they are victors or victims of any political contest? Do not these affect the social fabric? And do these effects redound to the benefit and security of the African? If not, does it not prove that the African has not shown capacity for self-consciousness?

Again, look through the social institutions of the African. Do not nepotism and favouritism motivate the policy of Africans instead of efficiency and competency? And is it not a universal practice? Are these evidences of capacity to crystallize self-consciousness?

How about the tribal idiosyncrasies of the African with their by-products of tribal prejudice, hatred, contempt, spitefulness, and other vices which tend to disrupt, rather than solidarize, African society? Are these examples of ability to cultivate consciousness of kind?

These are some of the reasons which lead us to maintain the view that the idea of self-consciousness of the African, manifested racially, socially, politically, economically, etc., is more artificial than real, because the African seems to be enmeshed in the dregs of disunity.

It may be true that Africans have been able to enjoy certain privileges as a result of efforts towards self-consciousness, but this is an infinitesimal fraction, compared with what is possible for the African to achieve, if he would cultivate spiritual balance, become socially regenerated, become economically deterministic, experience mental emancipation and usher in political resurgence.

Why should Colonial Governments continue?

Rightist: Because certain parts of the world are so backward that it behoves the colonial powers to exercise their civilizing mission so as to effectuate peaceful and orderly government for the maintenance of law and order and security of the people.

Had the colonial powers not embarked upon this task, the backward peoples would have continued in their barbarism. Life would not have been safe. Property would not have been secure. There would not have been law and order. Instead, we would have had a sort of anarchy.

It is very essential that colonial powers should continue their mission of civilization so as to afford to the backward peoples an opportunity of tutelage.

Centrist: Colonial Governments should continue because it is their destiny. The backward peoples have some raw materials which the Colonial powers have not. The latter have the blessings of civilization which the former have not.

On a reciprocal basis, it is very essential that the Colonial powers should continue to civilize backward peoples so that in course of time the latter may be enabled to stand by themselves.

Leftist: Colonial Governments should continue to exist so long as the so-called backward peoples are so backward that they do not realize that all races, nations, and countries have a destiny of their own.

What is the future of the African, so far as the Mandate Governments and the Permanent Mandates Commission are concerned?

Rightist: We believe that the future of the African in so far as the Mandatories and the Permanent Mandates Commission of the League of Nations are concerned must be looked upon with optimism.

At the Paris Peace Conference it was thought fit to consider the lot of the backward peoples. Motivated by the spirit of humanitarianism which manifested itself in the Berlin Conference of 1885 and the Brussels Convention of 1890, Article XXII of the Covenant of the League of Nations was devoted to the backward peoples thus:

"To those colonies and territories which as a consequence of the late war have ceased to be under the sovereignty of the States which formerly governed them and which are inhabited by peoples not yet able to stand by themselves under the strenuous conditions of the modern world, there should be applied the principle that the well-being and development of such peoples form a sacred trust of civilization and that securities for the performance of this trust should be embodied in this Covenant.

"The best method of giving practical effect to this principle s that the tutelage of such peoples should be entrusted to advanced nations who, by reason of their resources, their experience or their geographical position, can best undertake this responsibility, and who are willing to accept it, and that this tutelage should be exercised by them as Mandatories on behalf of the League.

" The character of the mandate must differ according to the stage of the development of the people, the geographical situation of the territory, its economic conditions and other similar circumstances. . . .

" A permanent Commission shall be constituted to receive and examine the annual reports of the Mandatories, and to advise the Council on all matters relating to the observance of the mandates."

So far for the mandates of the League of Nations. It is very easily forgotten that the League as an international organization is also interested in the African colonies from the point of view of humanitarianism.

In Article XXIII of the Covenant of the League it is agreed by the signatories that " subject to and in accordance with the provisions of international conventions existing or hereafter to be agreed upon, the members of the League :

" (*a*) will endeavour to secure and maintain fair and humane conditions of labour for men, women and children, both in their own countries and in all countries to which their commercial and industrial relations extend, and for that purpose will establish and maintain the necessary international organizations :

" (*b*) undertake to secure just treatment of the Native inhabitants of territories under their control. . . ."

Thus it will be seen that the future of the African is optimistic. Before 1919, no attempt was made to regard the relationship between Colonial Powers and Africans as one of trusteeship. The colonies were looked upon as suppliers of raw materials to the Mother Country or field for exploitation.

We are sincere in the view that the attitude of the Mandatories so far has been to regard the interest of the Native as paramount and to so formulate their administrative policies in that light.

The reports presented to the Permanent Mandates Commission of the League of Nations, annually, show how careful and humanitarian have been the Mandatories, and there can be no doubt that Africans who live in the Mandates enjoy better security than those who live in a system which is devoid of international humanitarianism.

Centrist: We are of the opinion that in the system of Mandates devised by the League of Nations lies the salvation of backward races.

True, this system cannot be regarded as perfect since it is a human device, but there is no doubt that of all attempts towards international humanitarianism towards the backward races, the principle of trusteeship is the best yet adopted.

To point out the practicality of this principle, may we refer, again, to the declaration of the British Government in 1923 regarding its East African colonies:

" Primarily,.Kenya is an African territory, and His Majesty's Government think it necessary definitely to record their considered opinion that the interest of the African Natives must be paramount, and that, if and when, those interests and the interests of the immigrant races should conflict, the former should prevail. . . .

" In the administration of Kenya, His Majesty's Government regard themselves as exercising a trust on behalf of the African population, and they are unable to delegate or share this trust, the object of which may be defined as the protection and advancement of the Native races.

" There can be no room for doubt that it is the mission of Great Britain to work continuously for the training and education of the Africans toward a higher intellectual, moral, and economic level than that which they had reached when the Crown assumed the responsibility for the administration of this territory. . . ."

The above statements represent a sense of responsibility on the part of Great Britain, a member of the League of Nations, for its colonies. It is indeed encouraging to enunciate this policy because it gives those who believe in international humanitarianism hope for the backward peoples.

Under the circumstances, we see no reason for Africans to be apprehensive of the future. Whilst it is true that situations exist which make the relationship of Africans and Europeans problematic, as in the case of the Bondelzwarts rebellion in former German South-West Africa, yet it is very rare that the Mandatory assumed unnecessary prerogatives which may be contrary to the ideals of the League.

Therefore, we believe that despite the difficulties occasioned by a change of philosophy of imperialism, Africans ought to be optimistic of the future, because having been regarded as a sacred trust of civilization, the trustee will do everything possible to give the ward a chance to become full-fledged for manhood.

Leftist: Under the present system of international organization, the Mandate system is not a blessing to the backward peoples. On this premise we conclude that the African cannot be optimistic about the future because calamity awaits him.

It may be true that the mandate system was an acceptance of the challenge of international humanitarianism, but no signatory of the Treaty of Versailles doubts the reality that the former colonies of Germany were spoils of war.

In the language of an authority, " In its genesis, the mandate system was a weak compromise between Wilsonian idealism, self-determination, and the concept of trusteeship on the one hand, and annexationist ambitions, political subjugation, and economic exploitation, on the other. Like all compromises, the system is unworthy either of the highest praises of its apologists or the most severe condemnations of its critics. It can be only characterized as a short step towards the protection of the backward races from the evils of imperialism through international supervision."[1]

Moreover, the claims and counterclaims of European nations for colonies, and the attempts of Germany to regain its former colonies, make the future outlook of the African rather gloomy.

Where in these mandated regions have agitations for autonomy or for the exercise of the civil rights of man on the basis of equality, been recognized? Outside of Iraq and Syria, have not the aspirations of the people who live in the mandated territories, for independence and self-determination, been crushed with the same ruthlessness which characterized imperialism before 1919?

See the carnage and brutality perpetrated on South-West Africans during the Bondelzwarts rebellion! Notice the chronic friction between Arabs and Jews in Palestine! Read the insurrections of the Syrians against the French! In Western Samoa,

[1] Schuman, *op. cit.*, page 621.

punitive expeditions have been the rule instead of the exception. Is there any wonder that Professor Schuman writes: "Africans and Polynesians have been unable to distinguish the new modes of oppression and exploitation from the old"?

Germans, Americans, Turks, Russians, and Arabs have jeered at this principle as a sham. Is the mandate system not a make-believe, in view of the startling revelations in the reports of the mandatories wherein the people are often heavily taxed and yet are uneducated?

The system of mandates, like the system of the League of Nations is destined to be a failure, since the League itself, by its studious reticence and its inability to save the Chinese and the Ethiopians and other minorities from such imperialist countries as Japan and Italy and other Powers, has sealed its doom.

Is it necessary for the well-being of the African to have European missionaries in Africa?

Rightist: Certainly yes. Without European Missionaries, Africa, as a "Dark Continent", might not have progressed so far. The early pioneers of Missions traversed the continent in their mission of goodwill and evangelization and the result is an advanced country, culturally and otherwise.

One Livingstone was enough to civilize about one-third of the Continent of Africa. One Crowther was enough to make West Africa safe from the Slave Trade. The schools and Churches which dot this continent are eternal monuments to the sacrifice of the Missionaries who laid down their lives so that Africans might enjoy life more abundantly.

Indeed, there is no doubt that it is necessary for the well-being of the African to have European Missionaries in Africa, because they have aided in developing the man-power of this continent, and through their efforts the Slave Trade was abolished.

Centrist: Indeed, it is necessary for the well-being of the African to have European Missionaries in Africa.

We admit that there are certain faults which human beings are liable to, and since Missionaries are human, naturally they are also heirs to these faults, but the shortcomings of the few should not be used as a norm to judge the many.

It is also admitted that Missionaries were employed either directly or indirectly in crystallizing Imperialism, but that is one phase of the problem. Just as Imperialists used Missionaries to exploit the African, so have the Missionaries also used the Imperialists to better the conditions of the African.

In West Africa to-day, there are very few Africans who are educated and civilized, who do not owe the missionaries gratitude for educating and/or christianizing them.

The great Fourah Bay College at Freetown; the enviable College of West Africa at Monrovia; the historic Mfantsipim at Cape Coast; the necessary Presbyterian College at Akropong; the well-known Igbobi College at Lagos; the important St. Andrew's College at Oyo; the serviceable Hope Waddell Institute at Calabar; these are all institutions of learning which are *sine quâ non* in the intellectual development of the West African.

Search through the hall of fame of West Africans, and there are few names of persons who were not trained in one of the above institutions of learning, under the aegis of European Missionaries.

The leaders of opinion in Gambia, Sierra Leone, Liberia, Gold Coast, and Nigeria were mostly trained in the above-named institutions or those allied to them.

We may be generalizing (although we have to admit that there are certain Government institutions which were responsible for the education of some of the African leaders), nevertheless, it is a truism that most of the leaders of West Africa were trained in institutions operated by Missionaries.

Outside the educational achievement of missionaries, we turn to their evangelizing influence. Through the use of the Bible they had succeeded in modifying the "savage" so that the latter has adopted a more humane system of ethics.

The institution of the Church has become a leavening influence in the social *mores* of the African. Through Christian Communion and fellowship the doctrine of Universal Fatherhood and Universal Brotherhood has become a part of the mentality of the African convert.

This practicalization of the philosophy of Jesus, has influenced African ideas to such an extent that the African has arrived and has begun to question the right of Europe, the home of Christianity, to violate the preachments of man's humanity to man, as was enunciated by the first Christian, in favour of man's inhumanity to man.

We submit that whatever progress we may have made to-day in Africa, is due directly to the efforts of missionaries. Forget their shortcomings. Overlook their errors. Discard the crimes committed by some of them. Still, these could not overshadow the great emancipation of Africans, mentally and physically, through the efforts of missionaries.

Add up the faults of the missionaries, multiply them a million fold, divide them a thousand fold and subtract them from their good deeds to Africa, and the result will portray the missionaries as assets and not liabilities to Africa.

In view of the above, it is too evident that missionaries are a necessity and not a luxury in the growth of African society from a simple to a more complex civilization.

Leftist: We admit the views postulated by Rightist and Centrist schools of thought as reasonable; we admit that there are advantages and disadvantages in the rôle of Christian Missions in Africa; but we submit that, comparatively speaking, the lot of the African has not been improved by their contacts with missions.

Be it known that whilst Christian idealism was responsible for the immigration of European missionaries into Africa, yet these evangelizers of the African were a means to an end.

This is what we mean. Africans are a powerful race. Their physical capacity seems unparalleled. A race of this type cannot be controlled physically. Only mental control is possible.

With the gospel of the Nazarene, the physical resistance of the African can be broken down by an appeal to suffer punishment in this world with a view to eternal reward, hereafter.

This has worked out; and so, despite the good deeds of the missionaries which we do not dispute, the result of their being used as a tool of Imperialism has resulted not only in the disintegration of African society, but also in the mental enslavement of the African.

These are generalizations, it will be admitted, but they can be proved to the hilt if the verdict of history and academic freedom means anything to the seeker after the truth.

Now, how have these affected the African, deleteriously?

Instead of the bold and brave person that he used to be, he has become cowardly, applying what he was told—to forget the privations of this world so as to enter into the kingdom of heaven.

Again, it has made the African outlook on the great themes of life to be clouded and so the African has been forced, so to speak, to live in an atmosphere of uncertainty charged with the virus of the inferiority complex.

The African looks to God for everything. He wants God to help him in raising cocoa prices. He wants God to cause the firms to reduce their prices to suit his purchasing power. He wants God to soften the hearts of Government so that his will may not be ignored by an official majority. In fact, he wants Jahweh of the Jews to do everything for him.

In this process, he becomes less self-reliant, which is an important asset to national consciousness and racial capacity to carve a niche on the hall of fame of the world.

We admit that it is necessary for the religiosity of the African to be modified on a progressive scale. It makes no difference under whose auspices this happens, be it Christian, Moslem, or otherwise. But we have no alternative than to state categorically that most Christian missionaries we have known, in their contacts with Africans and other religious groups, are apt to be intolerant and dictatorial, and these evidences of human weakness are usually the means towards the undoing of the noble work done by pioneering and tolerant missionaries.

We submit that some European missionaries whom we know, are hypersensitive and intolerant. Any criticism against some inconsistencies in the Christian religion, as manifested by its cohorts, finds them assuming unnecessary prerogatives as if Christianity is the only religion that has been subjected to criticism since the world began. We submit that this evidence of intolerance has been responsible for the scepticism of some Africans regarding the practicableness of Christianity.

Now, our friends, the Rightist and the Centrist, may be right when they submit that missionaries have been responsible for intellectual emancipation of Africans, but to suggest even impliedly that this is a unique achievement in history, is to blast historical scholarship into smithereens.

Rome was christianized in A.D. 306. England was christianized by St. Augustine in 597. Ireland was christianized by St. Patrick. Wales was converted by David. France was christianized by 496. Spain was christianized by 587. In other words the Christianization of one nation by another is not a unique incident in history. It is therefore irrelevant to the issue.

In view of the apathy, intolerance, dictatorial attitude, inconsistent Christian ethics of some European missionaries, we are yet to be convinced that the present quota of missionaries (and we will be generous enough to make allowance for the inspired and Christian ones) are necessary for the well-being of the African who is faced with problems of existence in this twentieth century civilization.

CONCLUSIONS : *So far, I have considered some important questions raised from the point of view of the Rightist, Centrist, and Leftist. It is up to the reader to interpret intelligently each view and attempt to adjust his or her problems in the* kulturkrëise *of European and African civilizations.*

CHAPTER VI

AFRICA AGAINST AFRICA

28. *THINK*

THERE'S many a fire hidden in the word " think ". It has been responsible for a recreation of society. It has enabled many a completely demoralized and shattered sports team to gain victory after the half-time.

Thinking is a process which is beyond human comprehension. No psychologist can successfully analyse this process. The best than can be said by the Behaviourists is that thinking is " sub-vocal speech ".

Just as vocal speech has a charm of its own, so too does thinking. The orator may incite his audience to lawless or lawful deeds. He may inspire them. Indeed, the power of vocal speech is an enigma.

But before making explicit their ideas, men have so undergone a series of intricating psycho-biological acrobatics, that the result is amazing. Nevertheless, thinking is responsible for man's primacy on the earth of to-day.

Descartes glorified this phase of man's hegemony over his colleagues of the same phylum. Said he: *Cogito, ergo sum*, I think, therefore I exist.

Existence is thus conterminous with thinking. Whether thinking is collateral with existence or not is not clear. But it is too evident that the ability to out-think the other fellow, be he a friend or foe, is the pathway to victory and success in life.

Man has therefore out-thought the diplodocus, else the mammoth would have survived the Darwinian struggle. The same applies to the *Pithecanthropus erectus* or even the *Sinanthropus pekinensis*.[1]

[1] Ape-man of Java and Peking Ape-man.

Being, therefore, at the apex of creation, zoonomically speaking, man's thinking processes have proceeded to lead him on to a higher level of existence. Somehow, he has failed. It is generally accepted among reputable psychologists that the brain-power of man, so far as is known, as been tapped by less than ten per centum, in mathematical terms.

This means that man has been overrated. It can hardly be otherwise, when nine-tenths of man's brain power and brain-capacity are still latent and potential.

If man should ever reach the acme of perfection, so far as his mental precocity is concerned, the universe would be peopled by geniuses. By that time, mankind might have drawn closer to either Armageddon or Nirvana or Paradise.

Without belabouring my reader with further analytical sketch of the thought processes, let me turn to the expository and narrative phases of the same.

Think of the fact that without Brutus out-thinking Cæsar, the former might not have shared immortality with the man who crossed the Rubicon.

Think of the fact that had not Queen Boadicea out-thought her contemporaries she would not have made history, much more to be mentioned in the writings of Cæsar and Tacitus.

Think of the fact that had Canute allowed the waves to insult his royal mien continuously, he might have drowned. Think of Alfred the Great and the cakes, of William the Conqueror and the cantankerous Harolds and Tostig, of Bruce and the spider.

Think of the triumph of the mind over brawn leading to the Constitutions of Clarendon, the Magna Charta, the Petition of Rights, the Bill of Rights, the Corn Laws, and the other documents which have preserved British rights and liberties.

Think of the British Revolution (1688), the American Revolution (1776), the French Revolution (1789), the Russian Revolution (1917), and the great movements of history which are attributable to this psychological phenomenon—thinking.

Friend, if after thinking over these historical incidences you feel satisfied with your present-day condition, you ought to be skinned alive. You ought to be thrown into the unfathòmable depth of the Niger River and " stay put ". The world should be better without you. Africa should feel like an individual whose burden has been lifted from his head.

Think again, and make up your mind if your condition of life to-day has changed. If you are frank, you will agree with me that Africans have progressed from the stand-point of things material, but when it comes to thinking, think my friend before you agree with me that they have failed.

Africans are like a beaten football team. But the game is just half-over. The other half remains to be played. And the coach and captain are telling the players to think.

I remember a few years back in my athletic days. I was a member of a football team. This team had beaten all oppositions. It was now on its onward march to a national title. But before that, it had to face its arch-enemy, whose rivalry extended many years back.

On the day prior to this classic of Aframerican football, there was a public holiday in the university. At the centre of the quadrangle, a large white flag flew. It contained the word " THINK " in bold relief. That word was magnetic. It burned through the souls of the team mates, who went to battle to die or live for the 'Varsity.

At half-time, the score was 1—0 against the team. The opponent had lost over three games before meeting the team—the potential national champions. The coach of the team was not dissatisfied. He called the members and got them expectant for a long speech.

Then an ominous silence enveloped them, and after ten minutes the coach said, " Think." And that was all. The team won the game by the score of 3—1, and later won the national championship.

Africa is like an athlete out of condition. It is like a beaten football team at half-time. It is a potential champion, but it is afraid to use its head. It must not be. There's many a fire hidden in the word " think ". Let the Africans think, and think, and then *think*.

. . . . .

The African is a child of nature. He is so kindly disposed that he is apt to forget self in order that others may be comfortable. He is hospitable. He is friendly. He is forgiving.

In so far as these traits are made manifest towards peoples of other races, the above holds true, but let it be applied to the African, and the thesis totters to pieces.

Somehow, the African is generous to the members of a race which asserts its authority and proclaims its superiority from the house-tops. But let an African from Angola do likewise, and no matter wherever he may go, to Algeria or Tunis, to Dakar or Cairo, he is looked down upon.

Again, I venture to say that African hospitality has its limitations. In so far as it extends to peoples of other races, there appears on the surface that greatness which characterizes the average aboriginal African as friendly and kindly. But when it comes to extending the same facility to a black man, one meets with a different response.

Why should the African be an enemy to the African? Why should his society be so demarcated into various compartments that he would rather welcome a member of a strange race than his own race?

It would seem that the African is a victim of the inferiority complex. He has been educated to lose faith in his race. He has been taught to believe that other races are his superiors, and that his own race is a child and must necessarily travel the difficult road of progress before attaining manhood.

In consequence, the African mentality is a curious psychological phenomenon. Whilst the African fights against repression and oppression he engages in the same against his kith and kin. Whilst he uses all efforts at his command to glorify other peoples, he uses the same to debase his own.

Of course, I need not be categorical, but in the final analysis the above is generally the rule and not the exception. Charity begins abroad, so far as the African races are concerned, and this is one reason for the evident weakness of Africans as a race, much more as ethnic units divided into nationalities.

Let a European firm establish in Africa, all means at the command of Africans are used to patronize the same. Let an African establish a firm of the same nature and unless that firm is exceptionally organized and is superior to a greater extent than the one organized by the European, it will fail.

The African mentality sees evil in African undertakings.

It sees failure in the same. It fails to realize that in business nothing fundamental to its success is necessarily racial, much more hereditary.

The business man must administer his affairs for the best interest of his customer, who must always be right. Since other races are human, the foibles of Africans in this realm of human endeavour are not necessarily peculiar to the African races. It must be universally applied, else partiality or the inferiority complex must show their horrid heads.

Some of these observations are responsible for the incongruities in the African social fabric. Let a European write an article pointing out certain errors or defects in the African community and, generally, he is acclaimed as an authority and as a learned critic whose opinions must be respected.

Let an African do likewise, and immediately there is a chorus of denunciations, vitriolics, vituperations and what-nots pouring in print, not necessarily attacking the debatable points, but viciously slashing the personality of the individual concerned.

Such an exhibition of mental subnormality has become part and parcel of the lives of Africans, so that they are now victims of their impulses instead of their rational selves. In other words, the average African puts his *social me* in the background and his *individual me* in the foreground, that is, in the language of the psychologist.

On a subject of this nature, one must limit one's ambit, but whilst limitation is desirable it must not be interpreted to be an exoneration of all Africans, nor must the contrary be presumed. Yet a sort of cancer is so gnawing the vitals of the social equanimity of Africans that they are drifting into the miasma of uncertainty and unnecessary frictions.

To be concrete, the following examples will suffice to illustrate a phase of what I have been expounding. A report is made in the local papers that such an organization is faulty in certain respects. There may be two or more points of view either in favour or against the statement.

Because an avenue is allowed for the discussing of institutions which are of public interest, that does not necessarily involve the persons engaged in the debate, directly or indirectly. Yet the average African writer will compose meaningless dogmatisms in order to carry his *argumentum ad hominem* to its logical conclusion, and that is, a biographical sketch of his opponent.

Again, let a statement be made that this team is champion or that this individual is a chief or headman. The next day or week will find the newspapers flooded not with arguments to disprove the basis of such a contention, but diatribes abusing those who are directly or indirectly connected with publishing such a statement.

In fact these are revelations of impulsiveness. They demonstrate that Africans are still victims of sentimental emotionalism. Whenever an individual allows his emotional self to master his rational self, he cannot be trusted as possessing qualities of leadership. In fact, forbearance, mental composure, self-control, fortitude are the essentials for a foundation upon which such superstructures must necessarily emanate.

Let the foundation be a base imitation of concrete. Let it be a radiation of impulsiveness, and the superstructure becomes an edifice which lacks the structural material so essential to permanence and reliability, so far as human leadership is concerned.

The kindliness of Africans to members of other races, their hospitality and spiritual balance in their relationship with other races must be concretized and applied among themselves as well, otherwise protestations are artificial and superficial veneers of racial degeneration and ultimate extermination.

Whatsoever ye would that a Ga should do unto Ga, do ye likewise to the African, be he Zulu, Bubi or Kru. This is the greatest law of all. Think, Renascent Africans, think.

29. *CONFUSION AND MISERY*

There is confusion in the world to-day. Every State has to contend with problems which are vital to its existence. Every country has to consider the grave problems raised in international relations to-day.

Individually, the persons who comprise the population of these States and countries are confused. They do not know what the future holds in store for them.

Evidence of confusion is not lacking in all the world. It makes no difference where the searchlight is directed, there is confusion.

Economically speaking, I see the nations of the world steeped in unnecessary tariff warfare, dedicated to the ideals of economic imperialism and economic nationalism. They make regional pacts with the avowed aim of excluding the goods of the most unfavoured countries from certain territories. To put teeth in these pacts, the Closed Door policy is rigidly adhered to, and so certain States are offended thereby.

The result is a retaliatory policy which eventually must engulf the world in a series of cyclic phenomena, known by economists as prosperity, panic, crisis, and depression. And the cause of depressions is due to a lack of the human touch in solving human problems.

Politically speaking, there is confusion in the world to-day. Certain States are independent. Others are partially independent. And others still are not independent.

The States which are independent seem to be unaware of the fact that the verdict of history is immortal and recurrent. Consequently, the policy adopted by certain States in order to strengthen further their hegemony, has engulfed mankind in one of the most diabolical races in history—the armament race.

The States which are partially independent are prone to seek for complete autonomy so that their status may compare on an equal basis with the States which are wholly independent. The latter sees in the agitation of the former a challenge to the existence of the States which are prone to maintain their hegemony at all cost. The result is a conflict of opinions. And the final effect of such an example of indiscretion and obstinacy is confusion and discontent.

The countries which are not independent study closely the relationship of the countries which are independent and the relationship of the countries which are partially independent. They realize that the independent countries employ one of the most ingenious tools of humanity in engineering their plans. This is known as diplomacy.

They realize that unless one independent State is capable

of outwitting the other, by fair or foul means, international relations would continue to be in the Old Stone Age state.

They read of States taking stands which are, by all the standards of ethics, not only unfair, inequitable, and unjust, but which are also rationalized on the basis of expediency. They read of States which after having failed to outwit the other States, employ the most inhuman form of struggle, known as war or legalized murder, to attain their objective, which is to subjugate the recalcitrant States so as to make them amenable to dictation.

Then they have the opportunity of seeing how Carthaginian treaties are idealized and legalized. They read from authorities of these States, justifying such treaties in this vein: "In International Law, force and intimidation are permitted means of obtaining redress for wrongs, and it is impossible to look upon permitted means as vitiating the agreement, made in consequence of their use, by which redress is provided for."

Naturally, an acceptance of such principle of International Law which directly violates the fundamental personality of the ethical man, creates dissatisfaction and ultimately there is confusion. And this confusion is due to the fact that those who, because of their strength, preferred to strengthen their positions, at the expense of the weaker political personalities, failed to apply the human touch in the solution of human problems.

Socially speaking, the various persons who inhabit the world have been privileged to learn that the Darwinian theory is applicable to all phases of life.

They see the fully independent States stratifying themselves into compartments, and also doctrinating that their political and economic status was due to their social superiority. The effect of this is to stir up an hornet's nest, in so far as the persons who populate the partially independent States and the persons who inhabit the dependent countries are concerned.

And the result is discontent, agitation and confusion.

When will mankind cease to be a wolf to its component units? When will the world learn to put into practice the teachings of the Nazarene? Why must France regard Germany as her potential enemy eternally? Why must Italy regard

Austria as an essential State to the safety of Italy? Why must Japan regard Manchukuo as its manifest destiny? Why must Africa be looked upon as the footstool of the rest of the world? And why must the United States regard the Latin-American States as its protectorate?

Are these realities conducive to international peace and collective security?

There is confusion. States are at loggerheads. Partially independent States are discontented. Dependent countries are baffled by the intricacies of the West. Whither mankind?

Day by day, I read of preparedness as a means towards a realization of collective security, but is that the human way of settling international disputes? There is confusion, and only the practicalization of the principle of love for our fellow man will prevent this scourge which threatens the obliteration of the nations of the world.

It is written: "And when ye shall hear of wars and rumours of wars, be ye not troubled: for such things must needs be, but the end shall not be yet. For nation shall rise against nation, and kingdom against kingdom; and there shall be earth-quakes in divers places, and there shall be famines and troubles: these are the beginnings of sorrow.

"But take heed to yourselves: for they shall deliver you up to councils, and in the synagogues ye shall be beaten; and ye shall be brought before rulers and kings for my sake, for a testimony against them. . . .

"Now the brother shall betray the brother to death, and the father the son; and children shall rise up against their parents, and shall cause them to be put to death. And ye shall be hated of all men for my name's sake; but he that shall endure unto the end, the same shall be saved."[1]

There is confusion. The message of the Nazarene is the universal brotherhood of man. He that shall proclaim this message, and shall endure to the end, even though he may be persecuted, shall enjoy the heritage of a new social order.

Why is there so much misery in the world to-day? Why are some individuals finding it very difficult to live? Why must they be driven to anti-social acts?

[1] St. Mark xii. 7 *ff.*

It is becoming a sort of man's destiny to suffer misery instead of enjoying the beauties of the earth.

Some Africans are nonplussed at the turn of events in the world. Some question why Adam and Eve had to be cursed by a God who knew that they would fall from grace. Some question why man was made to suffer privations by an omniscient God who knew man's destiny?

It is not for me to enter into metaphysical enquiries into the *raison d'être* of creation, but it is my duty to find ways and means for the amelioration of the lot of my fellow man.

God must not have intended for man to suffer privation else man would not have been made, or claimed to be, the apex of creation.

Probably, the misery which exists in the world to-day is due to the fault of mankind.

Men are too selfish. Men are too greedy. Men are too myopic. Men are apt to be hemianoptic, especially in their dealings with others.

Why do men wish to make a profit of five hundred per cent. because others have not been privileged to understand the "intricacies" of modern finance?

Why do men prefer to employ workers to labour for ten twelve, or fourteen hours for a measly salary, simply because they have been fortunate to accumulate wealth?

Why must men continue to enslave their fellow kith and kin, simply because in the present economic system these persons must work to live and must live to work?

Why must the worker be subjected to unnecessary reduction in wages, unprepared-for dismissals, and other avenues which reduce man from a high estate to that of slavery?

Why must man be a slave to man, simply because the one has been able to accumulate wealth at the expense of the other?

Is it destiny? Can it receive divine sanction that man must be enslaved by man, just because man wishes to be gratified by the labour of others?

I defy destiny to answer affirmatively. I defy any force under the celestial hemisphere or in the planetary system to reply to the above in the affirmative.

Man is gifted in many ways. Those there are who have talents. Those there are who have the knack for accumulating wealth. Those there are who have brains. Those there are who are just born lucky. Those there are who are just born unlucky.

Therefore, in the name of humanity, let there be less misery in the world. Let those who are in position to help others think less of self and think more of humanity at large.

I cannot live happily in the world without being in love with humanity. It is this spirit of humanitarianism which must make or mar the future of humanity.

Go to the law courts. See the noble specimens of humanity who are driven to miscreant life because of the misery of life.

Here comes a prisoner at the dock. He is charged with having broken into a dwelling house unlawfully. He is asked for his plea, and he admits his guilt.

Search through his life-history and you will find that, at one time of his life, he lived a good and upright life. He feared God and respected the rights of his fellow man.

But as the days rolled by, the wherewithals of life were denied him by a society whose economic institutions have not only fostered the profit-motive, but have also been galvanized by a religious dogma, that he who has, shall be given, and he who has not, even that which he has shall be taken away from him.

Oh humanity, why must human beings suffer misery in a beautiful world like this? Oh mankind, why must human beings suffer degradation because of man's inhumanity to man?

"One year," is the sentence pronounced on the culprit. One year behind the bars of a gaol house. One year for labour and for repentance; and then one comes back into a life of misery.

Why cannot society prevent the cause of the miseries of the world? Why must one section of society become criminal and another become law-abiding?

Look at him. He is a young man of fifteen. He has hardly outgrown his childhood days. Companionship with irresponsible and forgotten men had dragged him into criminal life. He gets a "caution" or a fine or a sentence of imprisonment.

But is society not responsible for the increase of crime? Can mankind not be called to book for allowing the appalling conditions which now exist to continue?

There is so much misery in the world that all mankind should regard the existing conditions as a challenge to alter the present ethico-societal order.

Let those who have give to those who have not an opportunity to have something. Let those who have not, be honest and sincere in their attempts to have something from those who have.

When one section of the community is dependent on another section for its livelihood, there is the existence of a class system. This should not be allowed to thrive, because class system brings about a caste system which, in turn, brings about an aristocratic society.

No man is born inferior, and no man is born superior. That is the basis of the idea of the equality of mankind.

But if by their neglect and greed and selfishness, men allow the forces of man's inhumanity to man to becloud their views on the natural rights of man, they cannot escape condemnation for their responsibility for the misery which now engulfs mankind.

Are you a wealthy man or woman? Are you seeking to obtain more wealth, at the expense of the many who labour under very difficult conditions in order to obtain the necessaries of life?

If so, my friend, you are lucky or you are talented. But you should not be deluded to think that you are superior to those who are not as wealthy as yourself.

Your task, my friend, is to alleviate the misery of your fellow man. If they work for you, make them realize that they are engaged in a co-operative effort to make you and all the inhabitants of the world happier.

Are you talented, my friend? Are you seeking to impose yourself on others because they are not as talented as yourself? If so, my friend, humble yourself and be a sort of beacon to guide others to happiness.

There is misery in life. There will continue to be misery in life until man has developed into a stage where he will regard his fellow man not as a stepping stone, but as a corner stone, for the happiness of humanity.

May Renascent Africans become apostles to eradicate confusion and misery in the world.

30. *THE BLACK MAN'S ENEMY*

The black man is the black man's enemy.

An enemy is a foe who would move everything moveable and give his very life to move everything unmoveable, so as to attain his objective, and that is, to spite his rival.

The black man is his own enemy. He stays down below the first rung of the ladder. He wrangles with his miserable colleagues. But he is satisfied to pull down any of them who may attempt to climb up.

The black woman is the black woman's enemy. An enemy of this nature is only interested in scandalizing and in slandering. She sees nothing good in her fellow black woman. She would do anything to achieve her objective and also partake of the universal pie so adored by vamps of her nature, no matter if she had spent ten or fifty years in England.

The black woman is her own enemy. She stings others so as to soothe her vanity. But she fails to realize that such a sting is like a boomerang which must retribute the hurler sooner or later.

Why are some black folks made with small minds? Why are some black folks reminiscent of the incarnation of His Satanic Majesty? Is there any reason why the black man or black woman never forgets? Is there any reason why the black man or black woman nurses an injury for ten, twenty, thirty, forty years and even unto death?

The black man is vindictive especially to the black man. He will not progress, and, like the dog in the manger, he will not allow those who wish to progress, to do so.

The black man is callous and jealous. He is so self-complacent that he would dry the Congo River in the attempt to besmirch the character of his fellow black man and then smile that his life's ambition had been attained!

The black man is small-minded. He is petty. He is spiteful. He sees no good in the work of other black men. All he wants is for self, for family, for relatives, for immediate friends, and for those who accept crumbs from him.

Go to the public offices and you will see the black man there. He damns ; he curses ; he swears ; he orders ; he threatens. A vain monarch who surveys a table to-day and slips into oblivion as soon as he is retired or as soon as he is caught before leaving his misdeeds on the head of his successor.

Go to the law-making chambers and you will see him there. He will not co-operate. He will not allow those who will co-operate to co-operate. His task is to blacken the character of others and to paint them in sombre colours for his selfish delectations.

Go to the make-believe homes of the " society " folks. You will see the black man there trying to live as a lord in a manor. Debts upon debts are piled up on his head.

His very home is mortgaged. He will not scruple to sacrifice his daughter in order to maintain his " respect ".

He will not scruple to sacrifice his wife so as to " keep up with the Joneses ".

He may be lucky to be a professional man, but he is so busy conniving and contrapting that his professional achievements are to be likened to those of a bench-warmer.

He wags his head every time somebody says something which delights him. He nods his head angrily every time somebody says something good regarding another black man who may be his colleague. Oh these selfish black men and women! Black as the night and black as the depth of the continent of Africa.

Search for the black man and black woman in the churches and you will find them there. They can recite the *Te Deum*, the *Nunc Dimitis*, the *Cantate Domino*, the *Magnificat* (they will pronounce the latter as the " Magnificent Cat! ") from " We praise thee, O God " to " Let me never be confounded."

If you watch them singing you will think that Angel Gabriel and the angelic hosts (if they exist) are on hand to transfer these enemies of their race to regions where they will continue to perpetrate their atrocities.

Poor black men and women. How long will you continue to hinder the progress of black men and women? When will you cease to soil the screen of righteousness with your infernal sobs? Buzzards of Africa, your days are numbered.

Black men and women, when will you cease to be spiteful and think of the redemption of Africa? Are you destined to continue to exist as a hindrance to the realization of a new order, buzzards of Africa?

Socrates was sentenced to die because he was charged with the guilt of despoiling the youth and arousing them to disrespect their elders. Yet two thousand years afterwards, the world is still where Socrates left it, and black men would not scruple to intimidate the rulers by inflammatory speeches so as to destroy black Socrates who might be alive! Buzzards of Africa, your days have been numbered.

Joshua, whom the Greeks called Jesus, was sentenced to die because he was charged with the guilt of evangelizing for a new order, causing mother and daughter to be rent in twain, father and son to be at loggerheads, brothers and sisters to separate, so as to realize the ideal of man's humanity to man, and yet there are modern Scribes and Pharisees to-day who would orate in public assemblies about cunning foxes who aimed at despoliation of the country simply because they doctrinated the casting overboard of all the concomitants of man's inhumanity to man!

Black men and women, when will you cease to cut your noses so that others may live in your god-given land?

Black men and women, when will you cease to cut your noses to that your faces may be spited?

Black men and women, when will you cease to starve your stomachs so that the hands and the eyes and the noses and the mouths and the limbs and other parts of the human body may spite the stomach?

Black men and women, when will you cease to drift along the way which leads to the extermination of the black race?

You are sowing seeds of dissension. You are qualifying yourselves for immortality in the labyrinth of cursed men and women of "The Lost Generation".

The black man is the black man's enemy. The black woman

is the black woman's enemy. When will the black man and the black woman consolidate their interests so as to make the land of the black man and the black woman a better place to live in ?

Must black men continue to be spiteful and jealous of the achievements of their own race, in the face of overwhelming odds from within and from without ?

Where is the joy in a black man regarding it as a feat because a black man has injured a black man ? Will black men ever learn ?

What an herculean task for Renascent Africans ?

31. *DISCORDS AND HARMONY*

To the indigenous African, marriage between man and woman is a man-made institution for the social conservation of the group.

This is the view taken by *soi-disant* primitive peoples. They are right in their point of view, because they have cultivated a realist's philosophy of life.

Therefore, for purposes of practicality, let it be admitted that marriage is a man-made institution. In this light my approach will be more human and more practicable.

The primitive custom of the Native African, with reference to marriage is definitely *polygynous* (i.e. marital union of one man with more than one wife—not *polygamy*, which is a wrong definition, unfortunately popularized by those who have no pretensions whatsoever in the field of *Anthropology*).

Polygyny is the basis of African marital institution. Monogamy is also a part of African social economy, but only few African groups practice this form of marriage. The same is applicable to polyandry.

With the acculturation of the West, it became necessary for Africans to adopt certain customs of the West. This ushered in the European form of marriage. Had Africans understood the significance of monogamous marriage, it might have saved them from the record of family difficulties which arise from such unions.

But the African is an imitative species of humanity. Although his emulative capacity is not to be discounted, yet the picturesqueness and the quaint customs of the West, in respect of its marriage system, have gripped the imagination of the African.

Thus Africans welcomed the gospel of monogamy, hook, line, and sinker. This is not a treatise on monogamy versus polygyny, so it will be irrelevant to show the advantages and disadvantages of the one over the other. Nevertheless, the two must be placed before my perspective whilst I consider the problem of discords and harmony within the family of a married couple.

Why are homes shattered to-day as a result of marriages? Why are children abandoned to the fates as a result of marriages? Why are some human beings who formerly were respectable, dignified, and healthy, now scornful, undignified, and unhealthy, as a result of marriages?

Since the family is a unit of society, and marriage of man and woman makes family a reality, the family problems raised by marriage deserve more than a passing remark, so far as discords and harmony in families are concerned.

The African intelligentsia (I mean those who were trained abroad and those who were trained in Africa, who are generally recognized as being well educated, as signified by their educational or professional qualifications) have presented a problem to the social pathologist by being also a victim in the vortex of this whirlpool of social distintegration.

This is what I mean. Some of the African intelligentsia are either polygynous or monogamous. In either case, the woman remains the weaker vessel to the bread-winner of the family (who is, invariably, His Majesty the Husband).

In polygynous families, the husband is a monarch of all he surveys, and his rights therein there is none to challenge or to question.

In monogamous families, the same is the case. And since African women are mostly uneducated, marriage, be it polygynous or monogamous, has become a sort of sentence to indefinite servitude, so far as the weaker vessel is concerned.

Why all these discords in the attempt to have harmony?

A highly educated African gentleman hardly ever marries a highly educated African lady. Why? Some highly educated African gentlemen often prefer highly illiterate ladies. Why?

Probably, the highly educated African gentleman is a problem. And the highly educated African lady may be a problem also. And a highly illiterate African lady may be a necessary evil to save the highly educated African gentleman, and the highly educated African lady from the ignominy of a marital catastrophe.

Some Africans who are highly educated are not human in their domestic affairs. If they marry educated women, they expect them to maintain the dignity of the husbands, outside the home, but they must stay in their place in the home—and that is the kitchen.

Some African husbands of this type are too offensive in their attitude towards their educated wives. Naturally, the other half resents this offensiveness, hence there is a clash of temperaments.

But the ladies are just as blameable. Some of them, by virtue of their education, are too prone to be superficial in their way of life. They want to dress as if they live in Paris. Black beauties imitate white beauties, by coating their healthy faces and lips with unnecessary rouge and lipstick.

Some of them will drain the family chest so as *to keep up with the Big Guns*. Some of them will involve their husbands in debts so as to have the reputation of being good entertainers and hostesses. Some of them will give mental anguish to their husbands by being as fleeting as a butterfly when it comes to fidelity.

Even then, how many homes have been ruined by the shallow-mindedness of some of these so-called "England-ladies", who think that a stay of two, four, ten years in the backwoods of England is sufficient to make them ladies not destined to rub shoulders with their less-favoured African colleagues?

Of course I cannot treat this subject fully in one section, but these humble observations are indications of where the wind blows.

Whether marriage is a sacrament or not, the objective is domestic felicity. When an educated man marries an uneducated woman, he cannot have domestic felicity to the fullest, because of what the jurists would call a lack of *aggregatio mentium*. There is no meeting of minds. The two look at family problems from two divergent angles.

Again, when an educated man marries an educated woman, the latter by her wrong conception of values hinders, rather than encourages, domestic felicity, by not cultivating a sane and practical conception of her mission as a *mother*.

Mark you, I am not of the ilk of the *kill-joys* or the *light-headed Epicureans*, but I believe that why the African family is being disintegrated, is because African men and women have not been honest in regarding the family as a unit of society and also in studying the marital customs of the West, from a practical viewpoint.

Monogamy or polygyny, the goal is the same, and marriage is the route to social discord or harmony.

. . . . .

Life revolves around one axis. This axis has two poles—the forces of good and evil. Both poles are continually at war with themselves.

Between the two poles is the equator—the ethical norm. Its warmth helps to disentangle humanity from the frigidity of any vice or virtue.

The two poles represent two extremes. Evil rules the one, and good rules the other. The equator is equi-distant from the two poles.

The diameter of life is the environments of human beings who settle sparsely around the axis, and the circumference represents humanity as a whole. If persons dwell within the circumference of life, it is feasible that sometime they will be influenced by the ethos of one of its sectors.

As the poles widen, so too do the *mores* and morals of the persons present a variegated ramification. In other words, ethical ideas of people living in the pole of evil cannot be said to be consistent with the ethical ideas of people who live in the pole of good.

But what is good in one pole may be evil in the other pole, and what is bad in one pole may be good in another pole. Because the equator is equi-distant from the two poles, it does not lead to the conclusion that regions around the equator are half-good and half-evil.

Seeing now how flexible is the problem of morality, it is fair to qualify the same by saying that due to the various aspects of life, and the standard of ethics in different parts of the world, no criterion could be formulated without taking into consideration the mental development of the race. In this case, it is possible to be vindictive, sympathetic, apathetic. Whatever is the nature of one's outlook, the normative value is always a question mark.

Turn to Mother Africa. See how she had been battered from pillar to post. She had been the victim of unjustified aggression and carnage. She was led to the altar to be baptized with bullets so as to enter the kingdom of civilization.

How has this baptism affected the sons and daughters of bleeding Africa? Have they been equal to the task? Have they risen beyond the tactics of the big bad wolf? No. They have not. I find Africans still seeking vainly for Valhalla, whilst they have trained themselves for Hades. I see Africans undermining one another, to gratify their venality.

Let one of them arouse their lethargy. Let one of them brave the storm of conservatism and call things by their real names; and Africans will notice a cyclonic change in their social structure. Advocates of constructive criticism become zealots of destructive criticism.

Indeed, Africans live in a continent of wreckers. They wrecked Egypt. They wrecked Greece and Rome. They wrecked medieval Europe. They wrecked themselves during the Slave Trade, and now they are engaged in wrecking themselves for the extermination finale. All for the sake of gold or to satisfy their emotionalism.

Indeed, Africans form a part of inconsistent humanity. They praise, only to denounce. They tantalize, only to pacify. They grumble, only to keep mum. They ventriloquise, only to orate. And life rolls along to an unknown goal.

If Africans are not inconsistent, how can they reconcile the following fallacies in their contemporary life:

1. Italians are Roman Catholics. Roman Catholics love Africans. Ethiopians are Africans. Italians have invaded

Ethiopians and killed them. Therefore Italian Catholics love Africans.

2. The Pope is head of the Roman Catholic Church. The Press functions as sentinel of popular liberty. The Pope has or has not articulated. If he did, he was not direct. If he did not, he was guilty of a studious silence. But he is infallible and the Press must not belittle him.

3. The Press is the forum of the people. The liberty of the Press presumes a sense of responsibility. Academic freedom and the right of fair comment must not descend into licentiousness. A member of the Press criticizes a well-known leader to-day. To-morrow he becomes a turn-coat. Why? Because of the liberty of the Press!

4. Africans are prepared for a better Constitution. Gold Coastians and their ethnological group are aboriginal Africans. African candidates are rivals for an election. One wins, the other loses. This incident and its aftermath bring about a gap which shows the capacity or non-capacity of the African for a better Constitution.

To-day, Africans advocate for better conditions. To-morrow, they denounce others who advocate for a better Constitution *because these advocates form an extraneous element.*

To-day, Africans urge for unity among the various tribes of Africa. To-morrow, they widen the gap by detribalization. To-day, they preach of love. To-morrow, they practise hate. To-day, they praise. To-morrow, they denounce. To day, they curry favours. To-morrow, they become ingrates.

And this is the type of leaders that has been responsible for the static condition of Old Africa. And when these conflicting ethical ideas and ideals are challenged in the normal and scientific way, a speciousness of loose-thinking pervades their atmosphere.

Whither are Africans bound? To the madhouse which "Civilization" is leading the world, or to the abyss of Greece and Rome?

In the final analysis, there must be stock-taking. The squalls are shrilling. The storms are raging. Tornadoes and cyclones are deflecting the African ship from the harbour of consistency and goodwill.

But there will be calm. And when the calm comes, the débris will be cleared for a better edifice. Call that edifice New Africa, if you like. Compare it with the calm that must come after Old Africa has gone. Forget the inventor of that term. Forget the circumstances in which it was used.

Ever remember that humanity is inconsistent because life revolves around two poles—the forces of good and evil. If the latter must predominate your philosophy of life, your doom is sealed. If the former, then you stand a chance of surviving the struggle which is now in its titanic stage, but must pass away, so that Old Africa may yield its place to the New Africa.

You may take it or you may leave it. But "the moving finger writes ; and having writ, moves on : nor all your piety nor wit shall lure it back to cancel half a line, nor all your tears wash out a word of it ".

The Bantu World in its issue of July 4, 1936, reports the address delivered by Professor D. D. T. Javabu, B.A., President of the All-African Convention, which was held at Bloemfontein on June 29, 1936.

According to this paper, "'Segregation and colour bars must go,' said Professor D. D. T. Javabu, in his presidential address on Monday afternoon to the second Congress of the All-African Convention at Bloemfontein.

"Over 300 delegates from all parts of the country (South Africa) attended the Convention which was opened on Monday morning by the chairman of the Native Affairs Committee of the Town Council (Mr Lionel Nathan), in the absence of the Mayor (Mr A. C. White).

"Mr Nathan drew attention to the fact that the deliberations would attract the attention of various shades of opinion throughout the country.

"He pointed out that during the past few years tremendous strides had been made towards arriving at a better understanding of the inter-racial questions and exhorted the leaders of the black races to realize their responsibilities and to regulate their words and actions as not to retard progress.

"Professor Javabu said that in its treatment of the black races, Parliament (of South Africa) seemed to have superseded the ideals of Christianity by the principle of self-preservation.

" Since 1909 no fewer than thirty-six pieces of colour bar legislation had been registered against the black people.

" Segregation was being enforced and the black people were not given the right to dispose of the money they contributed through taxation. The interest of the white race was paramount.

" The Budget Speech had afforded the black people no joy. The Minister of Finance had lavished gifts from his surplus on the rich, relieving opulent groups of income tax and leaving the European farmers free from direct taxation.

" These farmers were privileged to buy maize at five shillings a bag for their stock, while starving Natives had to pay eighteen shillings to save their lives.

" Through their cheap labour in the mines, the blacks had enabled the Government to reap profits exceeding nine million pounds, but the Treasury would not let go the one million pounds odd of poll tax ' sucked from the blood of our people under distressing circumstances of poverty and even penury '.

" It was now for the Convention to decide what to do with the new Native laws, and how to consolidate their organization and promote its unity and efficiency and to devise schemes for improving the economic welfare of the black races by self-help.

" It might be felt by some that the new Acts should be *boycotted*, that reprisals and *bottled revenge* should be taken. That would startle South Africa and attract the attention of the world. But it might end in disaster, for it implied that every person, literate and illiterate, would obey the word of command.

" On the other hand, the Acts might be accepted unconditionally which would imply that the laws were accepted as just. Again, it might be agreed to use what could be used in the Acts and oppose what was not wanted.

" One thing the black people should strive to do was to escape from the poverty which they were suffering. ' We would burst our way into the vocations that create wealth among our communities,' he said.

" They should not confine themselves to teaching and ministry, but take up law, medicine, commerce and progressive farming.

" One of the tasks was to educate the Union's rulers to the

blacks' view of affairs and their reason for claiming equal rights.

" *Segregation and colour bar should go. Otherwise, there should be a separate State for the blacks in which they could rule themselves.*

" *Economic repression should go. If they exercised their power, they could hold up industries that depended on their labour.*

" Selfishness should go. ' In our primitive African tradition, we used to smell out and destroy acquisitive individuals as a danger to society. By this crude method we guaranteed all men a chance to have food and shelter and clothing without prejudice. . . .'

" The war between Italy and Abyssinia was referred to by Professor Javabu. ' All Africans,' he declared, ' as well as all other non-white races of the world, have been staggered by the cynical rape by Italy of the last (*second to the last*, what of the Republic of Liberia ?) independent State belonging to indigenous Africans.

" ' After hearing a great deal for twenty years about the rights of small nations, self-determination, Christian ideals, the inviolability of treaties, human warfare, the sacredness of one's plighted word, the glory of European civilization, and so forth, the brief history of the last eight months (i.e. October, 1935 to June, 1936) has scratched this European veneer and revealed the White savage hidden beneath.

" ' Two decades ago, millions of human lives were sacrificed at the altar of Belgian neutrality ; to-day, nothing has been done to stay Italy's determination to butcher in cold blood and asphyxiate our peaceful fellow-men of Ethiopia.

" ' Italy's defiance of solemn pledges has been met by hesitation, prevarication, caution dialects and pusillanimity in turn.

" ' In 1914, it was a case of a White European nation, Belgium ; to-day, it is only Black Abyssinia.

" ' As on other occasions, the churches of the countries concerned claimed that God was fighting on their side, and invoked His blessing to prosper their imperialistic ambitions.

" ' Organized Christianity has so far failed to curb the animal propensities of rapacity and selfishness in the hearts of men who rule empires.

" ' The present world muddle seems to be exactly what it

was two or three thousand years ago. Take away our scientific knowledge of tools and we are where we were then.

" 'One man did paint and illustrate a better way of living, but he was murdered by his Jerusalem contemporaries for doing so.

" 'His professed followers have ended in lip service to Him, so far as war goes. They have partly wished to effect the change, and partly failed to take the necessary risks.

" 'The governing ideal in human history is once more the law of the jungle. The modern system centres round the glorification of national empires.

" 'In so far as we are included as subjects within and under these empires, we share the blame for their tragic obliquity, even against our will.

" 'The structure of European political morality has suddenly tottered and collapsed from above our heads down to its pristine level of the jungle that obtained two thousand years ago.

" 'Might is still right, though it is no longer the might of the sword, but the vaunted science of aeroplanes raining dynamite bombs and poison gas.

" 'That, in short, is the pride of so-called White civilization.

" 'It constitutes a moral challenge to the rest of humanity.' "

And Renascent Africans are nonplussed at the existence of discords as an avenue to harmony !

32. *ALL IS VANITY*

Greatness can be achieved by an idiot just as immortality can be achieved by an ass. But true greatness and worthwhile immortality can be achieved by the select few.

Let all Africans who yearn for greatness and for immortality analyse themselves dispassionately. Let them ask themselves this question : Is it worth while to be truly great and immortal ?

I can only advise that the affirmative reply will depend upon the nature and native ability of the person involved. If a negative answer is inevitable, then greatness must not be pursued *at all costs*.

There are some men who impose themselves on others,

forcing them to acknowledge them as great, when it is obvious that the germ of true greatness is not in them.

There are some men who yearn to be immortal in history, whilst it is evident they have not the daring and the peculiarities which make some persons immortal.

In the face of these, what price ambition to carve a niche in the hall of fame? Is it worth while? Is it creditable to one's intelligence? Yes and no.

Yes, in the sense that he who realizes the fact that there can be no crowns without crosses, and that there can be no successes without failures, is travelling along the right path.

No, in the sense that some men are inclined to the belief that greatness and immortality can be thrust upon those who are capable of seizing the opportunity offered, irrespective of their temperament and native ability.

But what is greatness? Does it consist of establishing reputation as a wealthy person or as a socialite? Or does it consist in humble service for the benefit of the greatest number of people?

No matter how one looks at the subject, there is one conclusion which cannot be escaped, and that is, that greatness, be it true or false, is vanity.

Some persons who claim to be great delight in wickedly designing against the life and liberty of others. They think that by so doing, it is possible for them to impress upon the world their greatness.

Can this be regarded as true greatness? Does it not reveal pretensions of a crooked nature? Does it not demonstrate the wickedness which is the basic nature of these persons' ego?

It seems to me that whoever claims to be a great man cannot be truly great, if for any consideration whatsoever, he stoops to be a sort of backslider.

There are some persons who prefer to hit below the belt and to climax their blows with an exhibition of fairness. I cannot regard them as great.

These are some persons whose ethics hardly transcends the instincts of the brute, yet they are in high places in African society, and they pose as great men.

There are some persons whose wickedness is incomparable

with the alleged wickedness of the brutes of creation, yet they hobnob with the arbiters of the destiny of men without compunction.

There are some persons who will not scruple to compromise their honour and dignity, in order to vent their spleen on any object which they have reason to hate. Are they truly great?

There are some persons whose avidity for plotting against others goes so far as to make them so unscrupulous that they will dictate the death warrant of others, merely to gratify their whims. Another evidence of greatness?

There are some persons who, despite the fact that they are looked upon to wield power in order to shape the destinies of others, allow a moment of weakness to overpower them so that they yield to this type of *great* men.

There are some persons who are supposed to mould the future of others, and yet they allow themselves to be influenced by sources which are not only polluted with the venom of hate, but are destined to work for their ultimate downfall, even though they may be unconscious of its effect.

There are some persons who will allow other persons much more inferior to them in many respects, to dictate to them what should be their attitude towards certain questions, which must jeopardize the fate of the many at the expense of the few.

Can it be said candidly that these types of persons are not living *among and between* Africans to-day?

Can Africans deny that they do not exist side by side with them and that their only fate is to be likened to the house which was built on a sand only to be smashed to pieces by the forces of nature?

Look around you. Notice some professed great men and women. Probe into their private lives. Search through their activities with their fellow man and fellow woman. Are you satisfied that the moral fibre so necessary for uprightness and straightforwardness is there?

Again, glance through the panoramic biography of certain persons who are supposed to be the final cause of the mundane existence of Africans. Probe into their activities and search through their lives among Africans. Can you say quite frankly that they are not a disappointment?

Yet these very persons are those who take advice from the self-professed African great men who are lacking in moral fibre and whose general outlook is contaminated with the virus of selfishness.

Yet these very persons prefer to hobnob with those whose activities and general attitude toward the danger zones of life's intricate problems are warped and shrouded in social myopia.

There is only one consolation. The professed great men are not destined to live for ever, biologically speaking. Being human, they are allotted the usual span of existence.

Those who prefer to allow themselves to be used as a means to an end, are also human. To-day be theirs, but to-morrow will come when they will be no more.

In the final analysis, the problem reduces itself to this: *Man is made of clay*. And clay is fragile. That is why man is vain. That is why man is a braggart. That is why man is so forgetful of the wrath that is to come: *Death, the doom of all.*

A man may be great, professedly, yet one day will find him humbled in the silent chambers of death.

A man may be powerful to-day, yet one day will find him leaving this earth to an uncharted and an unknown region, humiliated and to be soon forgotten.

And the interesting part of the whole topic is that when death comes, it does so without warning.

Great or small, rich or poor, powerful or weak—the same destiny awaits them, death, the common fate of all. Yes, six feet of clay await all in the end.

Common clay, this man. Yet he brags as if clay were immortal. Indeed, vanity of vanity, says the Preacher, vanity of vanity, all is vanity!

33. *ETHIOPIA CRUCIFIED*

International Law reached a milestone in its development (or devolution) on October 3, 1935, when Italy undertook to contravene all the legal doctrines of international relations which made a reign of law between States possible, since the days of Hugo Grotius.

In view of the fact that unless the fundamental principles of International Law which were violated by Italy are clarified, inter-State relations will revert to " lamb and wolf diplomacy " of the days of Niccolo Machiavelli, an Italian political machinator, I am undertaking to present to the reader in this section some of the deeds of Italy in the realm of International Law and diplomacy.

It is true, this is not a technical treatise, but it should be useful as a discourse to clarify to the African some of the tendencies of the Italian.

On its own will, Italy invaded Ethiopia and fought for a period of seven months. Although Ethiopia did not really surrender, yet its Emperor had capitulated and abdicated.

Why did Italy invade Ethiopia? What was the nature of this invasion? How was the Italian objective realized? These are the points which should be elaborated from a legal point of view.

Italy invaded Ethiopia, in order to avenge the defeat of Italy by Menelik II, at Adowa, in 1896. Italy invaded Ethiopia because it desired expansion for its population. Italy invaded Ethiopia because it needed raw materials. Italy invaded Ethiopia because Fascism demands conquest and glory.

These are the primary reasons for the invasion of Ethiopia by Italy. There are other secondary reasons. For example, Italy was of opinion that Ethiopian subjects violated its territorial integrity by trespassing on Italian Somaliland, so as to create the *soi-disant* Ual-Ual dispute.

Then there is the point of view of some " humanitarian " Italians who believe that slavery was rampant in Ethiopia and that it was imperative that the beneficent influences of Italian civilization should be carried into Ethiopia for the good of the world.

These grounds may be justifiable, but to the international jurist, the point is whether the grounds for the invasion of Ethiopia are legal, and if so whether they conform to the tenets of International Law and jurisprudence.

I submit that the primary and secondary reasons for the invasion of Ethiopia by Italy are not legal, and consequently they are not in accordance with International Law.

According to an authority, "Treaties and State papers of whatever form (such as Declarations, Protocols, Conventions, Proclamations, Notes, etc.) indicate the state of opinion, at a given time, in regard to the matters of which they treat. Since they are binding upon the parties to them, treaties may be regarded as evidence of what the States, bound by their terms, accept as law. When the same terms are generally accepted among nations, treaties become a valuable evidence as to practice, and are regarded as proper sources of International Law, or principles may be so well established by successive treaties as to need no further treaty specification."

If it is admitted, therefore, that any treaty signed by Italy, bi-laterally or multi-laterally, towards the realization of the peace of the world is binding legally on the contracting parties, it follows, then, that an infringement of the same is a violation of International Law.

Now, it is unnecessary to refer to the various treaties signed by Italy and Ethiopia towards mutual existence, although they are pertinent to the subject, but I wish to refer to two specific multi-lateral treaties which were signed and ratified by both Italy and Ethiopia, in concert with the rest of the world, towards the peaceful settlement of disputes.

These two treaties are important documents in the realm of International Law. Any State which regards either as a scrap of paper, cannot be respected as a State worthy of existence in a world where there is a reign of law, order, and good government. They are the Covenant of the League of Nations and the Pact of Paris.

The Covenant of the League of Nations is a multi-lateral treaty which was brought into being by and through the co-operative effort of Italy. Its extension to other States was also practicalized by and through the instrumentality of Italy.

If, therefore, Italy, which was responsible for the birth and growth of the Covenant of the League of Nations, chose to violate the sacred principles and stipulations in the Covenant, no person is wrong to regard Italy, not only as an international criminal, but as an outcast beyond the pale of honourable international society.

In January 1919, an array of diplomats gathered at Versailles in order to decide the fortunes of the world following the Armistice. A League of Nations Commission was constituted with nineteen members, under the chairmanship of the late Woodrow Wilson.

Among the members of this Commission were: Lord Cecil and General Jan Christaan Smuts (British Empire); M. Bourgeois (France); Baron Makino (Japan); General Venizelos (Greece); *Vittorio Orlando* (Italy).

The Commission finally submitted its findings, which were adopted at its plenary session which was held on April 28, 1919, as a Covenant of the League of Nations. It is interesting to note that among the original members of the League of Nations were Italy, Liberia, Haiti, and the Great Powers.

It is also interesting to note that *Signor Vittorio Orlando*, Italy's representative at the Paris Peace Conference (which was responsible for the formulation of the League's Covenant), who was assisted by Signor Sonnino, *became disgusted with Italy's failure to secure more of the Dalmatian coast, and left the Conference in a very unceremonious and insulting manner*, just as Baron Pompeo Aloisi did during the preliminary discussion of the Italo-Ethiopian tangle at Geneva.

However, the Covenant of the League (which was signed by Italy and other States) has the following as its Preamble:

"In order to promote international co-operation and to achieve international peace and security—

"By acceptance of obligations not to resort to war;

"By the prescription of open, just and honourable relations between nations;

"By the firm establishment of the understandings of International Law as the actual rule of conduct among governments, and

"By the maintenance of justice and a scrupulous respect for all treaty obligations in the dealings of organized peoples with one another. The High Contracting Parties agree to this Covenant of the League of Nations."

Italy was a signatory to the Covenant of the League of Nations. This document aimed towards the promotion of

" international co-operation and to achieve international peace and security by the acceptance of obligations not to resort to war."

Through this reorientation of diplomacy, the States of the world believed that the era of " lamb and wolf diplomacy " was gone for ever, and international public opinion was re-educated to realize the dawn of a new day in the realm of international relations.

That the League of Nations is an international organization which represents a new deal in international politics, is an admitted fact. But it is not the organization itself that must be looked up to for practicability of its precepts, but its individual members.

Despite the vague and pompous statements in the Preamble of the League of Nations, Japan did not scruple to invade Manchuria in 1931. It was difficult to attach any blame to Japan, since Manchuria is not a member of the League.

Article 1, Section 2 of the Covenant of the League specifically restricts membership of the League to " Any fully self-governing State, Dominion or Colony." There are other factors in the Japanese invasion of Manchuria which are irrelevant to this article.

When now Italy chose to slice a piece of Ethiopian territory, another factor presented itself, making the case of Italians in East Africa different from that of the Japanese in Manchuria, from a legal point of view.

This brings me to the second phase of my discourse : *What was the nature of the invasion of Ethiopian territory by Italy* ?

Off-handedly, any student of world affairs will say that the nature of Italian invasion of Ethiopia was through warfare. But the legal technicality remains whether there was a state of war between Italy and Ethiopia.

I will admit for the sake of debating, that, for a state of war to exist, there must be a declaration of war. I will even concede that what Italy has done can be technically classified as " intervention ", " reprisal ", " retaliation ", or even " retorsion ".

But the fact remains that there was an organized attempt to invade Ethiopia, by the employment of military force by land and by air. All the manifestations of war are evident, and to define Italian aggression by any other terminology is to beg the issue, with due deference to the opinion of Italian international jurists.

Granting, therefore, that Italy employed war to achieve its purpose, it is now necessary to demonstrate how Italy has also violated International Law thereby.

On August 27, 1928, Italy signed a multi-lateral treaty, entitled the Pact of Paris (popularly but erroneously identified as the Kellogg-Briand Pact).

Behold the Preamble of the Pact of Paris :

" Deeply sensible of their solemn duty to promote the welfare of mankind ; Persuaded that the time has come when a frank renunciation of war as an instrument of national policy should be made to the end that the peaceful and friendly relations now existing between their peoples may be perpetuated ;

" Convinced that all changes in their relations with one another should be sought only by pacific means and be the result of a peaceful and orderly process, and that any signatory Power which shall hereafter seek to promote its national interests by resort to war should be denied the benefits furnished by this Treaty ;

" Hopeful that, encouraged by their example, all the other nations of the world will join in this humane endeavour and by adhering to the present Treaty as soon as it comes into force bring their peoples within the scope of its beneficent provisions, thus uniting the civilized nations of the world in a common renunciation of war as an instrument of their national policy ;

(Ten States) " Have decided to conclude a Treaty and for that purpose have appointed as their respective Pleni-potentiaries. . . ."

The Ten States which originally formulated this Treaty are Germany, United States of America, Belgium, France, Great Britain, British Empire, *Italy*, Japan, Poland and Czechoslovakia. *Count Gaetano Manzoni* represented Italy in the capacity of Ambassador Extraordinary and Plentipotentiary at Paris.

The text of the pertinent clauses of the Pact of Paris is as follows :

" ARTICLE I. The High Contracting Parties solemnly declare

in the names of their respective people that they condemn recourse to war for the solution of international controversies, and renounce it as an instrument of national policy in their relations with one another.

"ARTICLE II. The High Contracting Parties agree that the settlement or solution of all disputes or conflicts of whatever nature or of whatever origin they may be, which may arise among them, shall never be sought except by pacific means.

"ARTICLE III. . . . This Treaty shall, when it has come into effect as prescribed in the preceding paragraph (omitted), remain open as long as may be necessary for adherence by all the other Powers of the world. . . ."

On August, 27, 1928, a Note with reference to the above Treaty, with particular reference to the portion of Article III, reproduced above, was forwarded to forty-eight nations of the world, including Ethiopia, Haiti, and Liberia.

In this Note, it was observed *inter alia*, "That the Powers signing the Treaty have recorded in the Preamble their hope that every nation of the world will participate in the Treaty. . . . In these circumstances I have the honour formally to communicate to Your Excellency for your consideration and for the approval of your Government, if it concurs therein, the text of the above-mentioned Treaty as signed to-day in Paris, omitting only that part of the Preamble which names the several Plenipotentiaries. . . .

By September 12, 1928, Liberia was among the three States which "Officially adhered to the Pact." By the same date, Ethiopia and Haiti were among the twenty-five States which "signified their intention to adhere to the Pact." Later, Ethiopia adhered to the Pact, *in toto*.

The Pact of Paris is a multi-lateral treaty which was signed by both Italy and Ethiopia with the rest of the world. These two Powers agreed to renounce war as an instrument of national policy and to settle their disputes without recourse to war.

By invading Ethiopian territory through marching of its soldiers into Ethiopian territory, by bombing Adigrat and Adowa, by raiding Makale, by raining poison gases on civilians at Dessye, Harrar, Jijiga, Dolo, etc., and by marching into Addis Ababa, the capital of the Ethiopian Empire, the Italian

Government has, by its overt acts, desecrated the solemn stipulations of the Pact of Paris, and *ipso facto* has violated International Law.

War is undefinable, according to the present development of international law. Even if the Covenant of the League of Nations is studied with a view to a legal definition of war, one finds oneself in a quandary..

When does a member of the League " resort to war " ? Do the military sanctions of the League constitute war ? In the sense of Article XVI, are coercive measures war ? Do actions taken in self-defence constitute war ? These are problems which the international lawyer must solve in the attempt to define war, legally.

It is admitted that when war is defined, some of its elements must be considered, for example, force, intention. But it cannot be admitted that the law of nations intended that belligerents should have the right to define or to establish the existence of war. If this is allowed, Italy's claim that its use of force on Ethiopia was motivated by self-defence and that there was no intention to make war, would be correct. In this case, it can be justified, for in International Law, self-defence is good ground for proving a lack of *mens rea*. And no doubt, Italy is justifying itself thus.

However, Article XI of the Covenant states clearly that " Any war or threat of war is hereby declared a matter of concern to the whole League." In other words, the League has arrogated to itself the right to declare the use of force illegal, even though each of the belligerent parties denies the intention to make war.

The League of Nations has placed itself on record as condemning the use of force by Italy on Ethiopia. Therefore, the presumption that Italian aggression on Ethiopia is war, is correct, from a legal point of view.

This brings me to the third phase of this discourse : *How was the Italian objective realized* ?

If, despite the fact that Italy signed and ratified the Covenant of the League of Nations, it proceeded to violate the territorial integrity of Ethiopia, thus contravening International Law, and if Italy used war as an instrument of national policy, contrary to the Pact of Paris which was signed and ratified by Italy, thus violating International Law again, were the means used to invade Ethiopian territory justifiable, according to International Law?

In an editorial which was published in its issue of April 6, 1936, the *Daily Herald*, a London morning paper which claims to have the "largest daily net sale in the world" (about 2,500,000 copies of daily circulation) said *inter alia*:

"Horror and anger have swept the civilized world as the full story of Italian brutality and frightfulness in Abyssinia has been revealed and confirmed. The destruction of the pitiful homes and buildings of helpless unfortified towns with high explosive and incendiary bombs, the use of poison gas in the field against unmasked and half-armed tribesmen, the spraying of liquid gas upon women and children and babies—these are hellish things. And they must stop. They must stop."

It is also confirmed by Italy that Red Cross units belonging to Great Britain, Sweden, Turkey, Egypt, United States of America, and Ethiopia were bombed during hostilities, even though the emblem of the Red Cross was heralded and clearly indicated.

The Hague Convention of 1899 declared in Article II against the "use of projectiles, the sole object of which is the diffusion of asphyxiating or deleterious gases."

During the Washington Conference, of which Italy was a principal member, a multi-lateral treaty was signed regarding the use of obnoxious gases in warfare.

The preamble of this convention reads as follows: "The United States of America, the British Empire, France, *Italy* and Japan, desiring to make more effective the rules adopted by civilized nations . . . to prevent the use in war of noxious gases and chemicals . . . have agreed as follows:

"ARTICLE V. The use in war of asphyxiating, poisonous or other gases, and all analogous liquids, materials or devices, having been justly condemned by the general opinion of the civilized world and a prohibition of such use having been declared in treaties to which a majority of the civilized Powers are parties.

"The Signatory Powers (and adhering Non-Signatory Powers as well) to the end that this prohibition shall be universally accepted as a part of international law binding alike the conscience and practice of nations, declare their assent to such prohibition, agree to be bound thereby as between themselves and invite all other civilized nations to adhere thereto."

Having used poison gas of variegated classification on the Ethiopians, Italy has violated the Hague Convention of 1899, by employing projectiles which diffused asphyxiating and deleterious gases. It has also violated the Washington Convention of 1922, by making use of poisonous or other analogous liquids, gases, etc., on the Ethiopians. These, I submit, are tantamount to a violation of International Law.

The Geneva Convention of 1906 relates to treatment of the sick and wounded in war-time. In view of the bombing of Red Cross units by Italian aircraft, I shall now sustain my contention that Italy also violated International Law, in this regard.

On July 6, 1906, a convention was signed at Geneva "for the amelioration of the condition of the wounded in the field".

The Preamble is as follows: (Thirty-five states) "Being equally animated by the desire to lessen the inherent evils of warfare as far as is within their power, and wishing for this purpose to improve and supplement the provision agreed upon at Hague on August 22, 1864, for the amelioration of the condition of the wounded in armies in the field, have decided to conclude a new convention to that effect."

In Chapter 6, Article XXIII, it was agreed that "The emblem of the red cross on a white ground and the words *Red Cross* or *Geneva Cross* may only be used, whether in time of peace or war, to protect or designate sanitary formations and establishments, the personnel and material protected by the convention." Turkey, Persia, Egypt, Japan, China, etc., were also allowed certain national emblems peculiar to them.

Articles XX-XXII of this Convention grant a sort of immunity from attack to Red Cross workers. The second to the last paragraph of the convention reads as follows: "*In faith* whereof the plenipotentiaries have signed the present convention and affixed their seals thereto." (*My italics.*)

I will end this discussion by summarizing the legal aspects of the Italo-Ethiopian war, and also by restating my conviction that Italy had violated International Law. Since it is my opinion that these violations of a reign of law in international society were countenanced under the ægis of the League of Nations, of which Ethiopia is a member, it leads naturally to the conclusion which inspired the caption of this section.

Ethiopia reposed its trust in the League of Nations. Ethiopia placed its confidence in the system of *collective security*. Ethiopia swallowed literally the bunk of a new deal in diplomacy wherein the " lamb and wolf diplomacy " of *pre-bellum* days was alleged to have been abrogated. Hence the crucifixion of Ethiopia.

Consistent with the aim of this treatise, I do not wish to be emotionally motivated. There must be scientific objectivity in order to state my case effectively (a) against Italy, and (b) against the League of Nations.

I have stated the case against Italy. In the first place, I showed why Italy invaded Ethiopian territory. In this connection, I demonstrated that having renounced imperialism by acquiescence in a system of international mediation, arbitration, conciliation, and judicial settlement of disputes, Italy helped to create and nurture to its adulthood the League of Nations. Its invasion of Ethiopian territory is therefore a violation of the Covenant of the League and is *per se* a violation of International Law.

In the second place, I elaborated on what was the nature of Italian aggression, and I discussed the rôle of Italy as one of the formulators of the Pact of Paris, a multi-lateral treaty dedicated to the renunciation of war as an instrument for the settlement of international disputes. I proved that Italy employed military force to invade Ethiopia, and since the League was of that opinion, I concluded that Italy had violated International Law, by desecrating the Pact of Paris.

In the third place, I examined how Italy attained its military objective, by analysing the employment of noxious and asphyxiating and other deleterious gases to wage war on the Ethiopians. I also referred to numerous bombings of Red Cross units. These, I submitted, violated International Law, because they were contrary to the stipulations agreed to by Italy and Ethiopia in the Hague Convention of 1899, the Geneva Convention of 1906, and the Washington Convention of 1922.

In this latter part of my discussion, it is my task to consider the Ethiopian membership in the League and how the latter has betrayed and crucified the aspirations of a free people, by its questionable diplomatic tactics.

In 1923, Ethiopia applied for membership of the League of Nations. Great Britain and Holland opposed the application. The late Sir Arthur Steel Maitland, British delegate, emphasized the recrudescence of slavery in Ethiopia. France and Italy supported Ethiopian application.

Count Bonin-Longare, the Italian delegate, "considered that Abyssinia's request constituted a tribute to the League of Nations. This tribute was of great value as coming from a distant nation which had hitherto remained outside the great international movements, but which, by the remarkable tenacity with which it had been able to preserve its religious faith and national character throughout the ages, had acquired titles of nobility to which due justice must be paid."

M. de Jouvenel, the French delegate, in supporting Count Bonin-Longare, said: "The Committee ought to recommend the Assembly to admit Abyssinia to the League, and that any delay in the admission of that country might prejudice the cause of peace and prestige of the League. *If an incident were to take place within the coming year on the frontiers of Abyssinia and it was settled by force, the League would be blamed for such recourse to force because it had failed to come to a decision in time.*" (*Italics mine.*)

Having agreed to adhere to the sections of the St. Germain Convention of 1919, with particular reference to slavery and *the arms traffic*, Ethiopia was admitted into the League's membership.

On this occasion, Ethiopia declared itself "ready now and hereafter to furnish the Council of the League of Nations with any information which it may require, and to take into consideration any recommendation which the Council may make with regard to the fulfilment of these obligations."

Now, what has *arms traffic* to do with the admission of a prospective member into the League of Nations? According to an authority: "With the accumulation of great stores of surplus weapons during the World War, some new restrictions, imposed on the export of arms from Europe as well as import by Africa, etc., were imperative."

The St. Germain Convention prohibits the sale of war arms to individuals and controls the sale of arms to Governments by a system of licence and publicity. Moreover, the League was entrusted with "the general supervision of the trade in arms and ammunition where such control is necessary."

I submit that this was the first step of the League towards the crucifixion of Ethiopia. By making its admission into the League contingent on its adhering to the St. Germain Convention, which limits its arms supply, the League prepared Ethiopia for any "frontier incident" which Italy did not fail to capitalize on. Let this be handed down to posterity.

The part played by the League, immediately before and immediately after the invasion of Ethiopia, by the armed forces of Italy, is well known. The League imposed an arms embargo (immediately after the invasion of Ethiopia) on a State like Ethiopia whose arms had been limited by the Limitation of Arms Traffic Convention signed at St. Germain-en-Laye. This marked the second stage in the crucifixion of Ethiopia. Let this be handed down to posterity also.

Instead of enforcing Article XVI, Section 4, which stipulates the expulsion of any recalcitrant member, and instead of enforcing the Sanctions indicated in the same Article, Sections 1, 2, and 3, of the Covenant, the League's dilatory tactics have astounded the conscience of the world as to the moral bankruptcy of the League of Nations. This is the third stage in the crucifixion of Ethiopia, which must also be handed down to posterity.

In a Note addressed to the League, on the eve of the Committee of Thirteen, His Majesty Emperor Haile Selassie, wrote as follows:

"There is no doubt that had the State members adhered to their resolve to stop aggression by applying effective Sanctions, the war would have ended long ago.

"Italy, however, succeeded in sowing dissension within the League and has prevented the imposition of Sanctions, and secured the postponement of those it feared, especially oil sanctions.

"Now small States are asking themselves what protection is afforded by the collective security promised in the Covenant.

"The Great Powers are now experiencing the effects of the spirit of aggression. The moral confusion created by the practical impunity of Italian aggression is beginning to produce its terrible consequences."

I submit that the words of the Emperor clearly sum up my indictment on the League of Nations. Any international organization which is lacking in moral courage to do justice, no matter how altruistic may be its motive, is destined to drag humanity into the lowest degradation of international anarchy, and possibly spell the ruin of civilization, because its actions would and must intensify bitterness among the races of mankind.

I say that the League of Nations betrayed and crucified the Ethiopian Empire because:

(1) It disarmed Ethiopia before admitting it into membership of the League of Nations.

(2) It imposed an arms embargo on Ethiopia when a great military power like Italy attacked that African kingdom.

(3) It failed to grant Ethiopia, a full member, collective security, as guaranteed by Article X of the League's Covenant.

(4) It did not expel Italy from the League to vindicate a reign of law and order in international society.

(5) Its dilatory tactics in the imposition of Sanctions facilitated the conquest of Ethiopia, from a military point of view.

(6) Its general attitude during the beginning and ending of the Italo-Ethiopian war is a betrayal of the smaller States of the world.

(7) It did not energetically indicate that Italy had consciously violated the international law of peace and the international law of war.

(8) It had allowed international law to be a joke, so far as the coloured races of the world are concerned.

Q.E.D.

But the irony of the crucifixion of Ethiopia is that black African soldiers, officered by Italians, constituted about half of the Italian forces in East Africa which invaded and subjugated Ethiopia.[1] A clear example of Africa against Africa!

[1] Edward Hamilton, *The War in Abyssinia* (1936), page 4.

34. *JEALOUSY*

I am jealousy, the green-eyed monster. I feed on meat and I mock and jeer and deride and scorn at the very meat which sustains my life. I praise merely to flatter. I flatter merely to arouse the vanity of humanity. I preach love, but I practise hate. I am jealousy, the green-eyed monster.

In the royal domain, I make my habitat as well as in the worker's hovel. I work in earnest, but I am never sincere in my professions. My tongue is as deceptive as the liquid gun of the squid. I am always diabolical in my plans and no good can come out of me.

I enthrone myself in the minds of the statesmen of the world and so they regard me as their only leader. I speak to them in the language of the demagogue. I criticize. I wreck. I shatter. I am noisy and long-winded. I bully my opponents. I call them names. I raise cain. But I hate any rival because I am jealousy, the green-eyed monster who eats meat and derides that meat which sustains his life.

I am an adept in under-hand dealings. I cheat. I rob. I lie. I fabricate. I distort. I concoct. I contrapt. I connive. I make-believe, even though ostensibly, I brand myself to be a foe of injustice.

Search for me in high places and you will find me there. Search for me in the low estate and you will find me there. I lurk in the executive offices and I find room in the workshops. You will see me rear my horrid head whenever competition comes on. I brook no rival. I destroy so as to exist as the great powerful "I am", for I am jealousy, the green-eyed monster.

What though I shout of liberty and freedom? What though I rant of oppression? What though I grumble against evil; yet I delight in perpetrating evil to mankind so as to predominate. I oppress. I repress. I depress. I impress. I coerce. I blackmail. I hit below-the-belt. I bite behind the back, for I am what I am—jealousy, the green-eyed monster.

I advocate for domestic felicity but my home is a harem.

I practise all forms of moral turpitude. I have wives. I have mistresses. I harbour harlots. I apotheosize prostitutes. I worship strange women. And I denounce those who do the same, for I hate any rival, even to the death, for I am jealousy, the green-eyed monster.

I preach the gospel of live and let live. I disseminate ideas of equity. I oppose any unjust measure which may jeopardize the right to life, liberty, and the pursuit of happiness of mankind. But I practice the gospel of die and let me live. I prepare herbs to take away life or to affect the brain cells. I am a disciple of Zachariah Fee for I believe in making mankind unhappy for aye, for I am jealousy, the green-eyed monster.

I prepare cocktails with lemon and sugar and rhubarb and gin and whisky and brandy. I flatter my victim as to the deliciousness of the Hecatean concoction. But he knows not that there is an overdose of strychnine to facilitate his exit to the nether worlds.

I sow giant seeds and reap dwarf trees in return, but I flatter myself that I have done my part. I plough through rocky and sandy soil and I expect a big harvest. But I know full well that what one sows not, one reaps if one becomes unduly jealous.

In addition to a telegraphic tongue, and a telephonic ear, my pen is as witty as can be. Just as my tongue can flatter so too can my pen distort falsehood in the semblance of truth. Seek for me in the haystack and you'll find me smaller than a needle. Seek for me in the woodpile and you'll find me in the form of a stone. Seek for me among crooks and murderers and cut-throats and robbers and gangsters, and you'll find me in my glory, for I am jealousy, the green-eyed monster.

But the food I eat, the clothes I wear, the house I live in are the results of the efforts of others. Yet I envy them, and I do everything in my power to hamper them. Isn't it folly that I cut my nose to spite my face? Yet I don't seem to realize this anomaly, for I am jealousy, the green-eyed monster.

Here is my rival. He comes to me, as a friend. He teaches me how to live. He gives me ideas. He shows me the light and tells me to find my way. He helps to make life worth while by infusing in me the competitive spirit of live and let live, and yet I plan his end. And yet I make no secret of my efforts to ruin him, even to death. But then jealousy is a blind demon. Even Zachariah Fee with all his demons and wizards could not have been so wicked and so devoid of humanity.

Look at my triumph! I fan embers into conflagrations so as to enmesh my rival and burn him to death. Oh jealousy, what misdeeds have not been committed in thy name!

Look at my victory! I dispatch letters disclosing his secrets so as to involve him with his opponents or with the law and thus bring about his exit. I sigh with him, even though I am seeking for his liver. I smile with him, even though I am secretly weeping for his untimely demise. But I need not quiver nor need I surrender for I am jealousy, the green-eyed monster.

Wherever I go, I must dominate or know the reason why. Wherever I am, I must be the IT or know the reason why. Whenever I have a rival, I must dethrone that rival or besmirch his reputation or concoct his downfall or trap him in a burning house or betray him to his enemies or initiate suggestions for injuries to his name or body. These must I do, for I am jealousy, "the green-eyed monster which doth mock the meat it feeds on".

. . . . .

And to you, Renascent African, is it not a fact that one reason why the Continent of Africa has been, is, and may continue to be, the footstool of other continents is because *Africans* (just as the other races, but Africans are more pronounced) *are too jealous of one another*?

Why must the bat in blindness rant that he has creation in a jug? Why must elephants trample on rabbits and have a self-centred notion of their invulnerability? Why must the owl question the enslavement of aphids by ants? Are these not evidences of jealousy? Are these not a deviation from the gospel according to Kropotkin that *mutual aid* is a factor in progressive evolution?

Africans must become spiritually balanced if they must do away with jealousy and its concomitants. No leader can lead if he is a jealous leader. No man can direct others if any of the above instruments of jealousy are found in his repertoire, because they indicate warped mentality, tawdry intellectuality and supercilious vanity.

CHAPTER VII

REFORGING AFRICA

35. *AS THE TWIG IS BENT*

TRAIN a dog how to perform certain antics and it will become proficient. Train a baboon how to be comical, and it will be a first-class entertainer. Teach a child how to read and write and he will become efficient.

These are psychological realities. They tend to substantiate the point of view that any stimulus will elicit response for good or for ill.

If a child, at the age of five, is taught to abuse his seniors, he will grow up to become an abusive individual. In his adult days his phraseologies will betray his abusive propensities. In his days of manhood his speech and his writing will always betray this painful and catastrophic omission in his home training.

That is why I think that whoever is responsible for this aphorism is right: " Train up a child in the way he should go and when he is old he will not depart from it."[1]

Africans are getting to the stage where they will appreciate the necessity of re-educating their children. In fact, some of the children have cultivated a different outlook on life, compared with the outlook of their parents.

It is not uncommon to hear children discussing problems of a political, economic, social and religious nature nowadays. At the last election of the Gold Coast, children played no less an important part in considering the two candidates.

This is reassuring. It shows that the twig is being bent correctly and so the stem and branches of the tree will develop

[1] Proverbs xxii. 6.

and shape according to the ideas of the party who bent the twig or pruned the branches when they were pruneable.

The African has been described as an unthinking individual. To an extent this is true. In view of this hopeless condition, it is encouraging to know that some teachers have become so intellectually emancipated that they are now engaged in emancipating the minds of the children under their care.

A Gold Coast teacher has written to demonstrate how he has fared in his evangelizing mission for the crystallization of the New Africa.

In order to avoid needless persecution, neither his name nor his station nor his denomination will be mentioned or disclosed. Suffice it to say that he is a teacher in a school in the Gold Coast. Whether the school is Government, Assisted or Non-Assisted or not is immaterial to the point at issue.

This is what this evangelist of a New Order has written: " Sometime ago, in an issue of the *African Morning Post* appeared an article which urged on Teachers to be race-conscious, and to instil the same in school children. Now read the following to know how the children in a small school in the .... Province, were affected by stories from the Italo-Ethiopian war fronts.

" On the occasion of the burial of our late king (George V), the Headmaster of the school entertained the children with a short account of the life of the dead king. He pointed out many useful good works the King wrought for his people here in the Gold Coast and elsewhere.

" The children felt their heart breaking. Some were so affected that they kept their eyes on the King's jubilee picture on the school wall for some time, with a feeling to burst into tears. The 'smiling' picture of the new King, shown to the children, relieved them from their sad attitude, when they suddenly hailed and clapped.

" During the course of the entertainment, the Italo-Ethiopian war was referred to. The children were told of how black sodliers, aided by the invisible hand of God, were outwitting and overthrowing their enemies. The children were so heated up with pride that when the picture of Madame Wayzaro Abebath, the Amazon heroine who put an Italian column to flight, was shown to them, they applauded, cheered, drummed on their desks and raised such a huge cry that in a moment a crowd of onlookers had gathered round, and it was with difficulty the Headmaster controlled the scene.

"As for the pictures of Monsieur Pierre Laval and Ras Gugsa, they were almost torn to pieces. At the sight of them, the children stormed, hooted, and exhibited their little fists at them threateningly; some cuffed the pictures when they were passed round to them to gaze, and it was under such circumstance that part of M. Laval's picture was torn.

"This is what the Italo-Ethiopian war has brought about. And now, Mr Editor, how does this interest you? *Postscript.* These school children are reserving and contributing their halfpennies to be sent to the school children in Ethiopia who may have suffered loss in the war."

Indeed, this is one of the most inspirational and revered letters received by The *African Morning Post* since its inception. It is an indication that some Africans are thinking, and more so that they have decided to make the younger generation think in terms of the New Africa.

Who would believe that school children, *somewhere* in the provinces of the Gold Coast, would care to pronounce such names as Wayzaro Abebath, Ras Gugsa, and Laval, much more to connect them with attributes which masculate or emasculate awakened Africa? Yet that has happened, and I will stake my life that wherever these children go in years to come they will idealize Wayzaro Abebath and point to others what had been done to postpone the crystallization and the realization of an era of man's humanity to man, on this paradise of stately palms—Africa.

The task has just begun. There are 59,638 school children in the Gold Coast. If all the teachers of this country will pledge themselves towards this type of evangelism, their gospel will be a success and they will have facilitated the New Africa.

Wayzaro, Gugsa, Laval. Magic words these. Yet they are indices to constructive thinking. Verily, as the twig is bent so is the tree.

. . . . .

No word is so beautiful in human language as *mother*. The sound is stirring. It is inspiring. It is ennobling. It is the sound of assurance and hope.

Breathes there any person whose ears are not co-ordinated with the musical sound which emanates when the word *mother* is pronounced?

If there such breathe, go watch that person; he or she is not mentally balanced.

Mothers are worthy of respect and homage. They deserve the gratitude of mankind.

When in its prenatal and postnatal stages, it is mother who, by her activities, cares for the child. The food she eats, the water she drinks, the clothes she wears, the words she utter, —these have an important bearing on the child's life.

When the child is born, mother brings to bear femininity—woman's tender care for her child, a part and parcel of herself. Is it not a wonderful mission to perform for humanity, to give birth to a child?

Some mothers survive the ordeal of labour. They visualize, at the prenatal stage, the beauties of motherhood. And when the time comes, all things being equal, they are privileged to welcome into the world, the darling little person sent by God.

Some mothers succumb to the ordeal of labour. Despite the fact that they dreamt of the glories of motherhood and expected to enjoy these, they do not survive. Some die in the attempt to replenish the world. What martyrdom! Oh Benoni!

Some mothers neither succumb nor enjoy the prize of motherhood. This type may have the unpleasant experience of seeing their child dead at birth.

Those who have the pleasant experience of caressing the little person they beget into the world, are great heroines, because their task is not ended until fifteen to twenty years later.

In childhood days, who washes your face, clothes you, feeds you, lulls you to sleep? Is it not mother?

In your boyhood or girlhood days, who advises you when you seem to go the way of all flesh? Is it not mother?

In arriving at your majority who continues to fondle you as if you are a big baby? Is it not mother?

If mother cares for you in your childhood days, in your boyhood days, in your adult days when you reach your majority, is it meet that you should forget mother ?

It is not uncommon to hear of mother-beaters. What brutes ! This libel on the brutes is not even permissible in view of the fact that some brutes do care for their mothers.

It is not uncommon to learn of a former baby, having grown into manhood or womanhood, assume an atmosphere of arrogance and asininity to exchange words with mother and to go the extent of abusing or even beating mother. What an ingrate ?

And some persons there are who forget mother as soon as they begin to earn their livelihood.

Mother, who cared for you when you were helpless in the world, must be cared for when the wrinkles of age begin to swath her face with their indelible marks.

Mother, who fondled you and saved you from the forces of nature, when you were unable to do anything for yourself, deserves protection and appreciation.

But are there not some folks to-day who seem to delight in ill-treating their mothers ?

Are there not some folks who would not scruple to insult the very woman who braved the travails of life and death in order to bring forth them, the same thankless selves, into the world ?

Mother deserves due consideration and sympathy, for without motherhood life will not be what it is.

When mother sees her child in danger, she does not waver in helping him to be saved.

When mother sees her child ostracized by the world, she does not feel ashamed to call her son, her darling boy.

Yet some children are apt to disregard the womanly feelings of their mothers and to treat them so brutally that some mothers curse the day on which their children were born.

Let every one seek to make the crowning years of mother's life one of happiness and satisfactory reflection of years gone by.

Let everyone aim towards the stars, and if even one gets to the tree tops, and one forgets not mother, she will be happy to hear from others as they sing praises to her child, and when they see mother, they will not fail to say : " Mother, behold thy son ! "

To every mother upon this earth, her child is a perfect piece of humanity. To every mother on God's earth, her child is the best child in the world. Her child is honest. Her child is kind. Her child is brainy. And she does not mind to suffer martyrdom for her maternal convictions.

Therefore, in the name of all the mothers of the world, let every son and daughter try to live up to the expectations of mother.

Let all children remember the days of old when they were toddlers, and when they cried and mother had to breast-feed or spoon-feed them.

And if in all circumstances of life, one tries to do one's best and to remember that nothing short of the best would make mother happy, one would have justified the faith that mother had in one when one first opened one's eyes in this bewildering world.

And to mothers of the world, it is essential that their human failings should be brought to bear on this humble observation of mine.

Your son may be the best man in the world. Your daughter may be the best woman in the world. But, mother, do you realize that your son may be the worst son in the world, and that your daughter may be the worst daughter in the world as well ?

As a twig is bent so is the tree. Spare the rod and spoil your child. Spare the tongue and lay a sandy foundation for your son's house. Spare the axe and let the tree over-reach its confines.

Some mothers, by their affectionate regards for their sons and daughters, have made them failures in life.

Therefore, just as I appeal to the sons and daughters of the world to treat their mothers with respect and filial duty, so too do I humbly appeal to mothers to produce worthwhile sons and daughters in the world, morally speaking.

Let mothers inspire their sons and daughters with moral habits and instil in them sterling character for the conservation of the race.

It is up to the mothers to make or mar society, by the way they train their children. And if this world is transformed into a better place to live in, what mother will not be proud to hear the words : " Mother, behold thy son ? "

. . . . . .

Education is a field which is noted for some catch-phrases, especially among educationists of the old school, who refuse to be influenced by modern scientific methodology.

Some of the followers of this field of study prefer the old system of education and emphasize character training beyond all other phases of training.

At Eton, which is one of the most exclusive private institutions in England (although it is erroneously classified as a *public* school), time was when education was limited to playing cricket and learning to become a gentleman who was born to rule.

So long as a student came from the aristocracy and/or was wealthy enough not to reside in the " Long Chamber " where the poor boys were quartered, it was evident that the tradition behind Eton was character training.

This tradition was translated to mean becoming a good cricketer or a good sportsman and a perfect gentleman.

By wearing shiny top hat, trouserine, tail coat, and Eton collar, and becoming a student of Latin and Greek, for " the building of character ", the school which produced the Wesleys, Shelley, Walpole, the elder Pitt, Gladstone, Fielding, etc., demonstrates to an extent, the efficacy of its system of education.

Moreover, the emphasis on sports was supposed to inculcate in the young Etonian certain virtues such as " playing the game ", " fairplay ", " team work ", " endurance " and other virtuous traits of the playing field.

These traits, by the way, not only enabled England to build one of the greatest empires on earth, but they justified the remarks of the Duke of Wellington that the Battle of Waterloo was won on the playing fields of Eton.

Assuming, therefore, that Eton is regarded as typical of some British schools for the inculcation of character in the students, it stands to reason that those traits of character which dominate their activities reflect on the efficacy of the way the seed is sown at Eton, Harrow, Shrewsbury, Didsbury, Rugby, Kingswood, Winchester, etc.

If Colonial Government and Administration may be used as a criterion to test the results of this type of character education, then subject peoples must take a different outlook on what is meant by character education, for it means something different to the ruler and to the ruled.

For example, " playing the game ", to the ruler may mean that so long as he has the power, the game must be played according to his own rules of the game. Whereas to the ruled, it may mean playing the game according to the sensibilities of both parties and all lovers of righteousness.

It is for these reasons that I become very cynical about this whole business of character education. I appreciate character training as important in the upbringing of a child, but I will under no circumstance admit as final the concept of those in authority, be it religious, economic, social or political, of what constitutes " character training "

To the religious zealot, for example, character training implies a memorization of certain portions of the Holy Bible, an ability to recite some of the important liturgies, an avidity to commit to memory Psalms 1 and 23, and some portions of the New Testament. These are looked upon as basic foundations for the formulation of good character. Yet I know some very zealous churchmen who are conversant with the Holy Bible from A to Z and who are within prison bars to-day, notwithstanding.

Again, to the economic evangelist, economic determination alone can save the country. Efforts are made to prophesy what certain industries can do for the good of the country. Granting that it is an essential platform, is it not too evident that the main reason for all forms of man's inhumanity to man to-day, throughout the world, is due to greed, selfishness and all the concomitants of the *profit motive* ?

For example, a certain company sells shoes at 12/6 per pair, even though it may cost 2/- to produce a pair. But a middleman must make a shilling on it. A wholesaler must make a shilling on top. A commission buyer must make a shilling on top. A retailer must make two shillings on top. A combine or group of companies or a single company must make four shillings on top. The African must pay the balance in taxes, directly or indirectly, so as to cover imaginary "overhead expenses" and guarantee to the shareholders some dividend, in their attempt to inculcate character education in the African and to civilize him in the ways of the West!

And men who are in charge of all the various steps through which the raw materials passed to be manufactured into shoes and retailed in Africa may be men who were trained in the religious and solemn atmosphere of Eton or Oxford or Manyakpowuno! That's character education from the economist's point of view.

Now look at it from the socialite's point of view. Character, to him, means education in preparation for life in a certain "select" society. In other words, the character of an individual must be so formulated as to make him narrow-minded and conservative enough to fit a certain pattern which should fit a certain groove.

Lord Babcock's son must be educated at Cambridge, where he would associate with Lady Castledee's son, because both boys must have character, according to the Cambridge tradition, in order to strengthen the dynasties of the Babcocks and the Castledees. The same applies to Eton or to any other educational institution in the world. And to people who look on character education from their own social point of view, character training is a sum-total of their own idiosyncrasy.

Finally, let me examine the subject from a political angle. A student may "play the game" at Eton; he may cultivate "fairplay" at Harrow; he may be moulded to be a model of "teamwork" at Winchester; yet as soon as he leaves the playing fields where Waterloos are won and sails from England bound for India or for Africa, his character training assumes a different hue, and the strong are strengthened and the weak are weakened, and *Divide et Impera* is crystallized, and fairplay becomes circumscribed, and in the end character training becomes a joke, because it depends upon whose ox is gored!

By all means let Africans acquire character education. But it must be discriminately done. Character education from the point of view of an evangelist may mean the subservience of Africans to insults and oppression waiting for the reward which may or may not come, on Judgment Day, whilst certain missionaries and Westerners desecrate the idealism which sent them hither to give Africans character education.

Indeed, it is an intriguing catch-phrase for any form of educational propaganda, and it justifies the maxim: As the twig is bent so is the tree.

36. *MY BROTHER'S KEEPER*

The evolution of man is based on mutual aid. The evolution of animals is based on mutual aid. The evolution of trees is based on mutual aid. In fact life is based on mutual aid. That is the thesis of the fascinating book written by Kropotkin: *Mutual Aid*: *A Factor of Evolution.*

In this book Petrovitch Kropotkin proved that by aiding one another to live and let live, the animals of the forest had been able to survive the struggle for existence.

Despite the fact that species are directed against species, and among mankind there are warfare and other concomitants of social disunity, the end finds the survivors succouring one another and offering mutual aid.

If it is a tornado that inhabitants of an island experience, there is a reaction on the part of a section of the world to aid in alleviating the distress of the stricken people.

If there is an earthquake in Formosa or Japan, one notices the attempts of a certain section of the world to organize ways and means to relieve suffering of those who have become homeless.

This is also applicable to the case of a volcanic eruption or a heat wave or a cold spell or any aspects of natural phenomena which may tend to disturb the equilibrium of a peace-loving community.

It is evidence of the fact that man is not necessarily a wicked animal. There is in man a distinct evidence of love for the conservation of the species, no matter what may be their racial classification.

That is what Kropotkin means when he says: "In the practice of mutual aid, which we can retrace to the earliest beginnings of evolution, we thus find the positive and undoubted origin of our ethical conceptions; and we can affirm that in the ethical progress of man, mutual support—not mutual struggle—has had the leading part. In its wide extension, even at the present time, we also see the best guarantee of a still loftier evolution of our race."

Whilst it is true that according to Darwinism, life becomes a struggle for the survival of the fittest, yet it is evident that the struggle, although it is a mutual one, is not necessarily directed against the species itself.

The struggle has an ethical basis. All men struggle to exist. But in their existence, whether in struggle or in survival, let them be of aid to one another so that the ideal of humanity may not be lost for ever from the face of the earth.

The various organizations of society find their background in this prototype: that is, the factor of mutual aid among animals and the primates that necessitated the herd instinct and the more refined gregarious instinct.

Living together is thus an art. Learning to understand the point of view of a fellow warrior in the struggle demands an amount of self-sacrifice and a co-operative spirit.

Applying these self-evident truths to African society, there is much to be desired. The existence of Africans seems to be one of constant struggle, not with the forces of nature, but with themselves.

Africans struggle to reach the top of the ladder at the expense of those at the rung. They aim to become richer at the expense of those who are not wise enough to live by their wits as some of the rich.

There is an aim to profit by the inexperience or poverty of others. Instead of aiding the down-trodden and the weak so that they may rise and become stronger, Africans apply the steam-roller to flatten them and to make them weaker.

Thus African society has deviated from its moral foundations for one of the most unethical superstructures. Self becomes more important than the rest of the group, and so long as the individual is able to corral his or her £ : s : d., the others may go to the devil or its ilk.

African society of the twentieth century has thus progressed materially, like that of the West, but in their social relationship, Africans seem primed for cut-throat competition, circumvallating themselves in tribes, sub-tribes, clans, sub-clans, gens, sibs, families, friends, back-biters, gossipers, enemies, etc.

If this is not the height of folly; if this is not a sure means of committing racial suicide; if this is not a factor of devolution; if this is not one of the most important reasons for the present socionomic structure of Africans, why need the following be aliens, one to another, even though they comprise one nationality: Ga, Twi, Awuna, Ewe, Fanti, Ashanti, Yoruba, Ibo, Temne, Efik, Hausa, Joloff?

It may be redundant to harp on one topic often, but there is no other tangible evidence of the weakness of Africans as a community, than their inability to realize the importance of mutual aid in their social, economic, and political evolutions.

Africans have demonstrated how they are at enmity with one another socially, so that it is impossible to effectuate any concerted action potent enough to command the respect and sympathy of their rulers.

So too in the realm of economics. Point out to me, Sir or Madam, any tangible proof of the economic capacity of the African so far as mutual aid is concerned. The average African business man dies with his business. His social proclivities lead him to doubt the integrity of partners, and his experiences with contemporary African businesses which fail, support his ignorance.

Politically, I dare not multiply the examples. Social and economic forces are responsible for the political status of the African, and if these are devoid of mutual aid, there is no need to attempt political emancipation.

Behold the way out. If the African would only believe that he is his brother's keeper and would realize that what affects his brother at Yendi affects him at Offinsu, Lome, Sherbro, St. Mary, Labadi, Tudu, Ebute Metta, Obosi, Opobo, Creek Town, etc., there should be less of these disabilities which are being imposed on Africans by aliens, and of which they are the cause.

I agree with Kropotkin that mutual aid is a factor of evolution and I posit that selfishness, be it individual or tribal, has been, is, and will be the most potent factor in the racial *devolution* of the African.

. . . . .

Mutual aid is an important factor in the evolution of human society. Without co-operation, society will deteriorate. Each individual will be left to himself, and the strong will prey upon the weak.

Among subject races, it is very essential that this fundamental principle of societal life should be taken into consideration, else the future cannot be assuring.

It seems to me that one of the reasons why Western Civilization is declining is because it places too much emphasis on individualism. True, there must be liberty of conscience and liberty of action, etc., but the enjoyment of these liberties must be done with an aim.

I submit that no aim is more sublime than to so enjoy liberty as to make the lot of the underprivileged better. If Africans regard the enjoyment of liberty otherwise, it is due to misapplication of values.

In an ideal society, the stronger element assumes the task of guiding and protecting the weaker elements. There exists a sort of symbiosis which enables both parties to contribute fuller to the life of that society.

The strong does not seek to strengthen its position, at the expense of the weak. Rather, the strong aims at using its strength to protect the weak and to make life tolerable for both.

The weak does not seek to further weaken its position, to the advantage of the strong. Rather, the weak aims at proving to the strong that weakness does not imply an indefinite sentence to poverty and penury.

I believe that indigenous African society regards the weaker element of its society as a trust for the strong to protect against outside forces.

Despite the fact that there have been tribal wars in African history, it cannot be denied that the African, unadulterated by the extraneous ideas of the West, seeks the interest of the group, first and foremost.

If it is conceded that the African is *communalistic* in his societal relationship, then there can be no doubt that the ethos of individualism is an outside force which the African has had to contend with as a result of the impact of other culture-complexes. That being the case, it means that in the cultural assimilation thus occasioned, the African seems to be gradually effacing his original societal philosophy, in favour of an alien idea.

I need not regret this unfortunate dilemma, because the African has no choice in the matter. He is educated to regard himself as an individual who is distinctly different from another individual, no matter what may be his blood relationship with that individual. With this idea of individualism impressed on his mind, the African seems not to care for whatever that happens to other Africans, so long as he is not affected.

This is dangerous to African societal existence because whilst in their pre-Western contacts Africans were more *communalistic* and were brought up to regard the society as an end; in their post-Western contacts they now regard the individual as an end.

In other words, yesterday, the individual was regarded as a means to an end—this end being the *Leviathan*, the great society; to-day, the individual is glorified and society is relegated to the background.

I am not saying that African society is not *individualistic* in certain respects, yet I am not saying that African society has been *communistic* or *collectivistic*. What I am suggesting is that pristine African society was *communalistic*, in that the welfare of the group was paramount to the welfare of the individual. In other words, the welfare of the many predominated the welfare of the few.

Granting that I am not far-fetched in my glorification of the golden age of "the noble savage", I think that I am on safe ground when I state categorically that the tendency on the part of the African to be unduly selfish, avaricious, greedy, and inhuman is due to the forces of acculturation—impact of Western culture.

In the present stage of the evolution of West Africa, it is essential that mutual aid should be practicalized, else Africans shall devolutionize into something which is not only alien to their societal structure but also inimical to the progress of any people.

If Africans must evolve better forms of political institutions, certain realities must be faced, and unless they are prepared to bear one another's burden, their aspirations will never materialize.

The struggle for political emancipation has just begun. In

different sections of West Africa, the right of self-determination is being doctrinated and evangelized.

No matter whether political autonomy is desired, within and under the protective claws of the British lion, or the cosy embrace of Marianne, or the protective angles of the German Swastika, it cannot be doubted that elements of nationalism are from within and not from without. This makes it obvious that he who must enjoy liberty must first strike the blow.

If he who strikes the blow does so sincerely for the benefit of the many, then the many must rally round him, especially in time of distress. This is a practical way of demonstrating mutual aid as a factor of political evolution.

In the New Africa, mutual aid must be a corner-stone in the foundations which must be laid for the superstructure of posterity. Consequently, the Renascent African cannot but face the issues involved in a spirit of selflessness and patriotism.

Am I my brother's keeper? Thou sayest.

37. *THE STRANGER*

Life is a glorious adventure. It is thrilling to the babe as he opens his eyes to see nothing but beautiful trees towering majestically as the birds fly about and hum listlessly.

And as the child grows he begins to appreciate the sun—the source of illimitable power and energy. The sky above in its azure colour and the changing firmament must have impressed the child that life is an adventure beyond adequate description.

In this innocent stage of growth the child is all smiles. Generosity is his virtue. He cries, but smiles. He nudges to and fro, but he sleeps apparently in perfect peace. That is why some writers claim childhood as an ideal stage in man's evolution.

As in childhood so in the races and nations. Without subscribing to the erroneous theories popularized by Morgan and certain famous anthropologists on the growth of civilization according to set stages, Dr Oswald Spengler's modification of this idea, in so far as it pertains to man in political evolution, is acceptable to me.

Africans have always been regarded as children, due to their hospitality, generosity and naive mentality when it comes to practicalizing all that which leads to a realization of *man's humanity to man.*

Unfortunately, the type of growth Africans are experiencing makes life rather rambunctious. From their Socialistic society, where all live for each and each lives for all, Africans are drifting towards the sandbanks of rugged individualism.

Instead of " We ", the African begins to think of his ego. " I " comes first in his thinking and " We " last. To an extent, it is safe to preserve the individual before attempting to preserve the society as a whole, but once Africans give way to egocentric ideas it is evidence of national decadence.

Western civilization is not wholly responsible. The intercourse of peoples and exchange of ideals have aided to revolutionize the African ethics and laws, but kindness to mankind is a trait which is eternally intertwined with the African's finer sense of values.

From time immemorial, Africans have been noted for their hospitality and kindness to strangers. There are reports from the writings of explorers and adventurers regarding the way and manner Africans go out of their way in order to make strangers happy.

There were times when tribes lived in perfect peace. But somehow, human nature became so pronounced that the idea of warfare crept in the social *mores* of the group. Hence the origin of national and tribal differences.

Moreover, linguistic differences made the gap to widen so that language became a destructive instead of a conserving element in the African social pattern.

Admitting that racial differences are so overt as to warrant prejudices and hostilities, are cultural and linguistic differences not so minor as to make people better acquainted by understanding one another more sympathetically ?

With all the educational facilities in America, some Americans are as bigoted as they can be on the question of extending social and political privileges to the Negroid or the Mongoloid racial groups. No matter whether they are graduates of Oxford, of London, or of Cambridge, some English men believe that the black and yellow peoples are doomed to eternal servitude and that they are destined to be their masters.

These disunifying factors are responsible for the crystallization of the spirit of ethnocentrism—where the doctrine of racial hegemony is preached so as to inspire racial groups to fight for a place in the sun—and the spirit of nationalism—where peoples of different cultures, but of the same language and race, are aroused to fight for self-determination.

Because of *high* civilization, the twentieth-century human being is as wicked and cruel against peoples not of his race or culture or language as the proverbial and much-maligned yet innocent " hard-boiled " egg, with all the implications that go with that appellation.

Realizing these disturbing factors in the social economy of the West, Africans should have mapped a better course for posterity. Instead, they have crystallized a shameful imitation of the worst sides of Western civilization, and they have lost all sense of originality in so much so that they are gradually drifting to the shoals of the Armageddon, smiling on a glass of cocktail whilst Europe simmers.

Why should any stranger feel out of place in Accra or Lagos or any other African society? Why should any stranger be duped, surcharged, maligned, deceived, scorned at, and ignored? Is he responsible for his racial or cultural or linguistic attachments? Is this policy conducive to a better and more permanent society?

Africans are slowly but surely committing racial suicide. If their only means of cementing goodwill and fellowship fails to work out well, there is no need for them to clamour for self-government and its concomitants.

If under a benevolent European Government, it was possible for a Gold Coastian to settle in Nigeria or Sierra Leone to earn a livelihood, what guarantee is there that should the British withdraw, these " aliens " would not be victims of the worst form of oppression?

If under the benevolence of Great Britain, Sierra Leonians and Nigerians find it necessary to be domiciled in the Gold Coast to earn a livelihood, what guarantee is there that in the event of Gold Coast becoming free, these " foreigners " would not be oppressed?

It is therefore essential to the future well-being of Africans as a race to forget the tribal affiliations of their colleagues. "A man's a man for a' that," said Robert Burns to those who laughed at him because he was a Scot. Remember, therefore, the stranger that is within thy gate, for as ye treat the stranger in thy home, so shall thy countrymen be treated in that stranger's home. In the end, it will hasten and it will not postpone indefinitely the crystallization of the New Africa, if your treatment is fair and equitable.

. . . . .

Life with all its vicissitudes has its beauty. No matter how high or low a person may rate in the scale of his society, there is a universal possession, which is the virtue of doing good.

When you pass through a lane, and you see a person struggling with a heavy load, do you pass him by? Do you chuckle to yourself that it is not your business?

Has it ever occurred to you that the business of your fellow man is your business, if your colleague suffers through it? Have you stopped to think that a part of the whole makes the whole part and parcel of the suffering of its part?

Be a friend to man. Let your smiles ease off the burdens of any weary soul. Let your words of cheer drive away the cares and yearnings of any suffering soul.

Have you shown any kindness to your fellow man? Show it now and show it always. The virtue of kindness was not given to you alone. It is a universal possession. Pass it on.

Have you ever passed by an old woman who groans as she walks in the crowd, feeling remorse at the way she has to suffer in her old days? Don't you appreciate the fact that she was somebody's bonny sister in the days of yore? Don't you realize that she was somebody's darling in days gone by? Don't you realize that she might be somebody's mother?

So my friends, in all your experiences in life, in joy and in sorrow, be a friend to man, for friendship and kindness are a universal possession which helps to girdle the universe in a psalm of happiness.

How many Africans smile at the calamity of others! How many brag about how glad they are that some one whom they dislike is in trouble! If that is your fate, young man or young woman, desist from it, because it is wrong. Man's calamity is *man's* calamity. It is a universal sentence. To-day may be another man's calamity, but to-morrow will be yours.

How many Africans chuckle as they learn of the difficulties of some persons! That is not the ethical attitude. You cannot grin at the expense of your fellow man and expect to be happy.

No. Life with all its vicissitudes is universally the same, so far as its burdens and worries and calamities are concerned. Mankind is doomed to this fate.

Wake up, Renascent African. Realize the destiny that is yours. Hasten that destiny by becoming a friend to man.

You may be Ewe, and he may be Bantu, what difference does it make? Are you both not God's children? And do you both not live under the canopy of the universe, breathing the fresh air of God? Why not be a friend to man?

You may be Hausa and he may be Bubi, but are you both not black? Do you not carry and share the same burden, and experience identic trials and tribulations?

You may be tall and he may be short. You may be of light complexion and he may be dark. You may be fat and he may be thin. Yet, you both are children of God, and you both are heirs to the heritage of this balmy land of sunshine—this tropical paradise.

Friends, go out into the streets full of hope and full of cheer for the new life that is in you. Greet your fellow man with sincerity. Shake his hand with energy. Speak to him and let him appreciate that you are honest. Folks, be a friend to man.

No race of persons in this world has progressed without mutual aid. The catastrophe of one person within a race is a catastrophe of that race. By mutual aid, catastrophes can be averted.

Look at the situation in the world to day. See how vices are being rationalized and justified. See how brute strength predominates over the virtues of right and justice and equity.

Do you think, friends, that man is destined to a better existence when the vices of greed, avarice, selfishness, indeed, all the factors of man's inhumanity to man, predominate his social ethics?

Is it not time for mankind to retrace its footsteps—to solving human problems in the human way? Why should not mankind become penitent like the prodigal son and return home to moral relationship of man and man?

It is up to you to appreciate the ominous cloud of distrust which hangs over the world. You can lift this cloud by allowing a little sunshine of love to filter through so as to give light.

Go to your friend who is now your enemy. Tell him that you are brothers. Assure him of your sincerity. Challenge him to discard malice. You will find him amenable to your requests.

Like attracts like. Man attracts his fellow being. As in physical realities, so in ethical realities. Good attracts good. Kindness attracts kindness.

Let Africans be good one to another. Let them be kind one to another. Let them forgive the misdeeds and waywardness of the past. Let them think of the good that they can do in the future, by being good in the present. Unless Africans practicalize the virtues of goodness and kindness among the African races and humanity at large, woe betide their posterity.

Africans were not made to carry woods and to draw water for ever. But their inability to be friendly to their kith and kin has been responsible for this apparent doom of destiny.

Wake up, ye sons and daughters of Africa. Behold a destiny sublime for you! Can you attain it? Can you achieve it? Can you prove your mettle?

If the above must be affirmatived, then my friends, make up your minds to live a self-sacrificial life—yea, a life of self-denial—to make others happy.

If you find yourself on the streets, smile and greet your fellow man. Such a smile and such a greeting are contagious. Your fellow man will smile to you and he will greet you.

And your fellow man will smile to another fellow man of his. And this fellow man of his will smile to another fellow man of his, till the city of Accra, or any part of the world, join in this pæan of glory to smile, to greet, and to be friendly to mankind.

Life with all its vicissitudes has its beauty. Smile. Greet your fellow man. Cheer him on. Carry his burdens for him.

Appreciate his struggles and help him along. These are the greatest deeds that man can do to man. Be a friend to man.

38. *PHILANTHROPY*

Day by day it is becoming evident that the African must be likened to the man who built his house on sandy foundation which was unable to face the stormy weather. The result is complete collapse of the house.

Africans live in an era which is problematic to them because by coming in contact with a foreign country they are being influenced by its ideas and habits. This places them in an embarrassing position because they are groping. They do not know what to adapt to their mode of life and what to ignore.

In this process of social adjustment, Africans are also the underdog. Since all underdogs are usually under-privileged, Africans have found their lot increasingly difficult.

Is there a way out? Can Africans be saved from the ignominy of racial extermination or from the non-cherishable doom of being an eternal serf?

The modern African is a selfish being. The ancient and the medieval African might have been so; but then their condition of living cannot be intelligently compared with that of the modern African.

I say that the modern African is selfish and this is what I mean. Ability to earn a living does not exonerate a person from the responsibilities of society—an under-privileged society at that.

Moreover, the wealthy African is too prone to cultivate the *extra-ordinary* hoarding instinct. He saves the pounds. He saves the shillings, and he saves the pennies and the farthings.

I do not say that saving money is a crime, but I submit that the use of money is the only criterion which justifies its accumulation.

It seems as if the African who is wealthy looks at money as an end and not as a means to an end. Therein lies the crux of the problem.

Once the African is wealthy, and he is goaded into believing that by investing half-a-penny he can amass thousands, he forgets others; at times he even forgets himself. When, therefore, I say that the African is selfish, I do not mean that he is not unselfish, but that he thinks less of himself and least of others.

Now scan through the pages of West African history and notice the great men and women who have left their foot-prints on the sands of time.

Some of them were wealthy. Some of them were good livers. Some of them were comfortable livers. Yet they died without leaving any monument to guide and direct their followers towards the route of philanthropism.

It is true that some Africans were benefactors of their race, because in Sierra Leone and Nigeria certain institutions exist through the philanthropy of Africans, but I submit that in comparison with the obligations of the African to his posterity, these attempts at philanthropy are negligible.

There is need to-day for philanthropic Africans. I mean wealthy Africans who would give most of their wealth to certain institutions or to certain great national causes.

Recently, the story of an Indian patriot whose father was one of the wealthiest men in India was published in the *African Morning Post*. This man gave every penny he had towards the Indian Nationalist Movement.

There is another story in an English paper about an Indian physician who amassed great wealth and, besides having made a trip to prison for his political opinions, he also gave a large portion of his wealth to the Indian Nationalist Movement.

Gandhi was a successful lawyer in South Africa. Had he accepted the rebuffs of that prejudice-ridden country, he might have been wealthier than the wealthiest African barrister. He thought otherwise. He gave everything he had, but his loin-cloth, to the Indian Nationalist Movement.

Now, in West Africa there are some men who could be said to be wealthy enough to be worth at least £5,000, i.e. including certain illiterate traders and some Chiefs.

How many of these men have come forward with £1,000 each to aid the National Congress of British West Africa? How many of them have given half of their wealth for the general improvement of their country? How many of them have devised and bequeathed their all, outside of few allowances for their family, to the cause of African progress?

If I must be candid, let me respectfully and shamefully admit that the answer is "No, not one."

If none of them is capable of bearing the cross of others, why do they yearn to be leaders? Why do they yearn to enjoy a better life? Why do they hope for a new day?

Do you not realize, friends, that he who must enjoy liberty and the pursuit of happiness must be the first to strike the blow? Do you not realize, compatriots, that the hardest blow to be struck now is financial foundation?

When the delegations were sent to Lord Swinton, in 1934, how many wealthy Gold Coastians fought for immortality in history by offering to pay all the expenses of those delegations?

Am I wrong when I posit that there are more than ten persons in the Gold Coast who could have volunteered individually to bear all the expenses of those delegations?

And yet the whole country was appealed to, even the exploited labourers and overworked clerks and the under-paid manual workers, for support, in order to have funds to send delegations to England!

Shame on you, selfish Africans! You wax fat on the labour of others. You capitalize on the shortcomings of others, and yet you shout the loudest when it is obvious that your rights and liberties are being infringed, due to your apathy.

Are Africans not the authors of their doom? Africans must realize that he who pays the piper calls the tune. They should appreciate what this expression denotes and connotes. If Africans are not mentally matured enough to realize that only through African philanthropy can this continent be saved from its impending doom, then they are lost.

Philanthropy means the love of your fellow man. You are philanthropic if you educate your relative or your compatriot who may not belong to your family. You are philanthropic if you give some or all of your money and wealth to the cause of your country or to some cause which would make life worth while for humanity.

In Europe, there is an organization which aids the afflicted and distressed. The funds of this organization are made available by those who are wealthy or those who are philanthropic.

In the United States, there are various organizations which aid those who are in need and also plead the cause of the oppressed.

In Africa there is none.

When are Africans going to have an African Defence Foundation? By this, I mean an organization which would be worth hundreds of thousands of pounds and whose sole *raison d'être* is to protect the interest of the African, be it political, economic, social or otherwise.

If an African Defence Foundation exist, any question of national importance would be threshed by it, and moreover, it would not be necessary for Africans to humiliate themselves every time there is national agitation, to solicit for funds. And the result of this is due to improper use of wealth.

Some Africans are talented; and some have the knack for accumulating wealth; *but very few have the modicum of intelligence as to the proper use of wealth for the good of humanity. And this weakness represents the difference between the progress and backwardness of any race or people on God's earth.*

Throughout the course of history, the spirit of humanitarianism has manifested itself, and has stamped some persons as great men or women.

This spirit looks at self as a means to a better end; it regards self as an avenue for service to others.

Unless the individual is inspired from within, it is impossible for that person to be inspired from without. Where there is no spark, no amount of friction will bring about combustion.

The inward ego is the motive which propels the self towards good or towards evil. If the environment is adaptable to good deeds, the self will ultimately be. Otherwise, all is lost that is noble in the breast of humanity.

Why was the Good Samaritan immortal in history, even though his name is unknown?

Because he forgot self in the attempt to rescue the perishing and to care for the dying child of God.

Why is Florence Nightingale immortal in British history? Because she faced the arduous campaign of Russian warfare in order to succour the afflicted and to rescue the perishing fragments of humanity.

Miss Nightingale, the heroine of Santa Filomena, will ever be revered not because of her beauty, not because of her wealth, not because of her intelligence, but because of her humanitarianism.

She was philanthropic. She loved her fellow man. She aimed towards the alleviation of pain, of misery, of want, and of suffering. She worked all the night and she worked all the day. And she succumbed in harness, a martyr to the cause of humanitarianism.

There is another unsung heroine in history who rendered great service to humanity although her feats have been forgotten, principally because of her colour. But as long as history is undoctored, the name of Sojourner Truth will ever remain immortal in African history.

She lived during the days of slavery. She was a slave herself, and she saw the brutality and carnage perpetrated by man to man. Many a time her soul rebelled against the horrors and tortures of slavery, but she bore all with calmness and fortitude.

Sojourner Truth vowed to be a friend to man if such could be possible by her rescuing the perishing and caring for the dying slaves.

An old woman past sixty. She stayed somewhere in the jungles and savanna of the Southern States of the United States of America.

She passed word round to the suffering slaves that those who wished to escape were welcome to her "underground train." She meant by this that any person who was bold and daring enough to refuse to be a slave, and who could manage to get to where she lived, would be aided by herself, personally, to reach the free States. These were the Northern States in the United States of America which did not condone the inhuman practice of slavery.

This was a risk, for she could be charged with treason or conspiracy against the safety of the Southern States, inasmuch as Negro slave labour was essential to the production and distribution of cotton—Ole Kin' Cotton!

This old woman dared and she succeeded in saving the

lives of over one thousand slaves ere she died. This is a practical example of humanitarianism, because she gave everything she had towards the manumission of these unfortunate African slaves.

Some had no clothes. She prepared home-spun clothes for them. Some had no food. She prepared some sandwiches for them. Some knew not where to go. She sent them to the Abolition Societies of New England, of which she was an active agent.

And Sojourner Truth died a heroine of humanitarianism.

Now, Africans, blessed with all the material paraphernalia of the West, what good have you done to make the lot of your fellow African better?

Now, Africans blessed with all the security that a paternalistic Government could afford, what spark of humanitarianism have you evidenced in your contact with your fellow African?

Do you see a sick man in the streets and leave him to die? Is that evidence of humanitarianism?

Do you mock at the prisoner at the bar because he is not your brother or sister? Is that humanitarianism?

Do you slander your opponent because he disagrees with you? Is that humanitarianism?

Do you brag that you will see to the undoing of your fellow African? Is that evidence of progress in the ladder of humanitarianism?

Listen, fellow Africans, no nobler heritage can be left to man, than humanitarianism.

Make the burden of others your own burden. Make the cares of others yours. Be humanitarian. Be prepared to serve. Be willing to alleviate the sufferings of others. Be daring to stand by those who are exploited because of their weakness.

If you should rescue the perishing; if you should care for the dying, you would have stamped your name immortal in history, just as the nameless Good Samaritan, just as the heroine of Santa Filomena, and just as Sojourner Truth left their footprints on the sands of time.

Africans, rescue the perishing and care for the dying, for there is joy and contentment in rendering humanitarian service to make others happy.

There are some people in the world who devote their lives in capitalizing from the mistakes of others. They delude themselves in thinking that they are wise.

This kind of people are busily engaged in scheming for the calamity of others. Once their victims are being unfairly dealt with they seem satisfied, and they hope that a change will never come.

But life is a series of changes. The individual who depends on cheating others, to gain his livelihood or to accumulate wealth, will find out in the end that all that glitters is not gold.

People who indulge in this kind of life are usually lazy and mentally weak. They may appear robust in health but their mentality is clouded with dishonesty and avarice.

Every negotiation in which they are engaged, finds them insisting on their pound of flesh. They must always make profits, if even at the expense of life and limb of others.

They smile with those who are their unconscious agents in perpetrating this species of man's inhumanity to man. In their delusion they think that such agents are deaf and dumb.

They fail to realize that the hand that makes can also unmake. They fail to realize that as each individual totters, the particular fabric of society in which he or she is engaged in mapping a definite plan, naturally must take a turn in life's toboggan.

The same is applicable to those who must exploit others so as to make profits. They work their employees from sunrise to sunset. They pay them measly wages. In the end, neither the employer nor the employee gains the goodwill of the other.

This is exactly the situation with some of the mercantile houses in Africa to-day. Bent on making profit at all costs, they overlook the human factor in business. They discard the part that fatigue plays in the efficiency of workers. In the end, they experience such a labour turnover that they regret when it is too late.

Workers are human beings who are entitled to all the pleasant things of life. They are entitled to enjoy life, liberty, and the pursuit of happiness, but some organizations have made this practically impossible.

In Europe, the International Labour Organization, as an

organ of the League of Nations, is attempting to foster the idea of humanitarianism between employers and employees, but the profit motive makes it impossible for employers to hearken to the voice of this John in the wilderness of Western materialism.

In Africa, the Natives are beginning to imitate the European labour situation. Under the hot sun, labourers work and work and work. At the end of the month their measly wages are doled to them contemptuously.

There are some mercantile organizations which regard the human factor in dealing with their workers, but there are some which are business-like in their ideals to make money at all cost, through the sweat of African labour, no matter whether conditions are tolerable or not.

I submit that Africans are being gradually forced to the saturation point of labour discontent, in view of the forces of unemployment, on the one hand, and intolerable working condition, on the other.

Some persons are better off unemployed, because they have no cause for complaint outside the fact that they are unemployed and have no means of earning a livelihood.

Others are worse off employed, because they have something to do, yet the wages and conditions of work make labour intolerable and almost a sentence to servitude.

It cannot be doubted that employers of such type of workers are being unjustly enriched because they do not take the human factor into consideration in their dealings with their employees.

In the civilized world, and by this I am referring specifically to Europe and America, despite the labour problems which exist, due to the high standard of living, the relationship between the employer and the employee seems more humane compared with such relationship in Africa.

In certain American business organizations, efforts are made to encourage the best educated persons in all fields of human endeavour and to make conditions favourable to self-expression.

It is not unusual to find a business organization reserving thousands of pounds annually for the welfare of their employees. They make this welfare gesture a separate department with a special manager, named Personnel Manager, and his sole task is to see that employees are satisfied through his tact and courtesy to them.

In this type of work, employees are encouraged to be democratic. On the football field, an apprentice may find himself having as his team mate, a junior manager of a branch of the concern. On the tennis court, a junior clerk may find himself as the partner of a departmental manager. On the dance floor on any Employee Club Night, the wife of a messenger may find herself in the arms of the General Manager of the Company.

These little things which are generally overlooked in this part of the world, enabled and still enable any business organization with capitalization of £10,000 to soar to £10,000,000 overnight.

This is not mythical. It is not exaggerating. It is not rhetorical to make the above statement. I am speaking from actual experience, and I am pointing out to business houses in Africa why they are for ever grovelling down-below which is very crowded, whereas there are many open spaces up-above.

Most American business organizations are capitalized by the billions. Most European business organizations are capitalized by the millions. Most African business organizations controlled by Europeans are capitalized by the thousands. And most African organizations controlled by Africans or others are capitalized by the hundreds. Why?

Because the African is in a hurry for profits. The African wants to make a penny out of an investment of one shilling and so he gets it, but his business is stationary, and when he dies, his business dies.

Because the European is not always in a hurry for profits. He wants to make halfpenny or a farthing on a shilling and does not worry if it takes that business many years to make that profit.

Because the American is in a hurry to build *goodwill* firstly, between the Employer and Employee, and then between the business and its customers. And when profit starts coming in, it streams in by the millions.

How do American business houses build goodwill between Employer and Employee? By the principle of equity that no person should be unjustly enriched at the expense of the other.

Henry Ford illustrates this spirit. Every employee of Mr Ford's motor factory earns a minimum wage of one pound a day. There are five days of eight or six hours each day, in the week. Each employee has a certain amount of shares in the company so that at the end of the year, employees are also paid dividends and profits fractionally *promptly*, in addition to their wages.

There are other organizations whose systems may be better or worse than Mr Ford's, but the fact remains that when an employee is made to realize that he or she is not an extraneous element in a business organization, and that he or she is not being used as a tool to gratify the avarice of profiteers, that employee will give his best, and the business will be successful relatively speaking; and the community will be prosperous because a contented employee presumes a fairly reasonable wage and humane condition of employment which accelerate the purchasing power of the community. This is unadulterated Economics.

Africans are being unjustly enriched if they insist on becoming fowls and guinea fowls in business. Africans are far away from reaching the stage of the eagle in business, if they look at the immediate gain instead of building a sure foundation for gain which will redound not only to *the benefit of self* but also to *the benefit of the community*.

No man should be unjustly enriched, because the party who perpetrates this piece of inhumanity cannot, and will not, be regarded as an asset, but a liability to his community.

Let the businesses organizations in Africa realize the gulf which they are constructing through their short-sightedness. To make money is all right in a way. To gain profit is also natural. But the individuals who make the profit possible must be appreciated and encouraged by their employers so that the employees may redouble their efforts to make the business more successful. In other words, there must be mutual satisfaction.

Most organizations in Africa cannot be said to be very successful. It is not because the African does not patronize these business organizations. It is because those who have the money, European or African, have not the brains to run business on a modern basis, outside what they gained from old text-books or by experience as agents or what nots " down the coast ".

There are some good business men and women in Africa, it is true, but these cannot be compared with the trained and far-sighted bsuiness men and women elsewhere.

I submit that the human factor is responsible for the success or failure of any business in Africa, because no person should be unjustly enriched, when those who make the profit possible are parsimoniously remunerated for their efforts. Let all mercantile organizations, indigenous or otherwise, put this in their pipes and smoke it.

Africans as a race have much to learn regarding philanthropy. Unless Africans are prepared to help Africans, the future of Africans is doomed.

I make this statement not necessarily as an alarmist but as a realist. I have seen how the other divisions of the human race are helping themselves, and I know that they have been successful.

With the African the situation is entirely different. The African seems to take the writings of the Holy Writ literally. He seems to have and to hold, and to take from those who have not.

This philosophy of life is as strange as it is suicidal to the existence of Africans as a race, and unless those who profess to lead the African society revise their ideas of wealth, they are liabilities to the race.

Take the city of Accra, for example. There are more than sixty-five thousand souls. Of these there are men, women, and children. Of these, less than five per cent. control the wealth of the town; more than ninety-five per cent. have to work so as to earn a living.

There is a Government which rules by its own will, for the people. The latter are still unable to stand by themselves because of their social economy.

In a place like this, instead of having mutual forbearance and mutual aid, I see the people torn by petty and personal squabbles, thereby giving their rulers the opportunity to strengthen their hold on them, and thereby weakening their social fabric.

Now, if I say that the future of the African race lies in the ability of Africans to stand by themselves, I may be denounced as too theoretical, yet it is a fact which is unassailable.

If there are twenty men in Accra who possess not less than one thousand pounds each, why is it not possible for them to pool their resources together, for the good of the whole?

Granted that some Africans are dishonest and that some are greedy and some are selfish, are not some Europeans, Australians, Asiatics, and Americans, victims of these non-moral maladies?

Am I to take it that because some Africans lack foresight therefore the future of the African should be doomed thus?

I submit that those who have been fortunate enough to accumulate wealth are mis-using their wealth and abusing the same.

I make this statement on the ground that if wealth is not used to improve the wealthy person's country, such wealth is not an asset but a liability.

Now, I do not wish to step on the toes of any particular persons, but I am generalizing that so far as Africans are concerned they have been mis-educated in the use of their wealth.

Look throughout West Africa. See the number of people who are wealthy. Compare the conditions of their towns and also reconcile these with the conditions of those who are not wealthy.

You will agree that the African is as selfish as the dog who had a chunk of meat in his mouth, and, when he saw his shadow on a stream, jumped at it with a view to gaining two chunks, and lost both.

Why do I make these indictments without pointing where and how these shortcomings could be averted?

Firstly, the gauge of any country's greatness depends upon its schools which are independent of Government or any foreign control. How many private schools are there in West Africa that are independent of Government or any foreign control, but on their own endowments?

Yet I know that there are many Africans who accumulate wealth at the expense of their fellow Africans, and yet they are so selfish and so lacking in foresight that they do not think it proper to endow any privately-owned schools with money for maintenance and support.

Now, in civilized countries, I know of certain wealthy persons who give most of their wealth for the benefit of the children of those who made it possible for them to accumulate wealth.

Rockefeller, Carnegie, Rosenwald, Phelps-Stokes, Guggenheim, to mention five outstanding philanthropists out of over one thousand American philanthropists, have endowed universities, colleges, high schools, elementary schools, libraries, and other institutions which make for a better society, with millions of pounds.

They have offered fellowships and scholarships to students who have brains but have not the opportunity. How many Africans have been so broad-minded?

How many Africans have endowed schools so as to prevent them from becoming dependent on a Government which may have its own ideas as to what type of education is better for the African?

In Accra, Africans sing praises to His Lordship the Right Reverend John Aglionby, D.D., Bishop of Accra, because of his alleged philanthropy, but have they ever stopped to question what those of them who are wealthier than Dr Aglionby have done for the uplift of their country, comparable with the alleged Dr Aglionby's philanthropy?

Gold Coast people denounce Government because of Circular No. 2, and they criticize the Education Department as bent on restricting their education, yet they overlook the fact that some Africans are responsible because those who have the money are too selfish and too greedy and too inhumane with their brother Africans.

Indeed, if there are any traitors in Africa to-day, they are to be found in the class of people who accumulate wealth not for the good of all, not for their own good, but for the sake of being known as wealthy persons.

It is a silly notion, from an economic point of view, to accumulate wealth without spending it. Unless wealth is spent in a community, so as to increase the purchasing power of that community, the coffer of the wealthy person will never be what it should be.

Unfortunately, Africans who are wealthy are in a hurry for profits and that is why their wealth is ephemeral. A rich African accumulates wealth for others, because he spends his lifetime in accumulating wealth, only to die before he has the time to enjoy the same.

This seems rather reprehensible and an evidence of ignorance. There is no reason why one person should accumulate wealth, only to die, and make it possible for his children and relatives to fight and squabble over the division of his estate.

By all means let Africans accumulate wealth, but let this wealth be used in the community, so as to increase the purchasing power of the community, and so as to make it possible for the wealthy person to be of service to his fellow man.

I submit that so far, very few Africans are wealthy and educated enough to realize their folly and the harm that they are doing to the black race.

The fact that with all the wealthy persons in this country,[1] there is not one library or auditorium or school or swimming pool, or park or store or factory or technological institution or fellowship or scholarship available for the Africans, and made possible by Africans, shows that as a race Africans are prone to be selfish, greedy, miserly, unpatriotic, and short-sighted.

I may be too extreme in my indictments, but Africans are too noisy in things that do not matter, and it is essential that they realize their short-comings, now than later.

May Renascent Africans aim towards the reforging of Africa by becoming more philanthropic to their fellow man.

39. *WE ARE HUMAN*

Three-score and ten years may be the lot of man. Some may not attain to this figure and some may exceed it, but three-score and ten years are the allotted span, according to the Psalmist.

During this period of life, it devolves upon man to show his humanity to his fellow man, so as to justify the *raison d'être* of his existence; otherwise, he has no objective in life.

[1] Referring to the Gold Coast.

There is no doubting the fact that there must be purpose for man's existence, else he will not be better than the ants and the lower animals.

Unless it is possible to prove that man's *raison d'être* of life is mechanistic and determinable only by chance, then the present chaotic conditions of the world must not be criticized. Otherwise, let reformers and prophets continue to clamour and to look forward to the best of possible worlds.

In Africa, there are different situations. In some sections, the rightful owners of the land have been alienated and others who have no right whatsoever to these lands have settled, and are proceeding at a fast pace to exterminate the rightful aborigines of the land.

In other sections, chains are being tied around the inhabitants to regiment them to observe a code of social behaviour which must make them to act like soldiers who dare not reason why, but must march to the roaring cannon at the beck of their officers.

If the three-score and ten years which are the apogee of man's existence are utilized to further the *status quo* in Africa, I cannot say that life has been a blessing to Africans. Rather, life under such trying conditions is actually hell on earth ; indeed, it is a bane.

The African in his original state was "a noble savage". He smiled like a child of nature. His societal institutions were so humanized that all who came in contact with him found him to be almost an embodiment of human perfection.

In his humanity, he entertained his guests from other lands. He gave them palm oil, cocoa, ivory, gold, palm kernels, copra, rubber, and every imaginable product of the tropics. He gave them food, shelter and the wherewithals of life.

To his surprise he has found out that his hosts were not all true and sincere friends. Gradually he lost his sovereignty over his territory and over his population. And he found himself driven into the *veldts* in some sections ; and in others he was corralled into segregation-reserves ; whereas elsewhere he was allowed to live in his original habitation with restricted liberty.

I am not saying that the African enjoyed liberty licentiously before he was subordinated to the liberty conceived for him by his rulers. I am only explaining that the liberty which the African enjoyed before he was subjugated was consonant with natural liberty which is inherent in mankind.

Wherein then is the moral consistency of those who have come to lead the African aright? When you teach a man to wear trousers, coats, ties, shoes, singlets, shorts, felt hats, spectacles, gloves, socks, shirts, etc., and when you teach him to read, 'rite, 'rithmeticize and religionize, and you regiment him to follow your code of behaviour, and your code cannot be said to be perfect, do you expect this product of your stereotype to remain satisfied?

This is the crux of the problem when I take into consideration the clash of cultures in Africa and other so-called backward places.

Although Africans may wear ties, and wear trouserines and spectacles, and even become professional men as do their civilizers, they cannot be expected to be satisfied, if they feel that there is inconsistency between their past history and their contemporary history, comparatively speaking, with the history of the world.

Therefore, the criterion of success or failure of the means adopted to civilize Africans lies in the ability of their civilizers to appreciate the reality that Africans *also are human* like they.

If they are candid enough to do so, they will challenge themselves in the light of their history. They will place their patriots side by side with the African patriots, and they will realize that after all, outside pigmentation, which enables Africans to adapt themselves to the tropical environment, and which also enables the civilizers to adapt themselves to their temperate environment, the yearning to live and to enjoy life more fully and abundantly, is inherent in Africans and not alienable.

This yearning may be suppressed, due to the code of social behaviour which is forced on Africans, yet the yearning for liberty throbs in their breasts just as it existed in the minds of the patriots of their civilizers in the days when they were under the rule of their civilizers.

Chapter VIII

AFRICA AWAKES

40. *MAN'S BARBARITY TO MAN*

There were mingled feelings on November 11, 1935, when the Reverend Canon H. M. Grace, Principal of Achimota College, prayed at Accra, for peace and the cultivation of the spirit of goodwill among mankind.

It is challenging to all sane-minded persons that man should stage a sort of drama in order to enact legalized murder.

Think of the horrors of warfare. Think of the inhumanity, involved. Think of the savagery, the carnage, the barbarism, the animalism which this institution brings into play when war is on!

Can any nation claim to wear the badge of civilization when it sanctions war as an instrument of national or international policy?

Can any nation claim to be aiming at the cultivation of international and inter-racial goodwill and fellowship when it idealizes war as a pruning hook of civilization?

Can any nation claim to have justified its existence as a territory inhabited by *human* beings when it regards war as a means to the enjoyment of life more abundantly?

Is it not silly? Is it not selfish? Is it not the carnal passion that dominates the motives of nations which use war as an instrument for the settlement of disputes?. And are such nations civilized, in the real sense of that word?

Flanders Field! The Marne! Verdun! Names for ever accursed in the annals of *human* history, yet they have been so popularized that men look to these spots as hallowed.

And they memorialize these cross-roads where civilization

received its severest joltings and set-backs. "In Flanders field where poppies grow!" You mean poppies from dead men's bones. Such a slander! Such a libel! And yet the world has been so credulous as to sing of the brave who fell in Flanders field where poppies grow. And they say this is civilization!

Those who have been to war realize that there is no glory in war. The only glory that exists in warfare is the glory of being shelled, the glory of being blinded, the glory of being maimed, the glory of being wounded, the glory of being dead. If these be glorious, what price glory?

Is there glory in a German soldier who may be the spiritual brother of a French soldier, religiously speaking, aiming at the head or heart of the other?

Is there glory in an African soldier, under the British, who is the brother of another African soldier under the Germans, racially or culturally or linguistically, shooting to kill the other, according to the command of his British or German officer?

Is there glory in a soldier of African descent, be he a West Indian or an Aframerican, making a moving target of an African who may be fighting for his fatherland or may be fighting in the armies of European States?

Oh glory, what heinous crimes have been committed in thy name? To think that rational persons would commit such atrocities, such barbarities, such savagery, such carnage, such inhumanities, all for the sake of a brass, nickel, silver or gold medal! Yet that is the reward and glory of war!

How long will mankind continue in this folly of legalized murder? How long will mankind,which claims to be the apex of animal creation, continue to commit mayhem in order that glory may be the prize?

No, it must not be! Man was not made for war. Why should mankind be the bane of creation? What other animal, high or low, besides man, employs war as an instrument for the settlement of disputes? Have dogs a dog war? Do apes stage an ape war? In what relationship is man to dogs and apes? If men are inferior to these, then they are justified; otherwise, what they brag to imply progress actually indicates a devolutionary tendency in the ethics of man.

Think of the " glory " of warfare. The best specimens of humanity available are drilled and made to be smart and orderly. Their uniforms are kept immaculately clean. The brass buttons glisten and the individuals look beautiful, physically and aesthetically.

There is a leader, a captain, who tells a sergeant what to do. The soldier reasons not. The soldier asks no questions. The soldier dares not to retreat in the face of fire from the opposing lines, without the order of the commander.

" Advance " is the word. And like lambs led unto the slaughter the soldiers march into the jaws of hell. " Rat-tat-tat ! " one hears, as nets of machine guns begin to release their weapons of death. " Boom boom ! " one hears, as shells or cannon leave the heavy artilleries to shatter any object, in their mission of death.

Above may soar planes releasing bombs, gases, chemicals, etc. One, two, three. They fall. Soldiers of glory ! Four, five, six. They fall. Soldiers of glory ! In the hundreds and in the thousands. Then comes the command of " Retreat " or " Surrender " or " Continue the advance ", until the atmosphere is filled with all the evidences of Satanism.

The winner and the loser inevitably are the losers because there is no victory in warfare. Two opposing parties must lose their man-power and their material mainstays. In fact, the last war is an example that, at times, the loser is the victor.

And the saddest part of this exhibition of man's barbarity to man is that youth is *drafted* to suffer for the follies of others. The statesmen blunder. The diplomats err. The scheming politicians commit grave errors. Then to the youth they repair. They fire the imagination of youth with glory, with patriotism, with imperialism, in fact they urge the youth to revivify the glories of the past.

And youth, the cream of civilization, the flower of human society, is plucked in its bloom so as to satiate the greed, the avarice, the selfishness, and the hedonism of those who glorify war as the *summum bonum* of human achievements.

War is an exhibition of man's barbarity to man. It is an evil which has retarded civilization, from an ethical point of view. Youth must not be deluded into a belief that war is glorious. It is not. Tell the youth of the world the truth—that they are to be made cannon fodder, that they are to be made moving targets for the bullets manufactured by the munitions capitalists of the world. Tell them the truth and cease from glorifying Flanders field where the souls of millions of young men cry to high heaven of man's barbarity to man.

Indeed, Armistice Day is a day of remembrance. It is a day of international shame. It is a day which challenges man to love mankind.

. . . . .

At Verdun, Occidental civilization reached its zenith, because the people who lived in that part of the world lacked one thing : *Love of mankind.*

Since then, Western Civilization has been fumbling beneath the banal throes of materialism.

The invention of radio, aeroplane, and other evidences of machine technique seems to have forecast a new era.

Graft, selfishness, inter- and intra-racial prejudice with other standardized conventions typify the transitional stage of a passing age.

Fundamentalism with its catholic philosophy of universal fatherhood and brotherhood is on the wane.

The doctrine of man's humanity to man is wedged between scientific researches and theoretical hypotheses.

Whither mankind ? Towards Armageddon, or is man passing through another evolutionary process ?

This civilization cannot survive the material forces of the universe unless mankind abolished war as an instrument for the settlement of disputes.

This civilization is doomed unless the races of mankind became doers, and not dreamers, of the doctrine of man's humanity to man.

One thing the world is lacking. It is the doctrine of the Nazarene. It is the doctrine of man's humanity to man. It is practical Christianity.

Less than two score years ago, the most atrocious barbarity against humanity was committed by mankind, in order to make the world safe for Democracy.

To-day, the world is not safe for Democracy, but safe for Fascism and Communism and other *isms* of European civilization.

To-day, the world is seething with unrest. Nations are clamouring for war. The gospel of hate is extant.

To-day, the world is like a tinder-box. Races are rising against races. Fear, suspicion, hatred and prejudices are on the rampage.

To-day, man lives in fear of his neighbour. Man's thinking processes are turning towards the destruction of mankind through the use of the machine.

To-day, man is becoming a slave of Science instead of Science becoming a servant of man. To-day, war propaganda is rife.

The war of 1914-1918 has failed to impress upon man the solemnity of human life and association.

When I trace the history of mankind, from its genesis, I find its pages dotted with wars and brutal massacres. I find the paragraphs and pages and chapters of history tainted with war—man's barbarity to man.

Was man made for war? If nation wrongs nation, is war the only remedy available for the settlement of disputes? Can two wrongs make one right?

So through the ages, man has been guided by blind passion and his pugnacious instinct, for conquest and subjugation, has made him bellicose.

If the world could only regenerate! If nations could only trust one another! If races could only practise man's humanity to man! If mankind could accept the doctrine of Joshua whom the Greeks called Jesus, and live by the gospel of the Golden Rule!

Would there be more wars and rumours of wars? Would hate and suspicion becloud man's governmental machinery and international relations? Would there be any need for racial prejudice and arrogance? Would there be so much misery and confusion in the world?

Let mankind learn to love one another. Let mankind emulate the life of the founder of Christianity and apply the noblest ideals of Christianity so as to change this mad world into a paradise on earth.

Let the strong love the weak, and let the weak love the strong. Let the haves give to the have-nots, and let there be mutual satisfaction.

Let the rich help the poor, and let the poor help the rich. Let peace and harmony prevail over the world so that the world may be made safe for democracy—the democracy of all races, of all nations, and of all persons.

Let the millennium cease to be postponed and let this utopia become a reality :

" And righteousness shall be the girdle of his reins.

" The wolf also shall dwell with the lamb, and the leopard shall lie down with the kid ; and the calf and the young lion and the fatling together : and a little child shall lead them.

" And the cow and the bear shall feed ; their young ones shall lie down together ; and the lion shall eat straw like an ox.

" And the suckling child shall play on the hole of the asp, and the weaned child shall put his hand on the cockatrice's den.

" *They shall not hurt nor destroy* in all thy holy mountain ; *for the earth shall be full of the knowledge of the Lord. . . .*" [1]

" . . . The desert shall rejoice and blossom as the rose.

" It shall blossom abundantly, and rejoice even with joy and singing, the glory of Lebanon shall be given unto it, the excellency of Carmel and Sharon, they shall see the glory of the Lord, and the excellency of our Lord.

" Strengthen ye the weak hands, and confirm the feeble knees.

" Say to them that are of a fearful heart, ' Be strong, fear not : behold your God will come. . . .'

" Then the eyes of the blind shall be opened, and the ears of the deaf shall be unstopped.

" Then shall the lame man leap as an hart, and the tongue of the dumb sing : for in the wilderness shall water break out, and streams in the desert.

" And the parched ground shall become a pool, and the thirsty land springs of water : in the habitation of dragons, where each lay, shall be grass with reeds and rushes. . . .

" And the ransomed of the Lord shall return, and come to Zion with songs and everlasting joy upon their heads, they shall obtain joy and gladness, and sorrow and sighing shall flee away." [2]

May the time be hastened when man shall not be a wolf to man.

[1] Isaiah xi. 5-9. My Italics. [2] *Ibidem* xv. 1-10.

May the time be hastened when the fittest to survive will be those who have cultivated man's humanity to man.

This is the only way to make the world safe for Democracy.

This Democracy must not be limited to political spheres alone. *It is the Democracy of mankind. It is the acceptance of the fiat of the universality of mankind and the unity of human beings.*

There may be different races on earth. There may be different personalities on earth. *But all are part and parcel of creation.* The Democracy of the universe must be taken into consideration so as to achieve the peace of this world.

War must not be apotheosized as a pruning hook. War is a destructive factor both in the growth of the individual and in the evolution of nations.

The anomaly of this phase of man's thinking processes is that the strongest, mentally and physically, are usually sacrificed on the altar of Mars, so as to satisfy the selfishness and sadism of war-mongers and heartless Dictators.

The earth with all the fulness thereof belongs to mankind. Why must men kill each other and postpone the time when they shall enjoy the goodness and the fruits of this earth?

Man was not made to be destroyed. Man was made to live, and to enjoy life more abundantly.

That is what the youth-in-body and the youth-in-mind believed they fought for at Verdun. That is why they gave their lives as ransom for many, so as to make the world safe for democracy.

That is why John McCrae wrote:

In Flanders fields the poppies blow
Between the crosses row on row,
That mark our place; and in the sky
The larks, still bravely singing, fly
Scarce heard amid the guns below.

We are the dead. Short days ago
We lived, felt dawn, saw sunset glow,
Loved and were loved and now we lie
In Flanders fields.

Take up our quarrel with the foe;
To you from falling hands we throw
The torch; be yours to hold it high.
If ye break faith with us who die
We shall not sleep though poppies grow
In Flanders fields.

41. *PEACE ON EARTH*

The yuletide season is the time of the year when claptrap oratory finds its way in the pulpits and platforms of the world.

The leaders of the various denominations harangue their congregations on the message narrated by Luke, the physician: "Glory to God in the highest, and on earth peace, goodwill toward men."

They exegete this portion of the New Testament as if the Messiah's destiny was to bring peace to the world.

They comment on this verse as if mankind should not only glorify God, but should also exercise restraint in their relations, and bring goodwill one to another.

Because of this conception, the Christmas season has been over-emphasized in the parts of the world where Christianity is in vogue.

In addition to the popular notion of Christmas as the time of the year when exchanges of wishes on extravagantly-priced Christmas greeting cards should be made, I find that Africans, in particular, have been led to believe that Christmas is the period when goodwill should be made more vivid and realistic.

Christ did not come to this earth to bring peace. Christ was not sent hither in order to create a society where the sword will rust. Christ did not offer to expiate for the follies of mankind because he wished to create a pacifistic society.

Christ was not a pacifist. Christ was not a simpleton, as are the artistic portrayals of him on the canvas, on the screen, on the stage, and elsewhere.

Rather, Christ was a dynamic personality who was imbued with a mission—to challenge the forces of man's inhumanity to man, and to rid the world of these forces, if need be, by the power of the sword.

In this connection, it is my thesis that Christ was not a messenger of peace. In Matthew's gospel, Chapter x., verses 34-36, Christ said:

"Think not that I am come to send peace on earth: I came not to send peace, but a sword.

"For I am come to set a man at variance against his father, and the daughter against her mother and the daughter-in-law against her mother-in-law.

"And a man's foes shall be they of his own household."

This is an exhibition of a common sense way of viewing the advent of Christ. For a champion of social justice, and an apostle of a new order, to bring a message of peace on earth and goodwill to mankind, literally speaking, when man is inhuman to man, could not have been consistent with the mission of a Messiah.

Rather, Christ came to bring peace, after the inevitable chaos had taken place. After the flood, then comes the sunshine and the growth of vegetation. After strife, comes harmony. After the sword, comes the ploughshare. That is the verdict of history, and as an historical figure, Christ could not have done otherwise.

Bearing these factors in mind, it is anachronistic for the revered ministers of the gospel to preach the message of peace and goodwill, when they should know that Christ came to destroy the old, *by an imposition of the new*.

It is hypocrisy for any person to sing of peace on earth, when that person knows or should know that why Christ came, why he was not received, why he paid the penalty of humanity, was due to the fact that he believed that the only efficacious way to destroy the forces of man's inhumanity to man, was to use *force*, be it spiritual or materialistic, with a view to extirpating from the earth all the vestige of evil.

Is this possible in twentieth-century European civilization?

If it is possible, then the missions have failed, in view of the fact that their brothers and sisters and relatives are mainly responsible for the chaotic moral conditions of the world to-day.

If it is not possible, then why disturb the African with a theoretical formula of religion in this age of reality, when Africans are bearing the Black Man's Burden and the White Man's Cargo?

Why teach the African of a benevolent God, in whose image man was made, when the very handiwork of that benevolent God believes in the use of bullets, poison gases, chemicals, and other counterparts of bacteriological warfare, as a means of his baptism into the sanctuary of Western civilization?

Why talk of peace, when the atmosphere of Europe, Asia, and America is charged with intensive training and preparations —aerially, terrestrially, and aquatically—for the Armageddon?

Why tell Africans of goodwill to mankind, when their kith and kin have been butchered in order to satiate the greed and hedonism of an egocentric dictator, who is drunk due to the amount of unnecessary publicity and commendations given to him by the forces of the State, the Church, and the Army?

Why tell Africans of goodwill to mankind when they are still ruled by the velvet glove in which is the iron hand of imperialism?

Why proclaim from the pulpits of Africa, of goodwill to mankind, when the only goodwill Africans and their children had known through the centuries, is nothing but a baptism by rifle bullet fire, confirmation by machine gun fire, and communion by Ordinances and Regulations and Orders-in-Councils?

You may sing your *Gloria in excelsis deo.* You may preach of peace on earth and goodwill to man. But the only peace and goodwill the African has known, are the family tree of oppression, repression, depression, and other forms of forcible impression.

The angels are alleged to have sung: *Gloria in excelsis deo*! Glory be to God on high, peace on earth, goodwill to mankind.

It was the message of the birth of the Messiah. The occasion was important in the history of humanity, for it brought to light a delicate issue in the realm of human relations.

Let me overlook the problem of the existence or non-existence of angels. It is impossible for me to conceive of human beings in wings. But if the theory of evolution is not far-fetched, it may be possible that such animals as Saturns, Pegasuses, Angels, Centaurs, etc., lived. These may be hybrids or what-not. They are beyond my comprehension, at present.

However, the message of these angels is more important than the probing into the existence of the messengers, although I know that the existence of a messenger is important in order to validate his or her message.

Glory be to God on high. Peace on earth. Goodwill to mankind. I believe in a final cause. I know that the universe obeys a final law. I know that the human mind cannot comprehend all the mysteries of life.

That is why I must glorify the final cause. Call it God, if you please. Call it Universe, if you please. It amounts to the the same thing: the supreme ruler, the omnipotent governor, the omnipresent creator, the omniscient deity.

Be you a Deist, a Pantheist, a Theist, an Atheist or what-not, there is a common ground, and that is, the existence of a supreme being.

That supreme being may be personified as the Theists do, and it may be mechanized as the Atheists do, and it may be ontological or teleological.

Nevertheless, there is no misgiving that that " I know not what " is the question mark which baffles human intelligence. Indeed, God is to be glorified!

But God is everywhere, celestially, terrestrially, aquatically, etc. Peace may or may not be there, because glory is not necessarily coterminous with peace.

When, however, I turn my attention to the earth, I meet with finite creatures whose intelligence is comparable with mine in many respects.

This earth is the home of human beings and members of the mineral and vegetable kingdoms.

The one depends upon the other, and so the cycle of life rolls along at a tempo which, at times, becomes slow and speedy.

In man's existence on earth, there is the urge to adjust himself to his environment. He must partake of food in order to exist. Consequently, he " attacks " the vegetable kingdom for food. He also " attacks " the mineral kingdom so as to obtain his medium of exchange and to beautify himself, etc.,

Finally, man turns to himself. Either he is so anarchistically inclined that he lives for all and not for himself alone, or he lives for himself, at the expense of others.

Here I come to the cross-roads of this great adventure of man called " civilization ". Man may be greedy, grasping, selfish, and godly. In that case he is in position to impose his will on the philanthropically minded. He may be unequal to the task, in which case he fails to survive the struggle.

No matter what happens, it is too evident that the earth is filled with conflicting interests that it is impossible to guarantee the existence of peace and goodwill to mankind.

Look at Europe with all its vaunted civilization. Can you read through European history without heaving a sigh at the "scientific" way their savagery and barbarism have been glorified, in order to bring about peace and goodwill to man?

Look at America with all its vaunted civilization. Can you read through American history without being shocked at the atrocities committed in the name of Christianity and civilization?

Look at Asia with all its vaunted civilization. Is Asiatic history not a record of bloodshed and of intrigues, all in the name of civilization?

Survey Mother Africa. What do you see? Behold the civilization that was Egypt's—barbarism, savagery, bloodshed, oppression. Behold the civilization that was Ethiopia's—slavery, inhumanity, repression. Behold the other sections of African civilization—Ghana, Melle, Songhai, Ashanti, Dahomey, Benin, Zimbabwe! What do you find? A record of man's inhumanity to man.

And this has been the lore of all civilizations from earliest times. Men speak of peace on earth as if man is, by nature, a pacifist. If man is so pacifistically inclined, why were the very Christians engaged in the Crusades, the Wars of the Holy Roman Empire, the Thirty Years' War, the Spanish Inquisition, the Marian Persecutions, the Massacre of Saint Bartholomew's Day. And men preach of good will to mankind!

Christmas comes but once a year. It seems as if the preachments of peace on earth and goodwill to mankind are to be practised once every 365 days and, at times, none, because some wage-earners, Christmas or no Christmas, have to work every day.

Peace on earth. What earth? God's earth or man's earth? If for over 1,936 years, despite the physical changes of the earth's contour, the human beings who inhabit the earth have not experienced mental emancipation so as to look through human problems in a human way, the messages that are preached from the pulpits of the world during the yuletide season are nothing but an exhibition of sham hypocrisy.

With the Italian annexation of Ethiopia, dare any Italian Church preach of goodwill on earth to mankind? With the Ethiopian military manœuvres, dare any Ethiopian Patriarch preach of goodwill on earth to mankind? And that is how Christianity has been prostituted through the centuries in order to gratify the banalities of a self-centred world.

There may be glory to God, on high. But to speak to peace on earth and goodwill to mankind, when Africans are still hewers of wood and drawers of water, and are cannon-fodder for the military plans of Europe; when Africans are still cutting one another's throats, is to make a mockery of the anniversary of the probable birthday of Joshua Emmanuel Benjamin David Joseph, the Christ, whom the Greeks called Jesus.

42. *REAPING WHAT WE SOW*

Æsop lived in the sixth century B.C. He realized the fact that mankind was so divided that any direct sermon to them might be unproductive.

Thus he used a simple method, which proved very efficacious. He employed fables to illustrate his messages. Through his efforts, the children of the world have learned to regard fables as an important division of imaginative literature.

Some historians claim Æsop to be an Ethiopian. There may be some historical evidence on this score. Others claim him to be a member of the Caucasoid races. This may be true also.

Whether he was black or white, Æsop made himself famous by fabulizing on the foibles of his times, and his tales were told so as to prevent mankind from falling into the same errors which were prevalent in Æsop's time, i.e. about 650 B.C.

One of his most important fables is that about the *fasces*. He narrated that an old man had sons who often quarrelled among themselves.

He called them and brought together some fragile sticks. One by one, he bent them and they were destroyed.

Then he brought another set of sticks, fragile and of the same size as the first batch. He put two, three, four, five, six of them together. And in each instance it was difficult to destroy them. The more they were together, the less it was possible to destroy them, whereas the less they were together, the more it was possible to destroy them.

Then he gave them a lesson which is a gem: "United, you stand, and all things being equal, no force under the earth will conquer you, collectively. But divided, you will fall, individually, and everything will totter to disruption."

Through this simple illustration, Æsop taught mankind a lesson on co-operation. He made men to appreciate the fact that a bundle of sticks is unbreakable, because of the strength found in the union of elements that are individually weak.

This lesson was followed by the Nazarene in his injunction: "Seek and ye shall find." If man seeks peace, he will find peace. If he seeks war, war will he find. For every man that asketh receiveth that which he asks for and finds that which he seeketh for.

In the present-day civilization, the education of Africans, to be fruitful and to be of lasting benefit to their respective communities, should indoctrinate in them the lessons of history.

If Africans are not mis-educated, they should realize the relationship of the *fasces* with the Roman political ethos of *divide et impera*.

If the sticks are to be bent or broken, they must be done individually. There must be division among the sticks. There must be lacking in the sticks that element of cohesion. Once the sticks are broken, one by one, just so would imperialism become triumphant.

If, however, the sticks cohere, and refuse to be separated, it becomes a problem to the breaker, because it would take more strength to *attempt* to break the *fasces*, much more the ability to break it.

Africans should, by now, learn a lesson in the implications of Roman diplomacy as exemplified in their philosophy of *divide et impera*, in other words, *divide and rule*.

The Romans applied this method efficaciously. They were rewarded accordingly. All Gaul was divided into three parts, at the arrival of Cæsar; but when Cæsar left Gaul, the forces of Roman imperialism made Gaul to be further sub-divided to be under the protection of the Roman eagle.

The same thing applies to the barbarous tribes outside the periphery of the Roman empire. The Danes, Goths, Picts, Scots, Angles, Celts, Britons, were hopelessly divided among themselves, in their tribal groups. It was, therefore, easy for Rome to impress its will on any of the tribes concerned. Rome was particularly successful in Britain.

After dividing the Britons and ruling them for many years, internal affairs necessitated the withdrawal of the Roman army of occupation from Britain.

The Romans were hopelessly divided among themselves. Hitherto, the Patricians were in power. But the Plebeians were not destined to remain at the foot of the ladder for ever. There were revolutions, dictatorships, etc., and the Roman Empire was divided, and so became a prey to the forces of Odocer, Attila, Alaric and other leaders of the barbaric (foreign) tribes. Thus was the doom of Rome sealed because, unlike the *fasces*, the Romans preferred to be broken, one by one.

England learnt her art of government (diplomacy) from the Romans. Everywhere the Union Jack flies, credit must be given to the Britons for their suavity and for their successful mission of imperialism.

In Africa, racial, cultural and linguistic forces have been responsible for the division of Africans. It is, therefore, easy for any foreign country to impose its will on them.

As long as Africans continue to be divided, so long will the dreams of the National Congress of British (why British colonies alone, when Liberia and other West African territories are groaning under the lash of imperialism as well?) West Africa be destined to be unfulfilled.

As long as university education will not enable African leaders and mis-leaders and pseudo-leaders to have social vision so as to realize a common brotherhood among Africans, be they Zulu or Bubi or Galla or Touareg; as long as professional education will not broaden the outlook of certain Africans to realize their folly and the crime they commit by demarcating themselves into "strangers" and "sons of the soil" (strange terms these !), so long must Africans continue to bear the brunt of the grinding wheels of the juggernaut of imperialism.

Seek unity and ye shall find unity, for every one that seeketh, findeth, provided one has experienced mental emancipation and social regeneration.

. . . . .

Materialism has so engulfed the world in general, and the African, in particular, that its cohorts are prone to forget that there is such thing as ethics in the relation of man to man.

Consequently, the world is enmeshed in the throes of materialism. Money, power, influence, wire-pulling and their concomitants form the basis of the greatness of those in control of them.

Whilst they are thus ensconced in the wilderness of materialism they forget that the day of reckoning will come. They are oblivious of the fact that what one sows one reaps.

Had mankind the foresight to be moderate in the pleasures that are coterminous with materialism, how many that now suffer might have been in a better mental or physical state ?

Had mankind the vision to realize that life is a co-operative venture and that mutual aid is a factor of evolution, how many communities that are now torn by strife might have been welded together by the forces of social solidarity ?

But men are too prone to overlook the finer instincts of the human race. They are too avid to enjoy the material aspects of existence, and in the end they regret when it is too late.

Look at the cherub-looking belle of to-day. She is pretty and beautiful like a butterfly. She flutters hither and yon. Men worship her and flatter her. She wades into the pool of corruption with them. And as the years roll on, the lily of yesterday begins to wither as the sun shines on her mercilessly and ruthlessly. She begins to question the justiciableness of nature and she seems bewildered.

But then, in days gone by, this self-same sun had been responsible for the heat which gave her vivacity, and for the light which enabled her beauty to sparkle. Then, she failed to realize that the sun is likened to a boomerang which could make and unmake. The sun gave and the sun taketh. Beauty came and beauty went, for it was and is the lore of creation.

Take the spendthrift young man. In his hey day, he earns as many times as did his father. But in his father's days, there were fewer luxuries and his father was old-fashioned, so far as money was concerned. But to-day, there are luxuries, not necessities, and the son must impress his colleagues with his modernity.

Let him be given an income of £120 per annum. This amount may be prohibitive for any young man to start life with in Africa, but then in such an age, it is necessary that the wage scale should keep up with the standard of living.

The young man needs a bicycle to carry him on his missions. Indeed, he needs a specially-made bicycle. This means about ten or twelve pounds. He must live upstairs or somewhere which is roomy so that he may be in position to entertain his "guests"—the fairweather friends. He must have six suits in addition to a dress suit, for he is now a "society" *gentleman*. He must have a variety of shoes, including a pair of patent shoes to match his evening dress. He must have large quantities of shirts including dress shirts, etc.

At times the wants of the young man exceed his earning capacity and he is forced to be victimized by the rapacity and greed of human leeches known as money-lenders who do not scruple to play the rôle of money-doublers, in the attempt to get-rich-quick. Then comes the show-down. Probably, with the urge to become one of the *élite* in town, the elemental principles of character have been exchanged for the conventions of "society". Trouble may come. Trials and tribulations may come. Imprisonment, unemployment, death may come. And then what?

Is it not a species of folly to be ensconced in the wilderness of materialism, without any thought for to-morrow?

The wealthy men did not become wealthy over-night; rather they put aside part of their earnings, regularly and religiously, for a period of years, and behold the reward they have to-day!

It is, indeed, a truism that what one sows one reaps. If in their youthful days, Africans prefer to flutter from place to place, like the butterfly, their wings must be singed one day or the other. It is inevitable.

If in their youth Africans prefer to place a high premium on their beauty, it is certain that in their old age, the policy would yield nothing.

Consider the birds of the air which fly hither and yon. Despite their fugal propensities, they are frugal. Their nests are exemplary of patience and foresight; yet man claims to be superior to the birds of the air!

Look at the fishes of the sea. They swim hither and yon; yet their abodes are replete with evidences of foresight and care for the morrow. Yet Africans are piscivorous.

What heritage are Africans laying by for posterity? Material fineries or ethical ideals or intellectual virility?

The forefathers of the African had ethical ideals. They respected the rights of the individual. They had intellectual virility. Through this, they were able to stave off the chicaneries of their assailants.

True, they had no fineries of a material nature; but, if owning a house or a business establishment or having a collection of meaningless titles or degrees are the seed that the African must sow to-day, then to-morrow will never be what to-day has been.

In the animal and plant worlds, the saying is as true, that what one sows one reaps.

Cross-breed a black rabbit with a white rabbit, the issue will have white and black characteristics. Cross-breed one type of peas with another type, and the result is a conglomeration of the two.

That is what Paul meant when he said: "Be not deceived: evil communications corrupt good manners. . . . Thou fool, that which thou sowest is not quickened, except it die. . . ."

"For he that soweth to his flesh shall of the flesh reap corruption; but he that soweth to the spirit shall of the spirit reap life everlasting."

Those who continue in evil deeds shall reap their rewards in due course, because nothing that is, is without a reaction.

Those who do good must expect to have their rewards too, for no good deed is ever done without its attendant reward in due course.

There are some persons in the world who delight in doing

evil, believing that nothing will happen to them. Some of them are of the opinion that in death no harm will come to them.

They may be justified in their point of view, but it is too evident that no person can escape from reaping what he or she had sown, because it is an immutable law of nature.

Let all who believe in the New Africa remodel their lives so as to be an example to others. Little deeds of kindness, little expressions of gratitude, little examples of magnanimity, these help to make the world a better place to live in.

According to Ecclesiastes: " Let us hear the conclusion of the whole matter: fear God, and keep his commandments, for this is the whole duty of man.

" For God shall bring every work into judgment, with every secret thing, whether it be good or whether it be evil."

And what are the commandments of God? According to Jesus: " Thou shalt love the Lord thy God with all thy heart, and with all thy soul, and with all thy mind, and with all thy strength: this is the first commandment.

" And the second is like, namely this, Thou shalt love thy neighbour as thyself. There is none other commandment greater than these."

And I say to the Renascent African: Do likewise; seek peace and unity, for one reaps what one sows.

43. *PLAYING WITH FIRE*

Fire burns. Fire heats. Fire scars. Fire is destructive. That is why fire is feared. But fire can be subjugated. That is why fire is a destructive, as well as a constructive, factor in the history of man.

People who have experienced forest fires know what to expect, and they appreciate the destructive qualities of fire. And they can tell yarns regarding their experiences.

Fire-fighters know that fire is an uncompromising foe. It takes brain and brawn and a stout heart to subdue fire when once it is on the rampage.

Electricians also have respect for fire because they realize that fire also shocks. Even then they have learnt to harness this type of fire for the use of mankind.

"Playing with fire", is therefore a maxim which is as old as human history. Because of the destructive potency of fire, this maxim has been translated to mean "taking a great risk".

Before considering the symbolic phase of this subject, a reference to Greek mythology is pertinent, with particular reference to the origin of fire.

You cannot play with anything unless you know how that thing came about, and unless you know what that thing is, and possibly where it came from and when and why it became a universal gift.

I am not saying that Greek mythology is the final authority on the origin of fire, but my aim is to illustrate how the Greeks regarded the origin of fire so as to correlate the same with the maxim which is the caption of this section.

Prometheus was a Titan, belonging to a race of giants who inhabited the world before the creation of man. He and his brother, Epimetheus were granted the office for creating man and other animals.

Epimetheus is reported to have been so prodigal in his resources that after bestowing gifts of courage, strength, swiftness, sagacity to some animals, and wings, claws, shelly coverings, etc., to others, he had nothing to give to man.

In his perplexity, he appealed to his brother, Prometheus who, with the aid of Minerva, went up to heaven and lighted his torch at the chariot of the sun, and brought down fire to man.

According to Bulfinch's *Mythology*, "With this gift man was more than a match for all other animals. It enabled him to make weapons wherewith to subdue them; tools with which to cultivate the earth; to warm his dwelling, so as to be comparatively independent of climate; and finally, to introduce the arts and to coin money, the means of trade and commerce."

For stealing this sacred gift of the gods, Prometheus was chained to a rock in the Caucasus, by order of Father Zeus, where an eagle during the day ate his liver which grew again each night. Hercules finally freed Prometheus from this rock, so that he became unbound.

Fire is therefore a gift from above. It was not expected originally to be toyed with by human hands, but since the Titan Prometheus braved the perils of the Greek Pantheon and brought down fire upon earth, it had been harnessed, and it is now man's foe, servant, and friend.

Playing with fire is therefore a problem. The party who plays with fire aims, like Prometheus, to harness that fire for the use of humanity.

Fire itself is a problem, since its constituents are liable to reduce solids and liquids into gas, i.e. nothingness, if ignition is allowed. Therefore, to handle fire presumes caution and care.

In human history, fire has become such an important factor in life, that it is played with, yea toyed with almost daily. But only the pure in heart and the brave in heart play with fire.

Fire is not necessarily an enemy of man. It is the way fire is handled that makes it man's enemy. Had Prometheus not handled fire with a spirit of bravery and altruism, he might have succumbed to this phemonenon.

But he was brave. And he was altruistic. He knew that with a stout heart and a pure heart, he could benefit the forgotten sons and daughters of the earth.

So he went to the heavens and stole or captured or took fire from the chariot of the sun and returned to earth. This proved to be of value to humanity.

Those who guarded this gift rather jealously preferred not to disclose its power to others. And since Prometheus was responsible for disclosing the secret, he was chained to a rock only to be saved by Hercules.

In life to-day, how many men are not trying to play the part of Prometheus, and how many are not so selfish and so self-opinionated that they are prone to play the part of Zeus?

Seek through human history. You will find that the persons who refuse to accept the *status quo*, the individuals who refuse to accept established institutions as unchangeable, have done so at times without any selfish desires.

Granting that patriotism is a sort of selfish desire, I think that its ideal is so noble in its objectivity, that this type of selfishness is almost a virtue and not a vice.

In that case, any person whose patriotism leads him to play with fire in order that others may enjoy life more abundantly deserves to be saved by Hercules, because Zeus was so jealous of his powers and the established order that he could not allow Prometheus to grant mankind such a gift as fire.

Why is it that those who are in power in the world to-day prefer to remain in power? Why is it that those who rule others prefer to dominate for ever? Why is it that those who are affluent prefer to be wealthy always?

It is because man is innately selfish by nature. His greed and avarice make him impervious to any challenge to his good nature, and the result is that he becomes a slave to his passions.

Consequently those who are under the command of this proud and haughty "I am the monarch of all I survey" are supposed to accept his word as law.

Any attempt to question the justiciableness or the morality of the decrees of this deluded mortal is looked upon as playing with fire.

Let me grant that I play with fire when I take chances. I have to admit, however, that without playing with fire the world would have remained where it was in the days of prehistory when flints were used as tools and weapons.

Some men are born to be afraid of fire. Some are born to play with fire. And some are born to be fire-fighters. Each must play his or her part, according to the talent which each person has.

To dread fire, simply because it is fire, is cowardice of the worst degree. To play with fire without any sincerity of purpose and without altruistic motive is to commit suicide. To fight fire without foresight and hindsight is foolish.

But fire must be fought, and fire must be harnessed and fire must be played with, if the evolution of man must not be deflected from an upward to a downward course.

Let Africans therefore, realize that some Africans are born to be fire-dreaders, and some are born to be fire-fighters, and some are born to be fire-players.

As long as Africans identify themselves according to their natural gifts, there is no necessity to bewail the lot of Africans.

This is what I mean. A natural fire-dreader deserves no

censure for dreading fire. It is in his or her blood to dread fire. Nothing can change that fire-dreader. That person has not the courage to stand the heat of the fire.

A natural fire-fighter deserves no censure for fighting fire. It is a part of that person's physical and mental make-up. Wherever there is fire, that person must fight so as to subdue fire.

A natural fire-player deserves no censure for playing with fire. It is in his blood. He looks at fire not necessarily as a potential enemy, but as a friend. He does not dread fire and he does not hate fire. He plays with fire in the attempt to show his respect for fire and also to let the fire show respect for him.

Government of human beings is like fire. Government may be for the good of all or for the good of some, depending upon the form and type of Government.

The fact that great men of history existed, and some of them accepted the *status quo* and some advocated for a change, and some sought to change the social order by challenge of ethical ideals, shows that there are fire-dreaders, fire-fighters, and fire-players in the world, at all times of human history.

There is no necessity to dread fire. After all, fire consumes solid, but that solid changes into gaseous form and becomes as potent as, if not more potent than, fire, which is itself subject to oxygenation. So there is no need to be afraid of a phenomenon which is capable of reducing one into the ultimate constituent of fire itself.

There is no need to fight fire. It simply engenders hatred and distrust and suspicion. It is a dissipation of energy.

Why not play with fire, according to the rules of the game, and let the better sportsman or sportswoman win or lose, only to shake hands and prepare for another match? Play with fire if you are a good sport, but play with fire according to the rules of sports. That is why Prometheus is immortal and that is why fire is immortalized in Greek literature.

44. *THE NEW IMPERIALISM*

Impero! I command! I rule! I control! I own! I subjugate! I conquer!

Imperialism! The state of commanding, of ruling, of controlling, of owning, of subjugating, and of conquering other peoples!

Colonies! Sections of the world which are being commanded, ruled, controlled, owned, subjugated, and conquered by those who are so capable.

Colonial peoples! Those who are commanded, ruled, controlled, owned, subjugated, and conquered by those who command, rule, control, own, and subjugate them.

Indeed, Imperialism is a wonderful word in the vocabulary of human relations and in the dictionary of human life.

But yesterday, Imperialism might have sufficed, so long as raw materials were obtained from the colonies for the upkeep of the Imperialist countries!

But yesterday, Imperialism might have sufficed, so long as the strong were strengthened and the weak were weakened!

But yesterday, Imperialism might have sufficed, so long as one nation did not, like a hog, poke its snout into the potato patch of another.

But the times have changed. Values have been re-evaluated. Empires and dynasties have fallen. New Empires and new dynasties have taken their places. And the world is in ebullition.

Instead of the Triple Alliance and the Triple Entente, there is now a Fascist Bloc, a Danubian Bloc, a Popular Front, Isolationism, etc.

The changes which are taking place in Europe to-day are due to a change of philosophy of life. Whilst yesterday, the Europeans were fascinated by royalty, uniforms, ceremonies, etc., to-day the *isms* are being disseminated in their stead.

Behold these isms—some of them, at least—National-*ism*, Chauvin-*ism*, Fasc-*ism*, Social-*ism*, Bolshev-*ism*, Nazi-*ism* Anarch-*ism*, Syndical-*ism*, Union-*ism*, Fabian-*ism*, New Deal-*ism*, Have-*ism*, Have-Not-*ism*, Mandate-*ism*, League-of-Nations-*ism*, Isolation-*ism*, Colonial-*ism*, and others too numerous and none-the-less important *isms* which have transformed world politics into a minced pie of *isms*.

In addition to the *isms* of Europe, there is now a mania for shirts in different hues so as to distinguish organizations which believe in a certain type of *ism* yet differ in the fetish of ceremonial-*ism*.

Thus are the *Black Shirts* (they do not belong to the black race !), the *Red Shirts* (no affinity to the red race !), the *Green Shirts* (anthropologists have not discovered the green race as yet !), the *Grey Shirts* (it will soon be *scientific* to term the offspring of black-and-white as the *grey* race !), the *Khaki Shirts* (since khaki is brownish, we will soon have a brown race !), the *Blue Shirts* (a blue race may be in the making since " Aryans " are supposed to have *blue* blood in their veins !), and other colours, imaginable and unimaginable.

In the mad scramble of Europe to impress upon the world the mission of European civilization, it has become necessary for each group of *ism* to select its best philosopher, its best cult, its best colour, and its best medium for the purpose of disseminating its opinion among its yes-men and yes-women.

This makes it necessary for a re-orientation of values in Europe.

In one section, the God of the Jews was rejected in favour of the God of the Aryans. Elsewhere, it was thought that books which praised the former conquerors of an awakened people should be burnt so that the ashes of these books might be diffused in the atmosphere.

In some countries, some persons were expatriated because their blood was not blue enough. In some countries some persons were blindfolded and they were compelled to stand in front of a fast-moving bullet, at dawn or at eventide, because their whiskers were not long or not short enough.

In some countries, wives and mothers had to offer their jewelleries to the State because gold was not sufficient to buy enough lead to pour into the veins and arteries of those who *have* and do not know how to consolidate their positions.

In some countries, leaders had to run a front and back race, so as to impress their people that they had political acumen.

Leader " A " sets the pace for the first quarter-mile, with Leader " B " in second place. Leader " B " sets the pace for the second quarter-mile, with Leader " A " in second place. Leader " A " then resumes the pace for the third quarter-mile, with Leader " B " in second place. And Leader " B " resumes the pace for the first mile, with Leader " A " in the second place.

Meanwhile, the spectators are thrilled because of the exciting nature of the race, even though amidst the din and shouting of the crowd they cannot hear both leaders talking to each other to slacken the pace so as to live and let live !

Is there any wonder that the world is like a merry-go-round since the leaders of opinion are forever running round and round in an endless circle, making their followers believe that the tape is in sight ?

Behold Europe with some of its leaders ! Behold men of flesh and blood like Mussolini, Hitler, Stalin, Baldwin, Ramsay MacDonald, Churchill, Lloyd George, Salazzar, Schuschnigg, Benes, Colijn, Van Zeeland, Léon Blum, Pierre Laval, Anthony Eden, Beck, King Carol, King Zog, and others ! Do not these people with all their idiosyncrasies show the fallibility of human nature ? And are they not trying to impress the world with their imperialistic ability ! Poor deluded mortals !

Certainly, these men are fallible. Certainly these *isms* are fallible. Certainly these shirts, no matter who wears them, are not indicative of infallibility. Therefore a re-orientation of values is necessary.

Imperialism is a tantalizing word. Its utterance suggests the stamping of boots and boots and boots. It makes persons think of those slaves of the uniform who are so up-to-date in their habiliment that they walk with stiff front, heads high, and their steps are usually knee-high.

And when these uniformed demi-gods come in contact with the African " savage " only a command is necessary and, unlike Canute the Dane, the sea obeys and there is perfect obedience for ever and ever.

I say that the new Imperialism must come. Yesterday, Imperialism reckoned less with the human factor. All that interested the worshippers of this cult were the raw materials of those who lived in parts of the world that were doomed to be partitioned by those who had arms.

To-day the reverse must be the case. For over fifty thousand years human beings have battled with the elements. For over five thousand years human beings have been undergoing a process of evolution—material, physical, mental, and moral.

The African is a human being. He is also an heir to this glorious heritage of mankind. The African is evolving and he is destined to arrive. And when he arrives, he will not be satisfied with the back seat.

Now the continent of Africa is God's country. This country is inhabited by peace-loving and ethical beings. These persons are friendly, hospitable, and godly. But a worm will turn if you insist on taking advantage of its apparent helplessness.

The new Imperialism must emphasize human values in the relations of man and his kind. The new Imperialism must not partition a continent which is peopled by human beings on the round tables of some out-of-the-way rural communities of Europe.

If Esthonia must rule a section of Africa, let Esthonia try. Because Esthonia presents a strong array of soldiers and armaments, that is no reason why a section of Africa must be given to Esthonia at a round-table conference held in the neighbourhood of Lake God-Knows-Where.

If Latvia wants an African colony, let Latvia try. Because Latvia has an army of one hundred million souls and is equipped with all the deadly instruments of warfare that science can afford, that is no reason why a section of Africa must be carved and given to Latvia at a conference held in the regions of Lake Give-Africans-the-Works.

Africans are human beings like Europeans. Africans can think just as Europeans can think. Africans can live just as Europeans can live. Africans can struggle just as Europeans can struggle. Why then should some Europeans think that Africans prefer to take dictation for ever, unlike Europeans?

The new Imperialism must be tempered with humanitarian outlook on the rights of man. Unless this is the case, Africa, which is the pivot of European politics and diplomacy, is being primed to be the scene of great catastrophes in human history.

Africa can do without Europe in many respects. Europe cannot do without Africa in many respects. Africa is self-sufficient in many respects. Europe regards Africa as its life-line. Africa can live without Europe. Europe cannot.

If these are substantially true, what is wrong with the mentality of some Europeans who prefer to kill the goose which lays the golden egg?

Africa and Europe are destined to live as friends, if Europe is prepared to crystallize the new Imperialism; otherwise, the world must be regarded to be too small to accommodate Africa and Europe as co-equals be it a century or a millennium hence.

45. *ARISE AND WALK*

The energy of Africans is untapped. Their energy is unharnessed. Their knowledge of their energy is minute.

Look at the African continent. It appears as a giant who is fast asleep. He is so involved in this sleep of the centuries that his head is inclined.

Around this giant are multitudinous strands. These are the strands of ignorance, superstition, inferiority complex, exploitation.

Thus Africa sleeps and sleeps and sleeps. If he happens to open his eyes, he is so sluggish that he sinks back into the labyrinth of sleep.

Will this giant ever awake from this sleep of the centuries? Will this giant ever arise? Will this giant ever walk?

If Africans believe in the possibilities of Africa awaking from its deep sleep; if they have faith that this giant will ever arise; if they believe that this giant will ever walk, then the destiny of the African must be looked forward to with optimism.

Why is Africa asleep? Why is Africa still tied down by the strands of ignorance, superstition and other concomitants?

Because Africa is situated in the regions where the gods dwell. Because Phoebus glows amidst heavenly psalms in its supernal nod. Because it is a paradise of stately palms—oh wonderland of God!

Behold the chanting wind amidst tropic qualms as it soothes the wearied sod of Africa! And you can realize the circumstances which make Africa sleepy.

The vegetation of the tropics! The rarefied atmosphere of the tropics! The aeronautical beings of the tropics with sundry colours and cadences which drill the soul of humanity—these are responsible for this tropical paradise being God's country.

And then the ignorance of Africans! They know not how to live, because they are God's children. They know not how to prolong their stay on this earthly paradise because they are too naive and too simple and too sincere. Sons and daughters of Eos!

And then their superstition! They know not that they know not, and they are prone to act as if they know that they know! Sons and daughters of the Dawn!

And then their inferiority complex! They seem to know some of the idiosyncrasies of humanity, but they are held back by inhibitions which prevent them from realizing their destiny. Sons and daughters of Ethiops!

And then exploitation! Africans yearn for man's humanity to man, and they appreciate man's inhumanity to man, because every man is a wolf to every other man. Sons and daughters of Memnon!

But are they destined to sleep for ever? Are they bound to be held in chains in the labyrinth of ignorance? Must they descend into the limbo of superstition for ever? Must they be bound in the abyss of the inferiority complex perpetually? Must they be victims of exploitation for aye?

Speak up, Renascent Africans, or forever hold your peace. Rise up, Renascent Africans, or be buried for ever in your sleep. Walk, Renascent Africans, or for ever be lame.

You are not born to carry bags of cocoa for eight hours in order to earn thirty shillings a month, for ever. Yet that is the fate of some of you.

You are not born to be automata at the beck of self-styled masters, for ever. Yet that is the fate of some of you.

How many of you, that are now commanded, commanded in the great days of yore?

How many of you, that are now used as boot-scrapers, enjoyed the majesty that was Ethiopia's in antiquity, and the splendour that was Songhay's?

Wake up Renascent Africans and walk. Your lot is not that of a corn grinder or of a servant or of a boat boy, for ever. There is a far nobler destiny for you.

Africa sleeps because he is ignorant that his strength is as yet untapped. Africa is asleep because, like a virgin, he is as yet ignorant of the joys of life.

Africa is asleep because he is a giant and he knows not that he has a giant's strength, and he knows not that if his strength were harnessed he would be a factor to be reckoned with in the world.

Africa is asleep because he is unaware of the vast energy stored in the vast recesses of his body.

But giants are not made to sleep for ever. Even the giant Steam slept for centuries until James Watt woke it up from its deep stupor.

Then the strength of the giant was tapped. Then the strength of the giant was harnessed. Then the strength of the giant was translated into terms of energy. And the giant arose and walked.

See the possibilities of Steam to-day. The train on the rails! The steamer on the sea! The tractor on the farm! These are few of the possibilities of steam.

And yet Giant Steam slept for centuries untapped, unharnessed, and inert!

Then there's the Giant Electricity. It slept for centuries, but some men woke it up from its deep stupor. And the result? Electricity! Telephones! Most amenities of modern life!

Africa is a sleepy giant. From Cairo to Capetown. From Jibuti to Cape Verde. This Giant of immense proportions sleeps and sleeps and sleeps.

But there is one consolation in this kind of sleeping. Since it is not pathogenic, it may work to the ultimate benefit of the African because when one sleeps, one also dreams.

The African Giant therefore sleeps and dreams and dreams.

He dreams of the past. He dreams of the present. And he dreams of the future.

Dreams of greatness, dreams of fame, how you taunt Renascent Africans day and night? Must they waver in their faith, dreams of greatness and of fame?

Renascent Africans dream of a greater Africa. They dream in their dreams and see visions of an awakened continent of wide-awake men and women whose blood is virile and whose aspirations are fired by noble objectives, to crystallize man's humanity to man: to enjoy life more abundantly.

Who disbelieves these dreams of a greater Africa?

Who doubts the crystallization of a greater Africa?

Who does not dream of a greater destiny?

If any such person lives, and pollutes this free air of God with his or her breath, mark that person well, he or she is worse than a slave. Yea, he or she is a shadow.

And I see this giant as he dreams of the past.

And I see him as he is called by an unknown voice: "Africa, arise, and walk. Behold, the heritage that is thine is being sequestered! Africa, arise and walk."

And I see him as he struggles to open his heavy-laden eyes. And I hear him groan. "I cannot."

And I see before him spread the victorious army of Piankhi when, in 713 B.C., he and his noble band of blacks conquered all the armies of the great powers of the world, to crystallize the black man's dominion over the world.

And I see him look with rapt attention as another mist was cleared and he saw the victorious army of Sonni Ali preparing grounds for the victorious Army of Askia the Great to establish the Songhay Empire.

And I see him open one of his eyes. And he shook his head. And the reverberation which followed led to the overthrow of Empires in the Near East and on the Mediterranean basin.

And I see him fall back to sleep and his manpower was divested from him, as strangers of a different hue tied strands of traffic in human beings around him and he slept and slept and slept.

And I see him gradually awaking to repeat history.

And as he shakes his hands and feet preparatory to waking up, I heard another voice which almost rent the firmament into twain, saying: "Africa, arise and walk, there's the chisel. There's the marble. Make your choice. You are the master of your destiny."

How long shall Africans be satisfied with taking dictation from human beings who are flesh of their flesh and bone of their bones?

How long shall they allow their energy to be untapped, unharnessed and bound by the shackles of the inferiority complex?

Renascent Africans, arise and walk. You have the feet to walk and the brains to think, and the body to stand the rigours of this tropical paradise.

If that be the case, why must you continue to sleep? Why must you continue to tear one another's throat for a mess of pottage?

Why must the black man or black woman be the black man or the black woman's enemy?

In the North, South, East, and West, Africans are still asleep. They are still dreaming. They are still visioning the morrow.

And to-morrow will come to lift the veil of this shadow which has enabled them to sleep so long. And when to-morrow comes, may Africans in concert with the rest of humanity march together towards the end of the rainbow, singing: "Lord, it is Africa, marching with the rest of humanity, realizing its heritage."

And may it so happen that the reverberation re-echo, "Africa, arise and walk, and realize your destiny. The mission of an African civilization that is to be."

46. *BE NOT AFRAID*

Amidst the concatenation of events in this world, man is at times faced with insurmountable obstacles. The odds seem to be against him. And it appears as if all is lost.

To surrender would seem to be the easiest way out. It seems discreet to yield so as to gain a purpose—possibly, individual protection.

But a careful analysis of the part played by the great men and women of history shows that those who surrender usually do so either because they lack the will to fight to the end or because they are forced by circumstances.

There are in this life, circumstances which force a man with stout heart to play the rôle of a coward. There are circumstances also which force a weak man to play the rôle of a hero.

Take a distance race, for example, say the One Mile Race. The runners toe the mark. The starter shouts: "On Your Marks," "Get Set," "Go," and bang goes the gun.

In the preliminary stages of the race, most of the runners are in front jockeying for positions. The man who has trained religiously and is sure of his stamina and speed, does not worry about position, if he is within striking distance of the leaders.

After the first quarter mile, the runners with the grasshopper mind, who flit from position to position every hundred yards, begin to drop back, and those who conserved their energy begin to move on the fore.

When the half-mile has been covered, the field is so thinned out that it is possible to locate the first six men who will ultimately finish the race.

By the time the three-quarters' stage is reached, the champions begin to "go places". The pace is speeded. The stride is lengthened. Though the flesh becomes weaker and the last quarter-mile looks as endless, the brave grit their teeth and put everything in their strides, to reach the tape, no matter who wins, satisfied that they have run a *heady* race.

The secret of success of distance runners is the ability to conserve and harness energy over a long distance, where stamina and some amount of speed are necessary to carry one safely over the route.

Those who drop by the wayside lack the energy, the grit, the stamina, the speed, and finally the spirit to dare. They are afraid. And that is why they fail to finish the race.

The African of to-day is becoming renascent. He is to be likened to a long-distance runner who has exuberant energy but is unable to harness it or conserve it with telling effect.

Yesterday, he only took part in the race, to run for about

half the distance and drop out exhausted and to feel, a few minutes later, that he could have gone twenty miles more.

To-day, the realities of this complex life are causing the Renascent African to begin to train himself for the race of to-morrow.

The Renascent African is realizing the fact that not only is energy essential to perfecting the technique of long-distance racing, comparable with the problems raised by present-day civilization, but that that energy must be harnessed.

It, therefore, devolves on the Renascent African to use his energy where the best results are obtainable.

If by his activities, an African spends his time in cutting the throat of his fellow African, it is mis-spent energy. Indeed, it is a dissipation of needed energy.

This compares with the fate of the runner who started the mile race at top speed and had to quit after covering the first 300 yards, with 1,460 yards to go.

If by his activities, an African destroys the best efforts of another African, simply because of jealousy or greed or other forms of man's inhumanity to man, it is only an exemplification of the type of runner who sets a very hot pace to impress the spectator, only to drop out of the race during its finishing stages.

If by his efforts, an African causes the downfall of another African, simply because that other African has won the affection of more Africans than did his detractor, it is another example of the type of heartless runners who jog along at a slow pace and then whine because faster runners placed in front of them.

Amidst these vicissitudes of life, the Renascent African must take courage, remembering that the race is neither always for the fastest nor the battle always for the strongest, but for those who do not only conserve their energy, but also harness and utilize it effectively.

The Renascent African must therefore shun cowardice. Let him look at the facts of history nakedly. Let him believe that he will and there is no force to stop him from achieving.

. . . . .

"Be not afraid, it is I," said Jesus.

Why did Jesus assure his disciples that he was present and that there was no need to be afraid? Because he knew that the failings of mankind made them to be victims of the inferiority complex. They are therefore afraid whenever any phenomenon baffles them.

That is exactly the position in Africa to-day. Many an African Horatius has failed to guard the bridge simply because of heartlessness.

Africans are afraid because they do not believe. They are ruled because they show that they are incapable of ruling. Africans are subject races because they prove what they are by how they live and by how they think.

Horatius is the type of hero who appeals to those who are not afraid: "How can man die better than facing fearful odds?"

Yes, the price of facing fearful odds has a reward—immortality in history.

Horatius had the energy. He knew that he had the energy. He was master of the geography of the Sublician bridge. He knew that the bridge could admit a limited number of combatants at a time.

Thus inspired with a spirit which defied death, he faced his task with such deadly coolness and skill that ere Lars Porsena of Clusium was on his march to Rome, the brave soldiers were killed and hauled into the River Tiber by Horatius, Lartius, and Hamminius.

Renascent African, be not afraid. Be faithful unto death. Strike whilst the other fellow strikes. Cease from striking when he ceases. Ask for no quarter. Yield no quarter. And the New Africa is a reality.

But if you must be afraid and must shun death, if even to die is to make it possible for others of your kind to live; if you must not strike whilst the other fellow strikes, and thus jeopardise your very existence, by your studied reticence; if you must not cease from striking when the other fellow, appreciating your bravery and gallantry, ceases to strike, so as to consummate a truce; if you must always ask for quarter and must always yield quarter, then the shame of the centuries which is on all Africans must be regarded to be an eternal doom.

The unity of mankind is indisputable. Africans are all endowed with human traits which may differ in certain respects but which are substantially and essentially the same.

Africans have flesh and bone and blood like the rest of creation. Africans think like all the higher animals of creation, graced under the name of mankind.

Africans eat and sleep and live and die, like others. Yet they are woefully behind the rest of mankind, because they are afraid.

Fear is the bogey of the African. Fear causes the African to become superstitious. Fear causes the African to believe in ghosts, in witches, in vizards, in fairies, in evil spirits, in Occultism, in Astrology, in Palmistry, in Horoscopy, in Mesmerism, in Physiognomy, in fact, in all the "unknowables" which have chained mankind in mental slavery for ages.

Be not afraid, Renascent African. Discard your chains, for they are only figments of the imagination. Look at the rest of mankind. See how they are becoming mentally emancipated from this doom of destiny. They are human like yourself. If they could, you could. And if they would, you must.

Be not afraid, Renascent African. This earth was made for the enjoyment of all the living creatures. Your face is the seal of sovereignty over all the "unknowables" and the minor elements of creation. Your brain is an open-sesame to government of the universe and all therein. Why must you be afraid of your shadow?

Wake up and claim your heritage or be for ever destined to draw water, to hew stone, to carry bags of cocoa, to row surf boats, to dig ditches—yea, to be the scavenger of the other races, for ever.

Africans are not born to die unsung, unwept, and unhonoured. Africans are not destined to be like a flower that is born to blush unseen and to waste its sweetness on the desert air. Far be it from their destiny.

Africans are born to live and to enjoy life more abundantly with the rest of mankind.

Be not afraid, Renascent African, go forth and claim your heritage and enjoy life more abundantly, like the rest of humanity, or for ever hold your peace, for by your dereliction of duty and apathy, you prove your unworthiness to enjoy this glorious heritage of mankind.

47. *AND I AM SATISFIED*

And the God of Ethiopia cleared my vista as I see a noble race of Renascent Africans. And the history of this great race was unfurled to me. . . .

And I see[1] the African in the confines of his habitation. He resides where nature has been kindlier to man. There are no cold wintry blasts to haunt him and perplex him with problems, social and economic.

And I see the African with the blessings of sunshine, of rain, of vegetation, and of a fertile soil. He basks in the sunshine of his primitive bliss. He lolls around his balmy atmosphere. He is happy. He smiles—not forced smiles.

And I see the African family as the quintessence of his society. It is the unity of his clan, sub-clan, sub-tribe, tribe. He lives for his family and his family lives for him. The fathers, the mothers, the children are in domestic felicity, be that family polygynous or monogamous.

And I see the African child as he goes to school in the bush. He is taught the applied sciences—biology, sociology, literature, arts. He is graduated by the celebration of festivals and initiation into the secret societies.

And I see the African youth as he shows his chivalry and manhood by defending the honour of his womanhood, laying down life itself so that the kindred may exist, so that the members of the tribe may live and enjoy life more abundantly.

And I see the African as a man. I see him delving into the mysteries of the infinite. I see him build his temples and pyramids. I see him teach others as he learns from them.

And I see the African marching into the Near East to offer protection to the weak, to succour the afflicted, to feed the hungry, to give water to the thirsty, and to conserve the life of the oppressed.

And I see him as the ruler of the world.

[1] I must confess that I was influenced by the style employed by Professor Kelly Miller in his great poem " I See and am Satisfied," which is reproduced in R. T. Kerlin, *Negro Poets and Their Poems* (1923), pages 207-209.

And I see him as he battles for supremacy, challenging, striking, asking for no quarter, yielding none, and looking forward to a better day.

And I see him as he falls heir to the mysterious doom of the nations, to decline and to degenerate.

And I see him in the " Age of Faith," crystallizing a new civilization, building more temples, creating empires, waging wars, influencing others, and becoming influenced.

And I see him as a victim of circumstances, going through the horrors of slavery—the " middle passage ", the torture of the deserts, the wound of the master's whip, the bitterness of servitude in America, the West Indies, Europe, and Asia.

And I see him as he sings his slave songs—" Swing low, swing chariot, coming forth to carry me home."

And I see him as he yearns for death. Hoping against hope that the cup of death may offer relief to his anguished soul and suffering body.

And I see him as he dreams of equality, of life triumphant, of the Kingdom of God.

And I see him once more at his native haunts, depopulated, demoralized, degenerating.

And I see him as he sighs at the name of William Wilberforce, Thomas Clarkson, and the rest of the immortals of 1807.

And I see him feel relieved when, at Berlin in 1885, he was looked upon as a sacred trust of European civilization. He believed every word of that Declaration. He welcomed Bismarck, Napoleon, Leopold, Schnee, Lugard, Cameron, McCarthy, Harcourt, Wolseley, Guggisberg. He believed them. He was too childish to doubt.

And I see him as he welcomes more of them—good, bad, or indifferent. " There is gold ; " he says, " there is rubber ; there is cocoa ; take them to your hearts' content ; live and let live."

And I see him as he sacrifices home, children, wives, relatives, and life, so that the European States may continue to exist. He fought in the Great War, believing that through his efforts the world might be made " Safe for Democracy ".

And I see him as he returned from the War—battered, tattered, and bleeding. He sighed for the good old days. His old hunting grounds were now city pavements. His homes were now assessed and he was to pay taxes.

And I see him as he is nonplussed. He asks himself: "Are they here for good or for evil?" He cannot answer. He questions his sons and daughters who have gone to Europe and America for education. They answer him not. They know not what to answer.

And I see him as he disappointingly disinherits his sons and daughters, for treachery. But Bacchus and Aphrodite have, like Delilah, lured these Samsons, so that they have eyes but they see not. They have ears but they hear not.

And I see him as he weeps for the "Noble Savage". Gone are those idyllic days. To-day is the day of imperialism. Of money. Of cocoa. Of gold. Of palm oil.

And I see him as he faces the realities of cocoa, gold, and palm oil. Someone must dig the gold from the bowels of the earth. Someone must pick the cocoa from the pods. Someone must extract the oil from the palm nut. That is why Africans were born.

And I see him as he petitions for redress. He is rebuked. He is rebuffed. He is humiliated.

And I see him as he looks back at his history. He shakes his head. He says: "I will not take 'No' for an answer." He stands up, head-high above the crowd. His head is bloody but unbowed.

And I see him as he looks to Europe for aid. It is in vain. He looks to Asia. It is not in the cards. He looks to America. He is given the cold shoulders. Australia is out of the question.

And I see him as he makes an auto-analysis. He is introspective. He takes courage. He will not be denied. He can. He must.

And I see him a changed man. He is a Renascent African. He is no longer mis-educated. He is a man. He is a regenerated man at that. He walks majestically with the other races of mankind. He has his hat on. He is red-blooded. He is no Uncle Tom. He does not genuflect. He is respectable. He commands respect and does not demand the same.

And I see the Renascent African. He is spiritually balanced.

He is socially regenerated. He is economically deterministic. He is mentally emancipated. And he is politically resurgent. . . .

Indeed, the scales fell from my eyes, for I see the Renascent African inhabiting the New Africa, and I am satisfied!